AA Gill was born in Edinburgh. He is the TV and restaurant critic for the *Sunday Times* and is a contributing editor to *GQ* magazine, *Vanity Fair* and *Australian Gourmet Traveller*. He lives in London and spends much of his year travelling.

By AA Gill

AA Gills Is Away
The Angry Island
Previous Convictions
Table Talk
Paper View
AA Gill Is Further Away
The Golden Door

AA Gill is away

PHOENIX

A PHOENIX PAPERBACK

First published in Great Britain in 2002
by Cassell & Co
This paperback edition published in 2003
by Phoenix,
an imprint of Orion Books Ltd,
Orion House, 5 Upper St Martin's Lane,
London WC2H 9EA

An Hachette UK company

10 9

A CIP catalogue record for this book
is available from the British Library.

ISBN 978-0-7538-1681-3

Typeset at The Spartan Press Ltd,
Lymington, Hants

Printed and bound in Great Britain by
Clays Ltd, St Ives plc

The Orion Publishing Group's policy is to use papers that
are natural, renewable and recyclable products and
made from wood grown in sustainable forests. The logging
and manufacturing processes are expected to conform to
the environmental regulations of the country of origin.

www.orionbooks.co.uk

I would like to thank the *Sunday Times* and *GQ* for making it possible for me to reproduce these pieces here and to all those editors who have helped make my prose, prose.

Contents

For Michael Gill, my father, who brought the
world home with him and laid it at the foot of
my bed.

Foreword

When I'm stuck, I walk. I pace the house, usually ending up in my children's room, unnaturally quiet with their absence. On the shelves at the head of Flora's bed stand a crowd of dolls — she has quite a collection now. Their bright, elaborate costumes and gimpy limbs hug and jostle each other for space. Whenever I go abroad I bring back a doll in national costume. I've been doing it for the short decade of her life. It's become a little family joke. I rummage in the case and hand her the package and she says portentously "I can't guess what this is,'" and then laughs, "Oh, a doll." And it's admired for a moment and then carefully shuffled into the throng. In pride of place at the centre is a large over-dressed, cupid-lipped coquette with a parasol that we bought together in Paris. If you lift her skirts she'll tinkle a syrupy *chanson* for you.

I spend a lot of time staring at the dolls; they've grown to be my mute diary. Bought hurriedly in airports and gift shops or street stalls, they still manage to carry a distinct sense of place and an extraordinary breadth of imagination, religion, culture and history. For me, if not for Flora, they bring back real places. Every one conjures shades. The strange little rag doll from Bukhara, her head covered by a coat that's made without a neck hole, her arms tied behind her back to symbolise ownership by a husband. The black Cuban, bright and vivacious, under whose long calico frock hide not legs but a white Cuban, equally symbolic and provocative. The austere Icelandic girl with her oddly phallic headdress and the beautifully decorative kneeling Singaporean with downcast eyes and a modest fan. An abstract Zulu corncob doll intricately covered in beads; the Ethiopians preparing *injiri* bread. An Israeli, breezy and confident in what appears to be her school uniform, waving a flag that's brought so much hope and so many tears. In a couple of years she'll sport her sad national costume of military green.

Together the dolls have the jollity of an international folk festival. They dismiss with childish glee the armchair wisdom that the world has become a homogenous place. Their gaudy diversity points out that the planet is more variegated and divergent now than at any time in its history. Progress has exaggerated rather than shrunk the differences between us. To travel from London to central Africa today is, in terms of culture, education, consumption, knowledge, experience and opportunity, to travel a greater distance than Stanley or Livingstone. Abroad is as foreign and funny and strange and shocking as it ever was and our need to know our neighbours every bit as great. The First World's media focus on a thin agenda of global politics and disaster "events", coupled with a comfy love of sybaritism and predictable luxury, allows us a wholly false sense of familiarity. It's a dangerous received misunderstanding that fosters silly eco-sentimentality on the one hand and a shameful contempt for "over there" on the other. Both inflict a malign distortion on the lives and homes of people we don't really know or understand, which is one of the reasons I wanted to rescue these articles from the bottom of a budgie's cage and give them a little extra life as a book. Not to offer answers, but to cast a few doubts.

Of all the things that abroad offers, perhaps the most salutary is the sense of being a foreigner, not a favoured holiday consumer, but a temporary refugee in a strange place. Nothing alters your perception of who you are and where you belong to as fundamentally, radically and permanently as being somewhere else. I'm endlessly astonished by the power and unfading brilliance of the memories of people and places I've met. They live with me like schizophrenic voices in my head. The Maasai herdsman offering a gourd of warm cow's blood and then asking if I'd ever read any James Hadley Chase. The third-generation Korean, stuck in the awfulness of Uzbekistan, extolling the wonders of his Volga saloon that was held together with gaffer tape. The Cuban boy, hawking cassettes of salsa music in a hotel lobby, who kept a secret love of American rock and knew every state capital by heart. The French nurse with an angelically foul temper, trying single-handedly to save the lives of 10,000 Dinka babies in a place the size of Belgium that had no roads. The pretty teenager in the guesthouse at

Bukhara who wanted me to help her with her English homework and solemnly intoned the correct tenses in "My cat hasn't eaten my other sock, the bear has."

Travel makes for intense companionship. These are people I will probably never meet again, many of whose names I can't remember, but they live with me and I'm constantly reminded of their parallel lives stumbling alongside mine, somewhere out there over the horizon. Travel leads us to the realisation that what connects us is far more astonishing and precious than what separates us. We are further apart than we think and closer than we imagine.

How it works

In front of me, through the open French windows, the end of Thailand slips down into the Andaman Sea. Coconut palms peg the edge of the land; a long elegant boat with a burbling outboard on a boom is queuing in the middle distance, taking what appear to be two local men to some local business. I don't know anything about the Andaman Sea. You can't tell much by looking at it. It's blue and placid and speaks the international language of seas. The 30 minutes it's taken me to write that sentence reminds me of the only piece of advice I've ever been able to offer aspiring young journalists with any conviction: never write with a view. Face a blank wall. The world is a distraction. And I suppose that's what this collection is about. The distraction of the view.

It's hot here. Hot and humid and bright, with just enough breeze to shake the frangipani and the water lily. Nicola, who's travelled most of this book with me, is breast-stroking slow laps wearing alizarin sunglasses and iridescent bikini bottoms. It's December. Back home yesterday it was raining. It's been whinge-ing with grainy rain for a month – for two months – forever. I wanted to come here, to Thailand, to look at the Andaman, eat small sweet mangoes, drink lime and soda, lie under a damp musk sheet in the flickering dark listening to frogs and doves. I wanted to come because it's a holiday. Holidays have no plot. If it were work, despite the sun, the mangoes and the bikini bottoms I wouldn't have wanted to come. I never do. The feeling starts a week before, like the first shivers of flu, and gets progressively worse as the going gets closer. It's a sort of stage fright. You're desperate for the part. You'd sleep with almost anyone to get it. But as you stand in the wings you want to throw up. Your memory crashes. You feel like you're gestating catfish.

Journalists perform on an invisible stage. A broadsheet

1

proscenium. We can't see the audience but we know they're there. Millions of them. Every Sunday I'm read by more people than will pick up a Booker Prize-nominated novel in a year. That's not a comparison of quality, it's a statement of impact. Almost every other bit of the culture may have more value but none has more importance. Without poetry, fiction, drama, music, art, dance and origami we'd be immeasurably poorer, but we'd get on. Without news, without information, we'd be back in the Dark Ages. There's no democracy without a free press. It's an absolute prerequisite for a free market. There is no global anything, just rumour and speculation based on ignorance. Freedom of speech is what all the other human rights and freedoms balance on. That may sound like unspeakable arrogance when applied to restaurant reviews or gossip columns. But that's not the point. Journalism isn't an individual sport like books and plays; it's a team effort. The power of the press is cumulative. It has a conscious humming momentum. You can – and probably do – pick up bits of it and sneer or sigh or fling them with great force at the dog. But together they make up the most precious thing we own.

"It's all very well for him," I hear you say, "on his high horse about freedom, but just look at the papers. They're full of lies and gossip and laziness. The theory's fine, the practice is disgusting." Well, let's just look at that. I don't know what it is you do, what you make or sell, but consider this. Consider starting each morning with three or so dozen blank sheets of broadsheet paper. And then having to fill them with columns of facts, opinions based on facts and predictions extrapolated from facts. I don't know how many facts a newspaper has in it. Thousands. Tens of thousands. Millions. From the Stock Market to TV listings by way of courtrooms, parliaments, disasters, wars, celebrity denials, births, deaths, horoscopes and the pictures to go with them. Now tell me, how long did your last annual general report take? Days? Weeks? And you had all that information to hand. How long did the last letter you wrote take? You just made that up. Newspapers are the size of long novels. They're put together from around the globe from sources who lie, manipulate, want to sell things, hide things, spin things. Despite threats, injunctions, bullets, jails and non-returned phone calls, journalists do it every single day, from scratch. What's amazing, what's utterly staggering, is not the things papers get wrong, it's just how much they get right. Your business, no other business, could guarantee the percentage of accuracy that a newspaper does. And what's more, if you live in Britain, you don't get just one, you have the choice of a dozen national papers. Oh, and a small boy will come and put it through your letter box before you've even got out of bed. Nothing, but nothing, makes me prouder than being a hack.

I never planned on being a journalist. For a start, I was – am – spectacularly unsuited to it. Disabled by dyslexia and worse, afflicted with a chronic Anglo-reserve when it comes to asking questions or making enquiries, I am by nature a man who stands in the longest queue and doesn't ask what it's for until it's my turn. I started out at a perambulatory age to be an artist. I never doubted that calling all the way through school and a brace of art colleges – where, incidentally, I had a fantastically good time. Apart from anything else there is no dyslexia in drawing. Academically, I was a dead loss. Not uninterested, just not any good. One episode from school stands out. I was rather good, as in interested, in history but was always marked bottom of the class. Finally, furious and close to tears, I confronted my history teacher. A cork-screwed sociophobic old git of the type that only boarding school and the Foreign Office can find homes for. He picked up my exercise book with gingerly disdain and said: "Oh your history's fine, you're probably the best in your year, but I mark you the way an examiner will – you've got a real problem with your writing." I looked at him holding my chronic scrawl and thought, "Fuck you, you miserable smelly old misanthrope. I haven't got a problem with my writing. To me it's perfectly clear. It's not my problem: you're the one who can't read it. It's your fucking problem."

What I actually said was probably something along the lines of, "Righty-ho then". This exchange only took on a shining resonance in retrospect; at the time I simply ditched history for extra sex and drugs. But it taught me – or rather I learnt – one truly inspirational, life-changing lesson. My dyslexia is not my problem. It's someone else's. Indeed, that's a lesson that can be applied to any number of life's speed humps – may all your problems be someone else's.

I went on being an artist. The best thing about art is that you're supposed to be useless as a human being. It's in the job description. Artist – aka feckless, inconstant, feeble, amoral libertine with dirty fingernails. In practice it extended the adolescent research longer than most of my contemporaries who seemed to take to responsibility and capitalist expectation in varying degrees, like ducks to plum sauce. "Artist" is also importantly a synonym for absence of ambition. No one can paint seriously in Britain and expect to be anything more than flotsam in the current of cultural events.

And that suited me fine. I did a bewildering number of stop-gap menial jobs: selling men's clothes in Kensington; pornography in Charing Cross; artists' supplies in Soho; pizzas opposite the *Guardian* in Gray's Inn Road; posters and tins of hairspray in Carnaby Street with labels promising the sweet smell of success. I also turned a reluctant hand to gardening, painting and decorating, stacking jeans in warehouses, being a nanny and being a dishwasher in a gay gentlemen's club. But what I did most was sign on – and on and on. Off and on for seven years. It was the golden age of benefit. No youth opportunity or back to work initiatives; no retraining or assessing; no three strikes and you're off. In fact, no pretending that this was anything other than a subsidy for the cash-exploited, unskilled black economy. Again retrospectively, I can see that it was an unparalleled training for journalism. The more things you've done outside writing the more breadth and scope your writing acquires. And the one constant poverty guarantees is that your time is worth less than everyone else's. Being poor means having to wait. And a lot of journalism is waiting – waiting and watching. Rather glibly, I usually say I failed upwards.

The art atrophied into the applied crafts of portraiture and illustration and a brief attempt at *trompe l'oeil* murals. The slow realisation that I wasn't going to be a great artist arrived with more of a shock than perhaps it should. Finally, I stopped saying I was an artist altogether and simply admitted to being unemployed. Then someone asked if I would interview a painter I knew for an art magazine. I said I couldn't write. The dyslexia. They said it didn't matter as they didn't have any readers and there were sub-editors to do spelling and stuff.

So, having failed as an artist, I drifted into art criticism and proceeded to fail at that. I was a truly terrible critic. But then so was almost everyone else writing in this airless, self-reverential, arcane little world in the late Eighties. Art had disappeared up its own catalogue notes and most critics were happy to keep it there in the foetid dark. And anyway, no one read contemporary art criticism and even fewer understood it. It cured me of wanting to have anything more to do with the art world and I've barely been able to go back into a gallery since. But it was useful in a couple of ways. I got to write a lot. I'm not sure that I improved but I got faster, speed being an absolute prerequisite for journalism. The difference between book writers and journalists is that hacks don't get writer's block. If they did they'd become novelists. And I skimmed off a lot of truly bad writing. The rhetorical flourishes. The paragraph-long sentences with multi-storey sub-clauses. The open-cast metaphors and allusions whose primary purpose was intellectual flashing. And it was while writing art criticism that I began using my initials in my by-line. I honestly can't remember what the exact reason was, I expect it was some silly Edwardian snobbery. Sub-editors always say a short by-line is better than a long one: God knows why.

Now I rather wish I hadn't. AA Gill sounds like a rural rambles, pipe-jabbing, pencil-stub-licking, hairy-eared sort of a bloke with a Tupperware box of cheese sandwiches, a trusty pocket knife and a penchant for showing small boys disgusting things under leaf mould. Mind you, Adrian Anthony sounds like an ageing Florida interior designer who once did Rock Hudson's pool house out as a Tiki-Tiki wet bar. Anyway, I'm stuck with it and for better or worse, we all grow into our names. I drifted from the obtuse to the ridiculous and started to write for the *Tatler*. I loved the *Tatler*. I wrote everything and anything and was exceedingly lucky to find a wonderful editor who made me do two things: write funny and write in the first person, both of which I resisted with a donnish petulance and both of which probably took my writing from being a part-time job to becoming a career. I found a voice at the *Tatler* and took it to the *Sunday Times*.

I got my first big piece while on holiday in Scotland based on the very feeble observation that Inverness airport in August resembled a Fulham cocktail party with tweed and feathers. I filed and the picture desk asked if I had a kilt. Looking like a shortbread tin I was on the cover of that week's "Style" section and the editor, Andrew Neill, noticed – principally I think because he's always been rather chippy about Real Scots (him) as opposed to Reel Scots (me). I was offered a contract. On such risible nugatory strokes of fortune – dressing up like a Rob Roy interior decorator – are our careers made.

The paper's deputy editor took me to lunch at the Savoy Grill to close the deal. He offered me the journalist's graveyard of TV criticism and a softly political whinger's column and asked in passing what I wanted to do in journalism. As ever with that sort of broad horizon question, I said the first thing that came into my head – I'd like to interview places. Naturally, he asked what that meant and I said to treat a place as if it were a person, to go and listen to it, ask it questions, observe it the way you would interview a politician or a pop star. I'm a spectacularly inept interviewer, so it didn't sound terribly convincing. I signed on the dotted line for more money than I'd made in a decade and went home to be a columnist and critic. Every so often, usually when my contract was up, an editor would ask what I wanted to do and I'd repeat – interview places. Having mentioned it without thinking, I began to think about it a lot. But journalists get typecast and they wanted me to type sweet acid. Other more competent, steely-eyed real reporters got to file from the outside world. I was there to file from inside my head. Finally, they relented and the editor of "Style" told me, "For Christ's sake go and interview Prague – go tomorrow." So I went.

By nature and nurture I'm a worrier; about this job I worried in 28pt bold. As I left for the airport (three hours early) I realised I'd never travelled on my own before, a particularly pathetic admission for a 40-year-old. In Prague the photographer who was supposed to be coming from Hungary never turned up, so I sat in my hotel room transfixed by the incredibly graphic pornography and the thought that I had two days to find a story and not the slightest idea how to go about it.

In the lobby there was a discarded English language free magazine written for ex-pats and tourists; on a whim I called the editor and he put me in touch with a young photographer who had been one of Vaclav Havel's student bodyguards during the Velvet Revolution. He showed me the city and together we found a story about young Americans who'd come to write the great American novel, imagining that Prague could do for them what Paris had done for Fitzgerald, Hemingway and Stein in the Twenties. There was even a bookshop that self-consciously imitated Shakespeare and Co.

It was a thin story and you won't find it in this collection because, sadly, it wasn't very good. In fact, it was pretty awful. But it taught me a great lesson – actually, it reminded me of one I'd already learnt in another discipline. Paul Klee wrote that the art of drawing was the art of omission and I realised that in interviewing a place, what you left out was as crucial as what you put in. Here I'd been fretting over finding a story and had been inundated with them. Every city is an anthology of stories. They fade in and out of each other. Stop and start. Places are an endless index of beginnings. Prague didn't work as a piece because I couldn't edit out what wasn't essential. I had too much to say and too little space. But I loved the place and I loved being a journalist in it. This experience was quite unlike being a tourist, it had been intense in the way it made me look and listen and I can still recall the smells, the particular quality of the light, the warmth of the heated tram seats and the fake fur collars of the fake blonde girls. I *really* wanted to do it again.

The next story went better and *is* in this collection. I was sent to Milan to cover the fashion shows. The editor wanted a view that wasn't a fashion writer's. I've always loved fashion. It's a mad industry that reaches from the most utilitarian overall to the most absurd ball gown. It's the one piece of culture that everyone in the world takes part in. We all, after all, wear something. But it's a multi-billion-dollar business run by über-neurotic men who you wouldn't trust to babysit a goldfish and here I learnt another valuable lesson. Every story has a key, an image that unlocks everything else. On the page it may not be obvious to the reader but for me it's a fixed point around which the story grows. I was walking with Nicola through the monumental Victor Emmanuel shopping terminus. We were between shows, thinking about lunch and I suddenly stopped. I knew I'd just seen something that was important. Turning round there was a woman. Incredibly elegantly and expensively dressed, perfectly accessorised. She was in a wheelchair. Thin useless legs in beautiful high-heeled shoes trying to negotiate the step up to the Prada shop. Through the window I could see the shop assistants watching her. They didn't move. Their faces were bored masks. And I knew that the story would grow around that moment.

The key thing about this stem image is that I can't force it, I can't go out hunting for it. I have to trust that it will come. And it always has. In Cuba it was a pair of prostitutes who slowly disengaged from their repellent drunken German pick-ups to dance ecstatically and obliviously with each other. In Germany it wasn't an image, it was a smell: the odour of asparagus piss that pervaded loos during the white spagel season. The stink beneath the apparent bosky heartiness. In Sudan it was a man starving to death in a desert who offered me a sip of water from a tiny gourd.

Sudan was my big break. The editor of the *Sunday Times* magazine asked me to cover the famine – a relief agency would get me in and facilitate passes from the revolutionary army who were in control of the south. Sudan had been fighting a vicious war for fifteen years and I nearly didn't go. As I said, I'm a worrier and this seemed to be something that it was quite legitimate to worry about. I had two small children – someone less encumbered than I could go. I didn't need to do it.

What actually made me get on the plane was silly vanity. Another editor on the paper (they are legion) called me off-the-record and said that to send a food critic to a famine was in the worst possible taste and would do nothing but harm to the paper, and almost certainly terminal damage to me personally, and that in his considered professional opinion I should stay at home and do what I was good at. Eat and watch telly. Well, that was it. In the event it wasn't very dangerous but I did take a very foolish risk. The passes never materialised and I had to make an instant decision whether to abort the story on the border, go back to Nairobi and try again or carry on into a war zone without a passport or safe conduct pass. I went – and realised that stories get a momentum of their own. The desire, the need to go with them, transcends almost everything else and that's what gets journalists killed. The Sudan piece hardly needed me at all. In that deeply annoying phrase, it wrote itself. I just sat down and started writing and didn't stop until I'd finished. I never changed a word. On the page it was immeasurably helped by Paul Lowe's amazing photographs, which went on to win the Life Award. (I was bitterly furious that they didn't use one for the cover that week – we got Liza Minnelli instead.)

I'm neurotic about travelling light, so I take as little stuff in my head as possible. I never do any research. I know that this is not how they tell you to do it. You're supposed to go and find out as much as possible, talk to old hands, trawl the cuts and the clouds of chaff on the web. Well I've done that – been diligent and professional – and what happens is that you arrive with a mental I-spy list of things to tick off and yards and yards of preconceptions. You look for confirmation of what you've already been told. Of course I can't unlearn what I already know. We all travel with prejudices. I can't make myself a palimpsest. I just don't want to add other people's scribbles and ideas to my own. Actually, I greatly value my own prejudices – they're opinions based on a lifetime's random experience. What I have found though, is that the more I travel the less certain I am of anything. The more I see the less I know. What I write are essentially impressions. I need them to be as vivid and surprising as possible.

Once I've arrived, I'll talk to anyone, everyone, not unlike an insistent two-year-old. That old journalistic cliché, a quote from a taxi driver, is a cliché because taxi drivers invariably have a wealth of street-level knowledge. My sort of journalism is all about the surface of things. Travel writers all too often dig for stories, ignoring or mistrusting what's in front of them. What you get is the view from a hole. In India, for instance, I wrote a long bit about the Taj Mahal. Too many travellers and old India hands say ignore the Taj in favour of some other more obscure site because it is the alpha tourist attraction, so accessible and familiar it must be essentially, culturally, semiotically worthless: virtual kitsch. But the truth is the Taj is fucking stupendous. It's popular because it's supremely magnificent. It's all too easy to be bullied or blinkered by those who have emphatic prior knowledge or have got into print before you but you must balance that with the only rule of first person journalism. No one's opinion is worth any more than yours.

The other unorthodox thing about the way I work is that I really don't like to stay for long. First impressions are vital. There is an optimum time (and it varies) but you know that there's a day when you starting rubbing out rather than adding. I work best when I feel lost and wary – it makes the senses sharper, the vision clearer. After a very short time you begin to lay down thread roots, have breakfast in the same place, be greeted by the waiter, recognise street signs and bill boards, stop being surprised by the light fittings or the way people blow their noses, or the smell of the street. Familiarity does not necessarily lead to wisdom. Indeed it often grows into a wilful myopia – just go to South Africa and talk to whites in Johannesburg who have lived there all their lives to see how little you can understand while knowing everything. Time doesn't allow you to see further or clearer, or with greater insight, it's all just a matter of emphasis and importance. The reason I don't talk to foreign correspondents about places is because we do different jobs. Theirs is the explanation of events; mine is usually about the space between events. They do movement; I do colour.

On a job I don't carry a camera or a note pad, I never write anything down. Notes don't help. They are an interruption. Instead of being an aid, they dictate. You rely on them rather than what you're seeing and hearing. I do, though, collect things: bits of paper, maps, menus, tickets, newspapers (even if I can't read them), food wrappers, tourist brochures, receipts. I always return with a bag full of litter. I don't start writing immediately. The images are too bright and clamorous. I leave it a week or two, sometimes a month. I trust my memory to filter out what's important. And I talk about where I've been as much as possible. The act of turning it into stories, descriptions and anecdotes and having to repeat them, watching people react, begins to form an armature for the piece. This process of trusting memory is the most difficult of all. What if you went, saw, came back and forgot it all – or the most important bits? I just have to believe that everything is retrievable. That when you reach for an illustration it'll be there.

All this is only really possible in the first person. It's my voice, my view, my opinion. And just as no one's opinion is worth more than mine, so mine is worth no more than anyone else's. I'm often accused of being contentious. I suppose predictably and rather arrogantly I take that as a compliment. If my articles cause raised blood pressure, then good – that's what first person journalism is for. We hacks do opposition. But while they may be the start of the argument, they're never the last word. There is no last word. No definitive view. The older I get the more I see, the more I'm convinced about nothing at all. Opinions, prejudices, theories and revelations are just the social and intellectual weather under which we live.

The view from the window has slipped into something more formal. Now in front of me is Captain Bligh's *Bounty* and beyond it Sydney Harbour and the segmented convocation of the Opera House, the southern hemisphere's Taj Mahal. So familiar, so barely worth a mention. But you see, no one ever tells you about the bats. There are thousands of them. Stuttering and stalling over the bay like bad animation. They're the size of Alsatians, the biggest bats in the world. And there's a surprise.

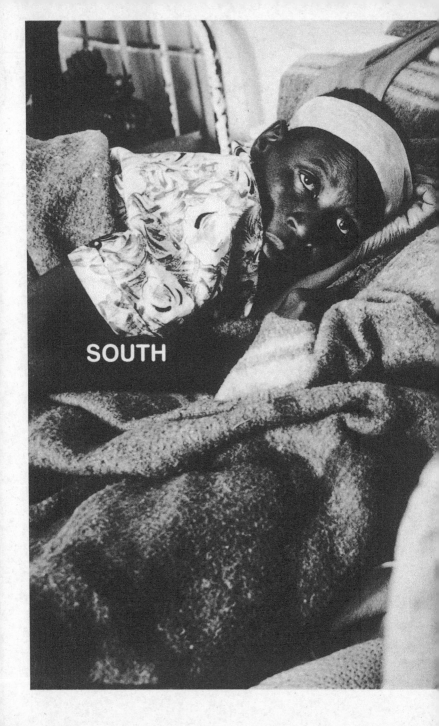

SOUTH

SOUTH

I have no more connection with Africa than an airline ticket, yet I'm continually drawn to it. I'm always missing it. I know that to talk lovingly of Africa has the spongy sentimentality of Americans who talk lovingly about Europe – which bit, pray? Stuttgart, Patmos, the Norwegian Fjords, Godalming? Africa is as varied and various as it is huge, but it does have a cohesion, a common beat that Europe or America has lost. It's something to do with living close to the edge of disaster, but also of being so mutually dependent on one another, on family and tribe and neighbour and luck. We get the luxury of solitude and individuality as a by-product of riches and progress. Africans cling to a web of fraternity through poverty and hardship. Everything Africa achieves is done the hard way.

One of the things I emphatically don't want to be part of is the school of salacious disaster reporting that revels in unthinkable horror and then shrugs a hopeless shoulder. Africa isn't a hopeless case; it isn't the measure at the bottom of the barometer of human suffering. The commonly held belief that Africa was far better under colonialism is a nasty nonsense. Just take Tanzania for instance. The British left it a poor country of 11 million souls. It's now a poor country of 40 million. The poverty is the constant, but Africa grows apace and despite the worst that nature, rotten government, sickness and cynical exploitation throws at it, it still explodes with enthusiasm, energy, laughter and entrepreneurial creativity. Africa is not a bad or cursed place. It's a good place where cursed and bad things happen.

The first job I did in sub-Saharan Africa was to write a piece on big game hunting in the Transvaal. I got off the little plane in the shadow of the Drakensberg Mountains and was shocked. For some ignorant reason I'd expected it to be the Serengeti: wide grassy plains with flat top acacia and koppies. This raw red tip that looked like God had gone mad with a pickaxe and had more thorns than everywhere else on earth put together, was a shock. Still wearing the clothes I'd left London in, I got into a truck with a rather sad Afrikaaner hunter. He wanted to farm his family land but as there'd been no rain for five years he was reduced to selling the sparse game that occasionally wandered in off the Kruger National Park to American dentists and German car dealers who wanted to be five-day Hemingways and had rifles that were worth more than his house.

In the back were a family of Spanish sherry heirs – a father and his three sons. They wanted an elephant and they'd paid an astronomical, non-returnable sum for it. This was their last day. They weren't happy Iberians. Every so often, they'd loose off at families of warthog that trotted through the bush in decreasing size, like families of Russian dolls. The white hunter drove with a depressed silent benevolence. Perched on the bonnet was a Shangan tracker. I'd never seen anyone with skill like his before, he could read dust as if it had motorway signs. Hunched in an army greatcoat covered in the red earth and ripped by camel thorns, he sat and tracked the elephant at 30mph. Raising a hand, we'd stop and he'd go off and squat on the earth with a cocked head. "One bull walking this way . . . he's eating . . . an hour ago." I stood beside him and saw absolutely nothing. Then he showed me the shallow shadow imprints of big feet. They emerged like magic out of the earth. Soft round pads . . . here . . . here . . . here. The Spaniards grew excited. There was a faint line like a dragged stick. "Look at that . . . tusks, huge tusks . . . to the ground." They high-fived. The tracker stood up and as he turned away said softly: "Penis." I caught his yellow malarial eye for the briefest moment. It was as blank as an eagle's. There was not the slightest intimation as to whether he was referring to the hunter or the hunted. It was a look I came to recognise in Africa.

They didn't get their elephant, which was fine by me. It crossed an invisible line into the sanctuary of the Kruger Park and stood still, slowly chewing branches. The Spaniards swore and complained in a huddle. I went and sat under a bush and drank warm Coca-Cola, my head was splitting, my back hurt: this wasn't the Stewart Granger scenario I'd been promised. The Afrikaaner walked over and standing in profile coughed: "I know what you're thinking." "You do?" "Ah, yes man . . . You're falling in love, you love this place." As a matter of fact, this was about as far from what I was thinking as it's possible to think. So I smiled. And he went on. "I can always tell. This place, this Africa, will haunt you. You'll be drawn here forever and you know why?" He wasn't looking for an answer. "Because it's where it all began. This is where we all come from. This is where we started. You've come home."

It was the longest speech I heard him make and I thought he was mad. That night as I lay in my camp bed and listened to the hyenas crunch the rubbish, I still thought he was mad. But it slowly crept up on me that he was also right.

The end of the road

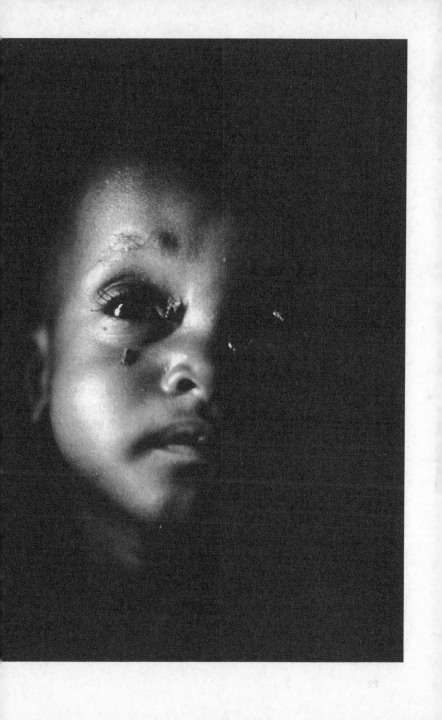

The end of the road

Sudan, May 1998

"There is no famine." Marc Hermant, the lugubrious Belgian head of mission for Médecins Sans Frontières (MSF), south Sudan programme, wipes his tired eyes and repeats himself like a patient schoolteacher explaining basic grammar to a thick nine-year-old. I am sorry, no famine? There must be a famine. "Not a Famine in Africa" isn't exactly news. I've seen the footage, it looks like a famine to me, Bob Geldof said it was a famine. "Bob Geldof said that?" Hermant gingerly sips his bright yellow mulligatawny soup. "No, what we have is a potential famine. If something isn't done now there will be famine next year." Ah, so it is the foothills of famine? The preview of famine? A promise of famine? "Yes, now is the hunger gap."

Don't you just love the hunger gap, such a great phrase? It sounds like an advertising slogan: "Mind the hunger gap", "Fill that hunger gap". One hundred years ago the hunger gap would have been familiar all over the earth. It is that lean time when the store food runs out before the harvest has ripened. In Britain, late spring was the time when it was dangerous to be young or old or alone. In Sudan, they plant with the rains, in normal years about now, and harvest in October. The hunger gap should be a month or so – nature's organic cull of the feeble and the halt and the sick and the unlucky on a species that has no natural predator but itself. This year the hunger gap has come early and the rains haven't come at all – yet. In the lexicon of professional aid, famine is a technical term. It squats darkly over the horizon, collating its misery, biding its time.

We're sitting in the terrace bar of the Norfolk Hotel in Nairobi, 500 miles from the Sudan. It is spitting rain emetically, and has been for a month. El Niño, this year's pan-global excuse for everything, suits the Norfolk, which looks like a down-at-heel Hampshire golf club, suburba-bethan: black beans and steak-and-kidney pudding, faded framed caricatures of long-dead ex-pats with smug grins and neat facial hair. In the lobby the souvenir carry-on of carved giraffes and smiley rhinos graze among the silver boxes of film crews, neatly encapsulating Africa's two great exports: anthropomorphism and bad news. The bellboy hurries back and forth, piling up the delicate technical kit and telescopic legs of investigation and concern. There are a lot of film crews here: the BBC has three; ITN has one, with another on the way. CNN and ABC and a host of others are passing through. Famine always draws a crowd.

Here's how a promise of famine works: people start to die. Charities on the ground blow the whistle, Khartoum wants to show international goodwill, so, despite a civil war, it allows strictly limited food drops. Thirty-six charities and the UN form an umbrella group called Operational Lifeline Sudan and make a deal with the guerrillas, who need to feed their soldiers, and then turn to the world media to provide the advertising. Khartoum says no one is allowed on a charity flight without its visa, which takes months, so forget it. The rebels won't allow anyone into their areas without a pass from them and they won't give it to anyone who has got a stamp from Khartoum, so the film crews have to charter their own aircraft and it is a very expensive operation. Bad news is the province of the rich. Charter prices have gone through the roof: the BBC has leased a Dakota; back home, editors are screaming about vanishing budgets, but like two bluffing poker players, ITN and the BBC won't back down. They need a story and so do the charities. Charities may work as a selfless consciousness of the world at the sharp end, but at the tin-rattling end, they exist in a deeply competitive capitalist market: an appearance by a logo and spokesman on the *News at Ten* means donations. An American religious charity went to an MSF feeding centre and put their T-shirts on the hungry kids to film them – cash in the tin back home. Someone sent a plane-load of anti-hypothermia suits made for Bosnia; ah, well, beggars can't be choosers. Brenda Barton made the front pages and the *Nine O'Clock News* in her logo T-shirt by feeding two malnourished children with her own breasts. It was a great picture. The fact that she had presumably taken up 10 stone of food space on an aid plane to transport a pair of pint-sized breasts to the starving wasn't mentioned. Nor was the horrible symbolism of a fecund European dribbling largesse over black babies, or the sensational tastelessness of flashing gravid teats in front of mothers whose own milk has dried up. "I didn't do it as a publicity stunt," she said. Barton is the press officer of the World Food Programme (WFP) and just happened upon a BBC camera crew in the biggest, emptiest country in Africa.

The journalists at the bar consider starting a charity called Lactaid and holding a red nipple day. Over the cold beers they talk about there not being enough "skellis": skeletal people. ITN coaxed an old woman into a tree to pick leaves. The humour is callous and black but it is forgivable, it is the flak jacket of people who have only their own hard-bitten cynicism to protect their dreams.

The press and charities have a mutually beneficial symbiotic relationship: hacks need the charities to find the eyebite-worthy starving; the charities need the publicity. Apart from the familiar charities there are some very weird organisations out here raising money while the sun shines. They have alarming names like Safe Harbour, A-Cross and Victims of the Martyrs. Because, at least in part, the civil war is religious: Christian and animistic south rejecting the imposition of northern Muslim law. There is an absolute prohibition on Bibles. It is a stipulation for continuing aid, but an air traffic controller at Wilson airport in Nairobi tells me she has seen American religious charities smuggling them in anyway. Now explain to me what sort of missionary zeal fills a plane with books when children are dying for milk?

Others smuggle guns, butter and psalms across the Ugandan border with the connivance of a bunch of bona fide foaming dingbats called the Lord's Resistance Army, who kidnap children, and give them Kalashnikovs and the belief that bullets can't touch them. There are rumours of CIA involvement and of links with the Tutsis. Saddam and Gaddafi have their fingers in this pie. Fifteen years of civil war, dislocation, drought, double-dealing, burnt crops and regular bouts of world amnesia have made southern Sudan a rich Petri dish for all the fungus and corruption of every conceivable form of apocalyptic, man-made misery.

Paul, the photographer, and I cadge a lift north with an ITN crew. From the air, northern Kenya could be the Scottish borders. This is *White Mischief* country, Isak Dinesen – I had a farm in Africa, the landscape of lachrymose colonial bathos and excess. But it exhausts the romance and the bedside literature to peter out into rough khaki scrub that stretches like mouldy pebbledash across the horizon. We are flying in a caravan, a squat, slow, single-engined workhorse, with a pilot who has aviator engraved on his shades. It's no comfort to be flown by someone who has to have their job description etched on their spectacles.

Bahr al Ghazal is a state twice the size of France with a population of perhaps less than a million, but no one's counting. This is where the worst of the proto-famine is. Six hours from Nairobi, it is like flying to Washington in a Morris Minor without a toilet. Tim Ewart, the ITN reporter, slowly does the *Telegraph* crossword, then gives up to read Mario Puzo (he's on page 20). Paul and I haven't got passes from the Sudanese People's Liberation Army (SPLA) guerrillas – the office in Nairobi was closed – but we are assured we can get them at the refuelling stop in Lokichokio. It's a formality, no problem. Lokichokio: crazy name, crazy place, a border town dropped in a fold in the hills between nowhere and nothing. The line that separates Kenya from Sudan is purely notional. A year ago this was a collection of huts baking in the wilderness, with a landing strip. Now it is a frontier town, a burgeoning collection of tents and hastily built breeze-block cantonments with bars and swimming pools and rooms with showers. It is a boom town, growing to service five Hercules aircraft, tied to the outside world by a thin, potholed, crumbling, rain-washed, bandit-harassed road that winds 1,000 miles to the coast at Mombasa. Everything – fuel, food, loo paper, Coca-Cola – has to be driven into Loki. This is Charityville.

In the West, we don't get to see the UN at work. We probably think it is a good idea, a bit wasteful, a bit blunt and slow. But we never get to see where all that money and effort actually goes. It goes here, into these ranks of Toyota Land Cruisers and bubbling Tarmac; and guards with walkie-talkies and gangs of black labourers, humping white sacks in the midday sun, and the pilots hanging out with a cold Coke in the Trailfinders bar. And the long lines of dusty tents, each the size of a football pitch, with the letters UN like a 20ft-high expletive painted on the sides. When this much neat charity lands on your doorstep, it changes everything: the economy, the social structure, the landscape. UN, the Ultimate Niño. Looking at Loki, it is impossible not to draw the trite conclusion that Africa has simply swapped colonialism for charity and there is very little difference. Both are buttressed with fine words, both in practice are paternalistic and divisive. It is still the white folk in the shade and the black folk humping the sacks.

There is a problem. A big problem. They won't give us a pass. The SPLA has changed the rules: it says it doesn't have authority, we've got to go back to Nairobi. "What do you want to do?" Stick here in Charityville, cadge a lift back tomorrow or the next day, then rent a plane sometime next week, or go on? "You're welcome to wing it," says Tim Ewart. "Basically, if we don't go now, there's no story." Someone says we'll risk it. Startled, I look round, what fool was that? Idiotically, it was me. As the plane takes off Paul says, "What can they do to us? Send us back?" I spend the next three uncomfortable hours thinking of all the things they can do to us. For some apparently good reason, we have left our passports behind. I am travelling across an international border into a war zone illegally, without a passport or a pass. I am going to a place that is 20 miles from the front line, that was evacuated a month ago because it was attacked by the Popular Defence Force. I don't mention the PDF, aka the Murahleen, light cavalry mercenaries employed by Khartoum to ride down the single, vulnerable railway track and do a bit of entrepreneurial terrorism on the side. They came at night, killed 200 and rustled cattle. No one has been up here since. What can they do to us? Plenty.

Suddenly I'm moved by an unarguable need to pee. There is nowhere to pee. We brought our own water (five inflated dollars a bottle from the hotel), but the bottles are still full. We land in Ajiep. I am hyperventilating with fear, the doors open and the heat greets us like a long-lost relative. "There is some bad news, I am afraid. Mawir Myok Lyal from the SSRA is here." That's bad? "That's bad." The SSRA is the political wing of the SPLA, sort of their Sinn Fein. This Lyal is Gerry Adams. That's bad. Tim Ewart says, "Look, no offence, but I don't know you, I can't risk my story." "We don't know you," says the charity worker. "We can't risk the team on the ground." Quite. "You can hide in the plane," says the pilot, "I'll fly you back." A court martial is better than another six hours in this thing. Sod it, at least I am going to stand in Sudan. Secretary Lyal is sitting at a roughly made table under a shade-tree. He is surrounded by lieutenants in T-shirts and bits of fatigued militaria. One bloke has a baseball cap that advertises *Men in Black*. Lyal is precisely what Central Casting would have ordered for *The Wild Geese*: imposing, cunning, tough. AA Gill, *Sunday Times*, London. There has been a bit of a mix-up, I'm afraid. I shake his hand with a firm confidence and squat at his feet, cod psychology. He opens his mouth to reply, but he hasn't got any front teeth and it rather spoils the effect. Have we got any identification, he lisps. I give him my press card. He examines it, flips it over and reads, "If found, please hand this card in at the nearest police station." Pauses for a moment. "Okay, you can stay, I'll fix it." Manfully, I restrain myself from French kissing his hand.

We look round for the first time. Nothing prepares you for mass starvation, for the promise of famine. Or rather, everything prepares you for it, years of photographs and terse newsreel, skimmed journalism, accusing posters and award-winning photographs. They all prepare you for it, but none of them protects you from the truth of it. The terrible, terrible, pitiful shock of it. It is not staring at the face of starvation that thuds like a blow to your heart, it is having starvation stare back at you. All our lives, we've examined these people and swallowed the lump, turned the page, been quietly moved, but protected by the one-way mirror of news. We have averted our eyes to the grinning photos of our own plump children framed on the mantel, and felt the shaming relief of the uninvolved. Nothing protects you from the quiet scrutiny of a thousand fly-blown, bloodshot, liver-yellow, starving eyes, and nothing protects you from the smile of welcome. What have the Dinka got to smile about?

Ajiep is where the buck finally stops. Having been passed from hand to mouth around the world it comes to rest in the shade of a thorn tree in this dry, hot earth. Here, finally, is that mythological, nursery tea-time place: "Remember all the starving people in Africa." This is what we left on the side of our plates. Here is the end of the longest queue in the world. "The people less fortunate than yourself." When the Dinka look round, there is no one behind them. They are refugees in their own land wandering in an arid, featureless plain, waiting for famine to organise its paperwork.

Technically this isn't a famine because the starvation is only patchy. Some of the Dinka, one of the three main tribes of southern Sudan, are less malnourished than others, but the hunger gap is working overtime. Ajiep is the worst any of the aid workers have seen. There has been no food here for a month. Lifeline Sudan flies its Hercules in broad circles over the area days before food drops. In this land without electricity or even the last century's communications, it is the semaphored signal for people to start walking. They walk enormous distances in an oppressive heat that makes every foot feel like a yard. Through a bush so bereft of natural features, I am lost within 50 paces; they do it carrying their children and with barely any water. We have to drink eight litres a day to avoid dehydration, but the Dinka carry only little carved cups around their necks and sip occasionally. The hardiness is beyond anything you have ever seen on a sports field or running track. And nothing can protect you from their awful beauty.

You couldn't have chosen a more handsome tribe to starve to death: they are tall and rangy, blue-black with high cheeks and broad foreheads with beautiful chevrons scarred on their brows. They wear elegant earrings and bracelets and simple silver crosses; the men carry orchid-leaf-bladed spears and stripling-thin cattle whips. They wear a mixture of swathed and swagged traditional togas and cast-off Oxfam rags. The young girls seem to like slips and nighties, and the mixture of beads and silver and silk petticoats in faded pastels disconcertingly makes them look like this year's Paris catwalk. Everyone moves with a slow grace. The Dinka are incapable of doing anything without a poised elegance. They arrange their limbs with fluid ease; you are always being drawn to the curve of a neck or the etiolated fingers cupping a child's head. They gather in tableaux, like Renaissance frescoes with occasional splashes of cerulean from the men's jellabas.

ITN go off in search of "skellis" and tree-climbing grannies, wrapping their poor-taste cynicism around them like a mackintosh against a storm of pity. I walk to the children's feeding centre, a collection of grass huts, where young mothers sit in the sun cradling their infants. The starving children are beyond words. They lie limp and exhausted in the young women's laps, eyes half-closed, limbs like so much kindling. Most are silent, and occasionally tears streak the dusty-sallowed cheeks, attracting the constant flies. Inside the longest hut in the stifling dark a French nurse tersely and efficiently logs the proximity of death. She does a MUAC test (middle upper arm circumference), where a calibrated circle of card is placed around the child's upper arm and slid tight. It is coloured green, yellow, orange and red. The orange section means the child is at risk, the red means the child needs therapeutic feeding. The circle is the size of an expensive cigar. She measures weight for height: children who have fallen to 70% of body weight are given supplementary rations. At 60%, they are kept at the centre and fed milk eight times a day under supervision. There are five-month-old babies who weigh the same as they did at birth. An infant who is 60% of body weight looks virtually dead. The fragile signs of life flicker like a guttering candle. Their skulls and joints are perfectly drawn through their baggy skins. The hair is as parched and sparse as an old man's, slitted eyes glint through well-like sockets. They exist from moment to moment, small bird-like gnarled hands resting on exhausted breasts. "A western child wouldn't live two days in this condition," the nurse says. "Here, the ones we can feed have a 90% chance of surviving. The transformation over a month is miraculous. They are very resilient, but of course they may have less resistance to illness later." Measles and diarrhoea are famine's little helpers.

She has seen 815 children under five: 167 are moderately malnourished by African standards, 404 badly and 234 severely. The centre works on a 5% higher threshold than anywhere else on the continent, otherwise they would be overwhelmed. All through the bush the Dinka are walking, moving in straggling lines to converge on an open, treeless plain where the food drop will be distributed. In normal days they are pasturalists who plant single subsistence crops and herd cattle. Cattle to the Dinka aren't food, they are everything. They're money, property, holidays, shops, golf clubs, arcades, multiplex cinemas, trips to the pub, walks in the park. A wife costs about 40 cows and five bulls. Cattle are life. And now they are eating them, or they are being stolen and shot. If someone took away your home, your income, and set you on the street in your pyjamas, you would still live in a place that was functioning and solid, in a society that doesn't even count hunger as a measure of poverty. Without their cattle, the Dinka have less than nothing. If these young people want to be homeless together, it has to be on tick, on the promise of future calves.

A gaggle of girls walk beside me, straight backs and high breasts. They move with an easy, undulating rhythm. Little plumes of dust are kicked up by their feet. They giggle and whisper to each other, as cool and direct and blushingly unnerving as any group of pretty teenagers. They flirt. Nobody prepares you for flirting in a famine. While there is life, there is still living. One strides close and does a rolling lumpen imitation of my gait, and her friends bridle and shimmy in peals of laughter. With long, strong fingers, she touches her heart and then her lips and gives me a glowing white smile.

On the plain the Dinka line up in a milling band. They stretch across the horizon like a David Lean panning shot. Facing them 200 yards away are the neat files of white sacks containing split peas and maize, each attended by companies of askari. Standing on a pile of food, a fat WFP officer with a plastic water bottle over his shoulder shouts orders and waves a fly whisk: a martinet that is depressingly familiar all over Africa. Small boys, self-important with red rags of office tied to their wrists, dart back and forth, prodding women with cattle sticks. This is the lottery of life, the rough end of charity. Not everyone will be fed. And considering its mortal importance, the choosing is remarkably good-natured. The sacks are broken open and each divided between nine women: they fill their calabashes with pulses and tear up the plastic to make bundles to put on their heads.

Each of these little groups comes from one village – the women are responsible for the food but the head man chooses who will be fed. There is a lot of shouting and gesticulating, and the process is meticulous and desperately slow. But the Dinka have nowhere else to be. They stand in the hot sun and wait: it is not so much stoical or fatalistic as a worn-out realism. Each of the women carries a small brush made from sticks to sweep the spilled grain. They are loaded with 28 days' subsistence and, balanced as finely as tight-rope walkers, they slowly move off into the bush, their small, naked children trailing behind. They will return to their villages if they still exist, or find a spot under a tree. An aid worker says, "I wonder what those women have to do to be chosen and how much of that food goes to the army." As the interminable business grinds on, I lie in the shadow of a termite hill with a group of men. They smile and nod. I hand out the last of my cigarettes, we sit for ten companionable minutes, watching. The choosing and reject-ing, the spilling of seed. There is a light touch on my shoulder, and a man about my age in a shirt that is just dirty ribbons, with bony elbows and ribs like the ruts in a baked road, leans forward and smiles. The taut parchment skin wrinkles over his cheeks, his eyes are the colour of weak tea. He holds out the little gourd that is slung round his neck: would I like a drink? It is a small epiphany of sorts, to be offered hospitality from the very back of the earth's queue. Think of all the starving in Africa. It was as if the Good Samaritan had been offered succour by the man overtaken by thieves, and it was the most gravely humbling gesture. I was glad to be wearing sunglasses. I didn't trust myself to speak, just shook my head and dragged deeply on my cigarette.

Biblical analogies come easily here, the exodus of the Dinka, the flight across the desert, the ancient heroic look of them, a chosen people. Every so often a flash of metal spikes the eye: invariably it is a silver cross. Unbidden, I remember the Sermon on the Mount. I never thought I would actually see it played out quite so literally or with such grace. "Ye are the salt of the earth." "Sufficient unto the day is the evil thereof."

I was dreading dinner: how do you eat in a promise of famine? Actually, it is not difficult; not to eat would be a silly act of self-mortification. And we are hungry. The relief camp was a collection of little tents set behind a low palisade of thorn bushes; on the other side the starving stood and watched as we shared out the contents of bags: trail mix, repellent muesli bars, apples, chicken legs, packed lunch from the Norfolk Hotel with weirdly surreal lamb sandwiches cut into triangles that Paul said reminded him of childhood. There was a bit of rather good boiled goat. ITN provided a bottle of whisky and told with glee of the American network crew who had set up a grand tent with an awning and a collapsible dining table, napery and candles, and toasted each other with claret while the Dinka stood in a silent circle. It was the French nurse's birthday: she slumped exhausted into a chair and ate a boiled egg. When next you hear someone talk sneeringly about the high moral ground, remember the field workers of MSF, the only charity to have staff actually living in Bahr al Ghazal. These are volunteers who work because MSF pays the lowest subsistence salaries of any international charity, not despite it. Who have to be rotated every two months because no one can bear it for longer but who sometimes have to because they can't be pulled out. Who have to sleep in their shoes with a water bottle because their camp may be overrun. Because if you do find yourself living at the very pinnacle of the high moral ground, there are any number of people who would slit your throat for a moral and a watch.

We turn in. I haven't brought a tent so I lie under a mosquito net. Sleeping out in the African bush under a sickle moon is one of the most awe-inspiring experiences – as long as you have a choice, of course. Men have lain here in the hot wind looking at the stars for as long as there have been men. This is where we come from, this swathe of thin earth, brittle grass and thorn stretching from the Rift Valley to the filigree marshes at the source of the Blue Nile. This is our ancestral home. The sour-sweet smoky body smell of Africa drifts on the breeze. The cooking fires of the Dinka flicker like earthed comets. There is a sound of crickets and a distant drumming and the exhausted wailing of hungry children. And the temazepam-induced snores of an ITN reporter. Just as I was dozing off I turned over and came face to face with a wild beast. I made a noise not unlike a stuck heifer. The bone-questing dog and I were frightened in equal measure. Paul in the fastness of his tent laughed so hard his film rattled.

Southern Sudan is the line in the sand where Arab and black Africa meet, but it is also the place where the First World, north world, blue-eyed haves meet the Third World, south world, dark-eyed have-nots. It is the front line, the raw edge of our conscience.

I had expected to feel guilty, angry, horrified and depressed, and in varying degrees, I am. But the abiding sense is one of dignity. The dignity of a Dinka standing patiently in the sun and the workers who risk so much to help them. It is not that suffering is dignified, it is that here the fat and panoply of life is stripped away to reveal a fragile but resilient shared humanity. When I got home, I tried to explain to my young daughter where I had been and what I had seen. "Are they dying?" she asked. Yes. "Where do they bury them?" Where do we bury them? In Monday's rubbish, in the commercial break, in the turned page and the changed subject in Sunday lunch and under the prune stones on the side of your plate.

In the grey light before dawn I woke and saw a line of women pass silently in single file with calabashes on their heads going to collect water from the muddy hollows of a drying river. They looked like so many ghosts. As the sun rose it caught the shadows of a thousand bare footprints in the dust. A mother was washing her son. He stood in an enamel basin, his arms raised, and gently, with a tin cup and infinite tenderness, she sloughed the dust off him. In the golden light, he glowed and shone like the child in an icon.

Out of their element

The Kalahari, January 1998

The great thing about the Kalahari is that it hates you. It doesn't have a welcome mat or a lei to drape over your shoulders or a glass of complimentary sangria. It doesn't have a hospitable grin or an information centre or translation earphones or a scenic walk. Between you, me and the vultures, the Kalahari loathes us. It makes no bones about it, or, rather, it does make bones about it. It is not generic, you understand, it is personal.

It wants you dead. In the Kalahari the only good tourist is an ex-tourist and there are plenty of good old boys that could do a lot with your corpse. Apart from all the usual Attenborough things that are waiting to mug you, there are hordes of ingenious little fellows eager to turn you into a resource. Ticks that can lay dormant for a decade underground and, catching a whiff of your carbon dioxide, emerge to suck you dry. Spiders the size of a fingernail that can turn your leg into an agonising black bolster, a beetle that has a binary arsenal in its bottom and can deliver a payload of boiling acid. And there are more thorns here than anywhere else on earth. Things with thorns have thorns on their thorns and they all have poison tips. Everything has a unique and ingenious and unambiguous way of telling you to sod off. Forget all that slow-motion-sunset in-touch-with-your-spirit Van der Post nonsense, there is no romance here. The Kalahari is an amoral, unregulated market force, a pure vicious capitalism practised by professionals. I love it here. I love it as the last truly honest place on earth.

"Owing to local custom, we don't wash underwear," said the footnote on the laundry list in my tent. Now you see this is the sort of tradition you want, a timeless prohibition on wringing out strangers' smalls. In the mists of time, some wise man called together the tribe and said, "Look, in a few thousand years, strange pale men will arrive wearing Calvin Klein tanga briefs, just don't have anything to do with them."

Twenty hours ago, I got on a huge aeroplane with a thousand other people at Heathrow and flew to Johannesburg, then got on a smaller plane with half a hundred people and flew to Muan in Botswana, and then on to a tiny plane with just God, a girlfriend and the pilot, who had thighs like hippopotamus babies, and we flew to the big tree on the left in the middle of the Kalahari desert. Botswana is the flattest country in the world; if Dolly Parton lay on her back in Botswana, she would be a triangulation point.

San Camp squats in a reef of palm at the edge of the world. I am sitting on my canvas chair holding the laundry list. There is that delicious moment where your clothes, eyes and ears are still tuned into concourses and crowds and the 20th century, but your skin knows you are somewhere else, the weird sense of being suspended between two utterly different places. And this place could not be more different from everywhere. The camp is the Stewart Granger Memorial Collection of 1940s safari tents, with no running water or electricity but with four-poster beds and mosquito' nets and cambric sheets and bucket showers and paraffin lamps and butlers. Through the tent flaps I can see the Makgadikgadi Pans run over the horizon like the mother of all Norfolk beaches.

This is one of the least-known places on earth. It is still a black hole. When it rains, three million flamingos live here, the biggest, pinkest migration of Barbara Cartland wannabes on earth. But now it is dry and nothing lives here for hundreds of miles, and it is why I came. You can see the curve of the earth here. Turn 360° and nothing crosses the eye but the bowl of the sky. It is the nothingness that attracts. This is God's own minimalism.

The best way to get across the saltpan is to fly like the kites and the crows, otherwise it is a quad bike. Fat-wheeled two-man lawnmower things. And you need kit. Kit is very important on holiday. This is the best. You have to cover yourself completely. The cocktail of sun and salt can flay you and peel your eyes like a blind grape, so we looked like crosses between Lawrence of Arabia and Mad Max. It is a vast style improvement on beach wear or ghastly Babygro ski wear.

We set off early in convoy, four bikes carrying bedrolls, food and water, a long-range desert patrol driving Indian-fashion. This is low-impact trespass. You leave as little behind you as possible.

We are guided by Ralph Bousfield, who owns the camp. He is the guide straight from Central Casting by way of Mills & Boon, a fifth-generation white African; all his ancestors were wanderers, explorers and hunters, and washed their own underwear. His father holds one of the few Guinness world records that Roy Castle didn't attempt: shooting 43,000 crocodiles. Ralph has lived here in the bush since he was three. He smoulders like a cross between Daniel Day-Lewis and an Ibiza deckchair attendant, and has an unsentimental awe and as deep a knowledge of this place as anyone. It is winningly half western-scientific and half bushman-folklore.

The Makgadikgadi was once a great inland sea. Around its edges are incongruous dunes of seashells, thousands of miles from any coast. Neolithic axes, arrows and scrapers glint blackly on the crest. There is the clock-stopping *frisson* of picking up something that was last touched 10,000 years ago by a man who looked over the horizon and could not imagine that his chipping this flint would lead to jumbo jets and skyscrapers. Holding the arrowhead somehow closes the circle. There are also tiny beads here, glass and stone and ostrich shell that the bushmen have used as decoration for thousands of years. Some of them are Phoenician and Roman and even Chinese; beads were currency for salt. The salt cakes that glisten like icing sugar on the pan have been traded by the red people – the bushmen – for millennia.

We bowl across the scorched earth. As the day heats up, the mirages swim and eddy. Topiaried bay trees appear to hang above shimmering lakes – actually families of ostriches. We pass flocks of swallows that fly in ragged formation in bas-relief on the parched earth, and perfectly preserved in salt where they fell to earth with exhaustion. Past the elephant tracks that walk in a circle and then enigmatically disappear, past the skulls of zebra and on and on. You can open the throttle and close your eyes and travel Zen-like, knowing there is nothing to crash into until you fall off the edge of the earth.

There are small epiphanies to be had, sudden revelations of the true nature of our place on the wheel of things. Here you lose contact with time, space and direction. You hum along, travelling without perceptively moving, while all the power and conceit of commerce and position evaporate, the delicate network of friends and plans and diaries, all the human hierarchy of achievement and aspiration ebb away.

As the sun begins to drop, we see a smudge on the horizon – Kubu island. This is what we have come to see, a granite fist in the flatness. It rises like a green baroque elfin city. I have seen few things in this life that are well and truly awesome. Kubu island is one. Filigreed with baobab trees like fat red ballet dancers bigger than buses, older than God – well, older than Christ. The place is a natural wonder that beggars both wonder and any received concept of what's natural. It has been the holiest secret of the Kalahari bushmen for longer than anyone knows, a place of power and ritual. Kubu is suspended from heaven, above the crisp linen earth, or perhaps it is just a 1970s record cover from a bad Dungeons and Dragons band.

The camp boys have got here before us; a cauldron of water bubbles for the shower suspended from a tree. The dining table is set and the drinks tray, with Beefeater, and Georgian fobs on bottle labels, stands waiting. Our bedrolls have been arranged on the high places and there is this goat.

I asked for the goat, a young goat, not a kid but under a year. It is tethered to a tree, a rangy, brindled, flop-eared, devil-eyed billy that could have been a regimental mascot. This goat is so old it remembers colonialism. The smiling cook produces a knife that you couldn't cut atmosphere with, it is blunter than a head butt. I get out a Swiss army knife that has a bit of an edge. Killing, skinning and butchering a bad-tempered goat the size of a healthy Shetland pony with a Swiss army knife is not something I suggest you try at home. There is a lot of laughter and joking and blood splattering. Finally, by torchlight, I take a twitching haunch, cover it with rock salt and smear it with wild sage, and we've got dinner.

As the last of the sun departed for South America, clouds began to appear in the east, piled on top of each other. Like an angry cook spooning mashed potato, they rose and rose until the stratospheric winds whipped and flattened their tops into the characteristic tropical anvil nimbus. Storm clouds. But it was too early for rain, far too early. Round the camp fire, someone joked that killing a goat was trepidatious, hubris in such a holy and mystical place. We went to bed and lay and watched the stars that the bushmen believe are the camp fires of their ancestors. We smelt the evaporating heat and dust of the pan, cosy with hot-water bottles and down pillows.

The first thick drops fell at about midnight. The next six hours were the most terrifying of my life. That is not a relative statement, it is an absolute. If you have never been in a tropical thunderstorm, forget everything you know about rain, it is not the same phenomenon. European rain is flushing a loo compared to Niagara. The storm cleared its throat across the pan and then broke directly overhead, the thunder and lightning simultane-ously strobing and crashing. The water hissed and sang like a fusillade of rifles. The fear started as trepidation with a side order of concern that you could see off with a dose of common sense and half-remembered school physics. The bedroll flooded and the person I was with sobbed, and the crack and flash zigzagged hour after hour, echoing through the towers of rock. I saw the faces of my children flashing on the back of my screwed-up eyes and wondered if I would hear the bolt that fried me. I knew, and I wished I didn't, that granite is conductive rock with an unhealth-ily high metal content, and this place was the highest point for hundreds and hundreds of miles. There was nowhere to run, nowhere to hide.

My bowels, which for days had been cast in stone, decided they needed to do what the rest of me couldn't, and evacuate. Let me tell you that squatting naked, like a gargoyle on the roof of Chartres, with terrified diarrhoea is an image that will leach into my nightmares until I join the goat. The pan was lit up in faltering jags as if by an omnipotent arc welder. The baobabs ululated and leapt. Shards of light danced as if the sky was shattering crystal. It went on and on and on, lulling, then thundering down again. Slowly, though, the storm ebbed, the lightning exhausted itself and was put back in the box, and the wind rose, keening like a vixen.

The relief was like the end of an awful disaster movie. The sopping discomfort, a blissfully welcome token of life. We lay and hugged each other, teeth chattering, until the false dawn gingerly broke over the crags. I have no embarrassment in saying that I prayed with a more heartfelt fervour than I devoutly hope I ever have to again. Unfortunately, it was probably to the wrong god.

As the pan slowly heated up, and somehow the boys managed to make breakfast, and the rest of our crew emerged, we laughed with relief and I had the silly urge to shave with a mirror propped on a rock. I smiled at the face in the mirror, scraped at the pepper-and-salt stubble, and gave myself a very close shave.

On the way back, we stopped to collect salt. Under the thick layer of crystal, families of small beetles scurried. How could they possibly live here in salt? The beetles are tiny, resilient, lonely, a single-species ecosystem. I put a couple in a film box and brought them back to London.

I spent a happy day collecting dung (hyenas' is white, aardvarks' is made up entirely of termite heads) and watching love beetles, which looked like pairs of Tiffany earrings and marched around joined at the groin in permanent coitus. We ate snot apples, disgusting bushman treats that fill your mouth with slimy, vaguely fruity, viscous gob as if a sheep with influenza had sneezed in your mouth. And there is the letterbox tree, the biggest tree in southern Africa, a point of reference for hundreds of miles. Among the names of the first white explorers carved in its multiple trunks, you can just make out Livingstone. We went tracking with the bushmen. They follow invisible spore with the assurance of traffic wardens walking down Piccadilly, and become the animals they track. "Here are three lions. Mother, two young, one male, one female. They haven't eaten." I'm sorry, why am I following hungry lions just as it is getting dark?

The Kalahari is a place of extremes and metaphor and allegory, it shuffles your deck, rearranges the cerebral furniture, messes up your priorities. It is the perfect unrest cure.

Back in London, I took the beetles to the Natural History Museum. They knew the species – *Pogonus* – but the beetle does not have a specific name. We don't know how it lives or what it eats or why it is there. It will probably get into the collection in about 50 years or so. They could call it Gill's condiment bug, but I think I'd rather they named it the "God, I know how you feel" beetle.

Game boy

Tanzania, January 1998

The Serengeti: under the lowering anvil nimbus, electric storms stutter on the horizon. The shimmering burnt-orange African sun plummets, a hot wind sways the social weavers' intricately constructed nests in the whistling thorn. The heavy air vibrates with the cooing of doves and the creaking-gate single note of the tropical boubou. High above, a pair of bateleur eagles catching a lazy late thermal precariously balance like their eponymous tightrope walkers. And over the undulating dry surf of grassland the game teems.

It teems and it teems. It teems from left to right and from right to left. It teems up and it teems down and it teems round and round until you are dizzy with teeming. Will this damn teeming never stop? The Serengeti game is divided into two teams: those that eat and those that are eaten. It is one enormous game of kiss-chase with biting. If you only know Africa from the television, then this is the Africa you know. This is Attenborough country. The gnarly buzzcut acacias, the purple sky, the oily, pustulant sun that slides across the horizon, truncating the evening into 20 minutes of the most exotically beautiful light on earth.

The Serengeti stretches from northern Tanzania across the border into Kenya. This is where the annual migration of wildebeest takes place. Animals following the rains, pulling all the mint-sauce teams behind them. Wildebeest are God's extras. Individually, they are odd, humpy creatures with long, mournful faces that seem to be continually muttering "Nobody knows the trouble I seen" under their breaths; collectively on the move at a stiff-legged canter, they are one of the great wonders of the world, making the Serengeti Cecil B De Mille Africa. A wildebeest's only defence against the cruel market forces of a carnivorous world is statistics. There are so many of us, chances are it won't be me. They even arrange to calve all at the same time in the same place, providing the lions and hyenas with the largest canapé smorgasbord in the world. Wildebeest are nature's proof that communism works, it's just not much fun. Their bones litter the plains.

The great grey-green greasy Grumeti river, all set about with fever trees, runs through the heart of the Serengeti. It is home to turgid pods of hippo and crocodile you could land small planes on. Each big enough to make a set of luggage that would comfortably take Joan Collins on a world cruise. Hippos look and sound like the House of Commons. Fat, self-satisfied gents with patronising smirks and fierce pink short-sighted eyes in wrinkled grey suits going "haw-haw" and telling each other dirty jokes. They sit like backbenchers in their soupy tearooms and defecate copiously, lifting their vast buttocks out of the water and spinning their tails like Magimixes. At night you lie awake and listen to them chunter and canvass outside the tent.

The Ngorongoro crater is the other place you'll know if you've only been to Africa by armchair. Seven thousand feet up, it is a volcano crater with more microclimates than you can shake a meteorologist at. A perfect soup bowl of game. In fact, Ngorongoro is Africa's Mount Olympus of game. Purists with breath you could use for snakebite serum of the Outward Bound knit-your-own-bullet school tend to roll their malarial yellow eyes and harrumph like warthog farts at the mention of Ngorongoro, bellowing that it is Disneyland Soho on a Saturday night, St Tropez in July. And they have a point. It is the beaten trail. But then, imagine a life lived never having seen Disneyland or Soho or St Tropez and then double it and double it again. The Ngorongoro crater fair takes your breath away. It is a spectacle. It makes *The Lion King* look like a song and dance. This is the real thing.

You *will* see a lot of other Toyota safari trucks. But the view at sunrise from Crater Lodge perched on the lip of the volcano silences all criticism. And visitors too are part of a safari's rich ecology. Crater Lodge looks like Portmeirion designed by Danny La Rue and Puccini. A fabulously camp camp, a collection of individual ethnic *petit palaces* on stilts, where you get your own butler, savanna beds, a log fire and rose petals in your bath. It is the natural home of one of Africa's most ubiquitous and photographed denizens, the honeymoon couple. I could sit and watch honeymooners for hours. They are endlessly fascinating and rewarding. The main reward being that I will never ever have to be one of them again. Africa is a perfect postnuptial ecosystem. It has danger, nature, adventure and the Tiffany of night skies. All the subliminal triggers for a really good "Me Tarzan, You Jane" sex life. For newlyweds, this is as good as having sex gets. A brief two weeks of libidinous malaria (sweating and shaking). Nothing in the world makes you feel younger, more alive, more fecund and vigorously, expansively free than other people's honeymoons in Africa.

The problem, and it is a problem with safaris, is that many tourists get to see Africa, experience Africa, fire off enough film to garland an amphitheatre to prove that they've done Africa, but never actually set foot in Africa. They step from camp/lodge to converted long-wheelbased Land Rover without ever getting dust on their new Gore-Tex safari boots. Viewed from a truck, it is all as real and special and awe-inducing as most north-world people could ever want.

But looking through a window frame stutters the image into being a sort of stamp-collecting. You go in search of things: the big five (lion, elephant, leopard, rhino and cape buffalo), a kill, a view. You find yourself asking endless questions like "What's the gestation period of a Thomson gazelle?" "How far in kilometres will a hyena walk at night?" as if you are swotting for a Third World pub quiz. You record and tick things off in the anecdote album. Getting out and walking is a whole other thing altogether, the snapshots allied into a great rolling panorama. You stop being an invisible, omnipotent observer and take your place as part of it. Both watcher and watched. Stalker and stalked. Meet it eye to eye. Danger is a big part of Africa's turn-on. Travellers love travellers' tales. The most commonly asked question is "Will it eat me?" And the guides have endless routines of blood-clotting stories. It's all fun, but it misses the point. In the wildebeest's statistics of danger, Africa is no more risky than most cities at night. "Will that bus eat me?" "Yes, if you stand in front of it."

You either get the point of Africa or you don't. What draws me back year after year is that it's like seeing the world with the lid off. You can see the works, the intricate engineering, that fantastically complex and beautiful series of cogs and wheels and springs and checks and balances that makes the globe work. Africa makes sense of all that ecology-biodiversity-sustainable-habitat stuff that sounds so like the special pleading of socially inept, bearded weirdies when applied to a field in back-garden Britain. Here it has the depth and grace of a religious conviction.

So if you want to walk, you must, simply must go to the Selous, an area the size of Denmark, the largest untouched reserve in the world, named after the greatest of all white hunters, a mythic figure who was the basis for Allan Quartermain. It is a vast area of thorn and cliff and sand and jungle, bisected and filigreed by the Rufiji river that runs through sand and cuts a new course after the rains every year, leaving behind lakes and deep gorges fringed with doum palms. Here is the world's largest collection of hippo, of crocodile and elephant. It is home to some of the last wild black rhino and the biggest packs of wild dog. Seen from the Sand Rivers camp on a bluff of sandstone, the river glides through a view that remains perfect and pristine for a decade of million years. You can camp out under mosquito nets on a dry river bed and listen to the great game being played out in the inky shadows thrown by a moon as bright as a Wembley floodlight. You can count shooting stars around the ironwood fire. You can travel up rapids on little flat-bottomed boats, being chased by bull hippos like furious tugs, and cast for fearsomely aggressive tiger fish while watching for crocodiles, being both fisherman and bait. Or walk quietly and with the pounding heart of a peeping tom to watch elephants bathing. You can be one of the pitifully few people who have ever seen wild dog, the painted wolves of Africa, dappled patchwork resting in the shade of an acacia. Don't think of any of this as frightening. It's exciting. And if this all sounds like Mills & Boon travel writing, then I make no apology. I don't know how to impart enthusiasm other than enthusiastically. But if you imagine it's all too purple to be true, then fine. Stay at home. Nobody would be happier than me.

For westerners, Africa is a place that happens despite Africans. In all the yearning literature this place has spawned, the only indigenous characters are servants and bearers and extras – and that's shaming. This is the one continent where travellers rarely say they want to meet the natives. Africans themselves spend precious little time enjoying or worrying about their game. The only giraffe most of them have time to care about is on their banknotes. But Tanzania in particular is a fantastically friendly and interesting human place, lively and complex. To come here and see only wilderness and animals is to see only half the story. In one-street towns there is an entrepreneurial imagination and energy that beggars Silicon Valley.

Stone Town is the main town of Zanzibar, the Muslim island that was the centre of the Arab slave trade. Zanzibar is the island of cloves and ivory and it is where Livingstone and the other Victorian explorers began their treks into the mapless nothing. Built out of coral, the winding streets and courtyarded houses feel more North African than sub-Saharan. I sat in the English church that was built on the old slave market with the altar directly above its whipping post and listened to Anglican evensong in Swahili, "The Old Rugged Cross" sung with that unmistakable mournful, soft sound of African voices.

Mnemba Island, off the coast of Zanzibar, isn't actually Africa at all. It belongs to that other world of travel-brochure covers. I have never been anywhere that so completely encompasses every dream of the perfect desert island. You can walk round it in 20 minutes. It has just ten huts hidden in jungle. There is a bar and frankly miraculous food served on the beach by candlelight. It is always in the sunny 90s, but the coral-white sand never gets hot. The sea is the colour of Paul Newman's eyes, and there is a reef within doggy-paddling distance. Nothing in the place stings or bites, and there are more laid-back staff than punters. All you ever wear is a *kukoi*, a sort of grown-up's nappy. Indeed you regress into it. After flopping about for three days, I'd unstressed into a five-year-old. I became a gurgling, smiley, supine, oily lump of wants and simple desires, moving from sun to shade like a happy, nutbrown maggot. Snorkelling over tropical coral reef is exactly like watching the cartoon channel with the sound turned down. Weightless, intellectually neutral colour and movement. In the other huts the sated honeymooners done Tarzanning in the bush lazily played mummies and daddies. In the eaves, doves' coos beat the intro over and over. The tune preyed in the back of my memory. What was it? "The Mighty Quinn"? No. "Here We Go round the Mulberry Bush"? No. Finally I got it. It was "Swinging Safari".

I don't know what makes you angry . . .

Uganda, October 2000

Nowhere wakes up with a greater sense of optimism than Africa. Good morning, Africa is one miraculous experience. The sun arrives bright and smiley as a kid's magician, there's none of the somnambulant slow-fade greyness of the north. A fresh gold light slants through the palms and acacias. The air is clear, the dust gauze and thermal shimmy are still a few hours away, the country glows with a new-minted radiance.

The early-morning sounds of Africa: kung-fu cockerels straining to out-crow each other, frantic weaver birds in the thorn tree like an immigrant tenement, mnemonic doves, bleating, hungry goats, chuckling children being bathed in tin buckets, men coughing and spitting into shards of mirror to shave outside daub-and-thatch huts, radios searching the static for distant news and Mali pop songs. Gaggling women at the wheezing water pump filling the first of interminable four-gallon plastic cans, and the smell, that most evocative essence of this bright continent: hardwood smoke, hard-work sweat, animal fat and the yawning breath of the hard red earth. Nowhere starts each day with more hope than Africa. Or needs to.

Uganda, the garden of Africa, is a shock of greenery. Compared with its neighbours across Lake Victoria, Kenya and Tanzania and Sudan in the north, it's a revelation of fecundity. Everything grows. Lean too long on a walking stick and it sprouts. Travelling north, you cross a faintly familiar patchwork of fields, a rare sub-Saharan glimpse of promised bounty. Up in the corner, where the country marches with Congo and Sudan, the cash crop is tobacco. Strip farmers' plots are mixed with maize, cassava, potatoes, bananas and leafy green vegetables that only have indigenous, sonorous names. In the margins of fields are tethered shiny, fat goats; chickens and ducks peck at the earth.

Every family steading of low, thatched huts has its own broad, shady mango tree. The fruit is small, sun-coloured, dizzyingly sweet. On its smiling face, Uganda is the African dream, a self-sufficient mixed agrarian economy, but it's only skin-deep. In its short independence, it has also been cursed with a brace of top-of-the-range monsters. Even by Africa's unimpeachably high standards, Milton Obote and Idi Amin stand in a class of their own. But progress is all relative, and after years of terror, pillage, civil war, invasion and the nightmarish buffet of bones there is now a sense of stability, a fragile hope for peace.

I'm in Omugo, a one-street town. There's a hospital, a collection of half-finished, half-started grass-roof barracks that is the town's biggest building and the biggest employer. As well as being a vegetative Eden, Uganda is also a medical theme park that can send the pulse racing and the temperature soaring. The hot, damp climate incubates some really world-class illnesses. There are, of course, the old rollercoaster favourites – malaria, TB, river blindness, and a comprehensive selection of parasites – and there's something for the kiddies: measles and diarrhoea to keep infant mortality rates right up there, and poliomyelitis, the experience that stays with you for life. But what really draws the enthusiastic pathology tourist to this corner of the continent are the specialist haemopathic diseases: Ebola and Marburg disease, the Ferrari and Lamborghini of sickness. You go from feeling fine to repulsive death within days, something that in the rest of the big-girl's-blouse world only toxins can do. An outbreak of Marburg will bring private jets from medical centres in the United States to Africa, then executive helicopters up into the bush, carrying men in all-in-one, head-to-toe anti-contamination suits breathing bottled American oxygen. Hell, it's not just don't drink the water, it's don't breathe the goddam African air.

Fearlessly they'll go right up to the no-hope, infectious poor bastards whose internal organs have turned to sludge and who are bleeding from every orifice, crying blood, and who, as a finale, will ooze claret through their pores. The First World billion-dollar experts delicately swab for souvenirs, seal them in nitrogen-cool attaché cases, and then get back on the whirlybird and go home to Atlanta or Boston in time for breakfast and some really thrilling, reputation-making research. They're thoughtful eco-disaster tourists, so they leave nothing behind except a rubber-gloved wave. Not even an Elastoplast.

And there's the big one, the crowd puller, the disease that made Uganda famous, an immoral dictator that beggars the puny efforts of Amin: Big Slim.

Aids. Africa is where it all started, it is the Wembley, the St Andrews, the Grand Ole Opry of sexually transmitted diseases. Aids has been granted the greatest accolade medical science can accord. It's officially a pandemic. And they got it here first. Actually, Uganda is now the only sub-Saharan country where HIV infection rates are falling, thanks to an open, energetic campaign of public health and precious little help from the rest of us. But Omugo's hospital doesn't deal with any of that good stuff. They see plenty, but this is a monogamous, one-disease institution.

Sleeping sickness. Look, I'm sorry, I know that's not sexy, not very cutting-edge. Nobody asks you to a ball for sleeping sickness, pert celebrities aren't wearing tight "wake up to sleeping sickness" T-shirts, there's no sleeping-sickness ribbon to pin with pride. Partly that's the fault of the name. You say: "Oh, do they just get drowsy and catch the zzz's?" It sounds benign, frankly lazy. Perhaps it would be easier if we called it by its grown-up name: human African trypanosomiasis – HAT on the form.

I'm up at dawn because we're going to find some. Up the long, red Ugandan road already busy with the great African herd, more numerous than even the migrating Serengeti wildebeest – the flocks of bicycles. Freedom in Africa is as far as you can pedal, carrying water, wood, maize, manioc, goats, your bed, the mother-in-law. South of the democracy belt it's the bicycle, not the PalmPilot, that's the greatest invention since sliced bread, whatever that is. Everyone waves at the white folk in the white Médecins Sans Frontières Land Cruiser, with the "No Guns, Thank You" logo on the side. Not just a polite how-do-you-do, but a big teeth-and-eyes hello before they're covered in our dust.

HAT comes in two flavours, *Brucei gambiense* and *Brucei rhodesiense*. *Gambiense* is what's here. It's caused by a parasite, an invisible worm that flies in the bite of the tsetse fly, in much the same way as malaria is carried by mosquitoes. First it works its way through your blood, and you feel a bit rough, a bit dizzy, sort of fluey, and then the lymph nodes in the back of your neck inflame, trying to deal with corpuscle corpses. But, seeing as a lot of Africans feel a bit sick a lot of the time, a bit of a lump is nothing to get on your bike about. Not many people get treated.

The second stage is when the little wrigglers break into your brain, and that's when life goes really mango-shaped. You get serious personality change, become violent, get delirious, hallucinations (always terrifying). Then you lose the use of your limbs, become limp as a rag, have to be fed, and finally you slip into a coma. Untreated, it's 100% fatal. With the right treatment, though, even in the final stages you stand a good chance of making a complete recovery.

Sleeping sickness is back with a vengeance. Across a swathe of Africa, from Congo and Rwanda, across Uganda and up into Sudan, it's back because this area has suffered great refugee migrations for the past 20 years. War, persecution, famine, acts of mahogany-faced gods, the usual stuff. And here's an interesting thing: it's the tsetse fly that catches the sleeping sickness from people, only 2% of the little suckers can carry it, and they have to get it on their first-ever blood meal. It's a more complicated life cycle than a Tehran transvestite's. So medical teams have to go out and find the focus for the disease, the place where a lot of people are infecting a lot of flies, infecting a lot of people.

Omugo is a focus. You're never immune to sleeping sickness. So they have to treat entire populations, not individual cases. MSF's 15-year project has been a success in Uganda, numbers are dropping. It's statistical, empiric, grinding repetitive work, one of the painfully small medical successes of Africa. But wait a bit, this is not a good-news story. But then you knew that.

Under a big, broad mango tree in a school playground set about with tobacco fields and cassava, medical orderlies trained only to find sleeping sickness have set up their trestle table, car-battery-driven centrifuge, their boxes of needles and surgical gloves and their recording ledgers. For a fortnight, men have been bicycling round the area, telling people to come and be tested. Under colonial rule, all this was easier. Public health could be maintained by coercion, farmers sprayed their water margins with DDT, the most effective and cost-efficient pesticide, and they made sure their workforce was tested for economic reasons. Now it has to be done with coaxing and explanation. It's difficult. It takes African time – why meet trouble halfway?

The medical orderlies are surrounded by a swarming crowd of schoolchildren shoving and laughing. The girls wear garish yellow and purple uniforms and push each other forward to have their fingers pricked. A drop of blood is put into an agent and spun on the little turntable. The white-coated orderlies work rhythmically and fast. The children feign bravado at the needle's jab and tease each other. From the classrooms, that universal tune that lucky kids the world over know and hate drifts across the packed mud playing fields: da da di da. The sound of tables learnt by rote is bizarrely familiar here in the bush.

Boys throw stones into the tree, trying to scrump the last mangoes. One lands on the classroom's tin roof with a percussive clatter. Mr Chalky rushes out shouting, flailing a cartoon cane. The boys scatter, whooping and screeching, and take their swift beating with a stoic, smirking grace. We watch and laugh. Unnoticed on the table, a drop of blood finishes spinning. It looks different from the rest. Not a lot, just a little. Separated like a vinaigrette. It's a sign, an indication that a child is producing the antibodies that fight trypanosomiasis.

The orderly checks his cards and calls a name: "Helen." The children twist their heads and a pretty girl with cropped hair steps out from the protection of the group. You can see in her face the dawning that this isn't good. The orderly makes her sit down by herself. The other children stare. She's separate now. No longer one of them. Her eyes are wide. She looks for help. With a prick, this sunny morning has burst into the worst day of her life, perhaps the first day of her slow death. Fingers twisted and knotting in her lap, her shoulders sag. Head bent, tears trickle down her nose onto the yellow and purple uniform.

At the end of the morning there's just one other suspected case, another girl of 14. They sit together but apart, finding no solace in each other, wounded souls hugging a lonely, choking fear to themselves. They have to go back to the hospital for more tests, they have to go now, right this minute. The first, Helen, raggedly crying, mutely refuses to get into the car. She wants her mother. If she doesn't get into the car, maybe they'll just let her run back to the happy, carefree boredom of the classroom. Perhaps they'll just forget all about it, and she's never been in a car before. The nurses gently but immutably stroke away her resistance and we set off back down the long red road to Omugo.

The last of the various tests for sleeping sickness is a lumbar puncture. Sticking a needle into somebody's spine is a serious deal. Back home only doctors can do it. Here, Helen, naked to the waist, sits on a table in a corridor, arms cupping her little breasts. A nurse bends her forward and holds her head with both hands so she can't look round. Behind her a technician runs his fingers gently down her spine, feeling for the point of her hips, swabs a spot on her lower back with rust-coloured disinfectant, then takes a long, fat needle and, with the practised eye of a matador, eases it between vertebrae into the narrow channel of spinal cortex. Too far and Helen's in a world of complications, too shallow and he'll have to do it again. He's yet to make a mistake.

He opens a valve in the shaft of the needle, and viscous, precious drops of spinal fluid glitter into a vial. It's an eerie, almost divine alchemy. This is our most precious bodily fluid. God willing, from birth to death, we never see it. If anything is the essence of who we are, it is these priceless drops. Helen can spare only a few, enough to check for parasites. On the iron beds of the wards, patients lie with a resigned boredom. Everyone comes with a family helper, who cooks their meals in a dark communal shed beside the hospital, fans flies and sits quietly. Mothers come to tend their children, children to tend their mothers. The extended family of Africa is its greatest health service.

The treatment works like this: for the first stage it's a series of seven to ten intramuscular injections of pentamidine taken daily. It's very efficient, has a commendable cure rate and is available throughout Africa for a reasonable cost. Did I say is? I meant was. The European company that makes it, Aventis Pharma, found that pentamidine could also be used for Aids-related pneumonia (in America, not Africa of course) and it became difficult to find here. The price rose 500%. Due to bad publicity and international pressure, 85,000 vials a year of pentamidine are being donated to the World Health Organization (WHO).

For second-stage sleeping sickness, the treatment is altogether more serious and problematic: melarsoprol. This is one of the oldest drugs still regularly being used, a 51-year-old blunderbuss of a treatment. I watched a nurse preparing it: wearing rubber globes, she carefully measured a dose into a huge glass syringe, like something from a Hammer horror film. They have to use glass because the drug is so toxic it melts plastic – and she's about to inject it into a woman's vein. The active ingredient is arsenic. The patient gives her arm to the tourniquet, turns her head. She knows what's coming. The injections are given in three sets of three, with a ten-day recuperation period between each. Here's why. The needles find the vein, the tourniquet is loosened, the woman's body stiffens and starts to shake as the plunger is slowly depressed. Her eyes roll up under crocheted brows, nostrils flare and her lips are pulled tight over her teeth in a fierce fighting grimace. She makes small hissing grunts like someone lifting weights. It takes about 30 seconds. The other patients watch and wait. They too know what's coming. They say that it's like having chilli peppers injected into your heart. The woman's small daughter brings a mug of water and sugar with lime juice. It's the only painkiller she'll get.

Melarsoprol is a colonial legacy. It kills outright 1 in 20 patients and because it's been used for so long there's a growing resistance, so something like 30% relapse. Melarsoprol is so poisonous you can't take it again. Nearly half the treated patients die anyway, one way or another, and that's not odds we'd shrug our shoulders at back in Berkshire. Ah, but it's not all bad: there is an alternative. An efficient, shiny-new, pain-free, plastic-syringe high-success drug: DFMO, or eflornithine. It has few side effects and is the best thing for second-stage sleeping sickness. It's the only treatment where melarsoprol has failed.

It should have replaced the arsenic, but it hasn't because, like so many other trickle-down First World gifts, it's been snatched away. Aventis, which also makes DFMO, has stopped making it, and you can guess why – you're ahead of me. It's not worth it. It wasn't invented as a sleeping-sickness drug anyway, they only got stuck with these sick Africans by accident. They were tinkering about looking for an anti-cancer drug (lots of rich cancer patients) and found it wasn't quite the thing for the big C, but, hey, it's just perfect for sleeping sickness. Hell, just bad luck really. Helen up here in the Ugandan bush doesn't see a dollar from one year to the next, so they stopped making it. Supplies ran out in May.

The WHO – which has to keep looking at its headed notepaper to see what its job is supposed to be, and most of the time appears to be suffering from self-induced sleeping sickness – actually stirred itself and asked Aventis nicely if they would reconsider. Well, no, they wouldn't. But they would have a look in the attic, under the stairs, and in the bucket under the sink to see if they could find some more. And they did. And that will run out at the end of the year.

Now, the men at Aventis aren't heartless, money-grubbing ambulance chasers, really. They know what sleeping sickness does, they found a cure for it, for Christ's sake, so out of the goodness of their hearts they gave – not sold, mind you, but gave – the patent to the WHO. Big hand for Aventis. Except that the WHO isn't in the drug-making business. It is looking for another pharmaceutical company who'll make DFMO, but it will cost. Estimates are two or four times as much as it costs now, for what has become for all purposes, if not intents, a bespoke boutique vanity drug.

Back on the ward there's a young man being treated with melarsoprol. It was going well but suddenly he's developed some serious secondary symptoms. He has another parasite. This is quite common, lots of Africans host lots of parasites. This might be river blindness. The arsenic is so powerful it will drive all other infections into the brain. They have to be treated separately first. Originally he came to the hospital with his sick mother. He cycled from Sudan with her on the handlebars. She died. They tested him. He's sick. He speaks halting, quiet English picked up in transit camps. He's been a refugee escaping byzantine civil war and famine most of his life. His ambition is to finish primary school. He's 23. In African terms, that's over half his life gone before he's started. His, and 300,000 other Africans', who are, as you read, feeling a little dizzy with a lump in their necks and worms in their brains.

That's how many people are estimated to have sleeping sickness, but it's really no more than a guess, like trying to guess the weight of the church fête cake or how many cornflakes there are in the box, and that, when you think about it, is even more shocking. Nobody really knows, because mostly Africans suffer and die in remote, mute darkness. I don't know what makes you angry, what induces that tightening of the stomach, the ball of fist, the roar in the ears; being cut up on the motorway maybe, rude waiters, queues at post offices, airline officials, Bruce Forsyth. Whatever teaspoon you measure righteous fury in, be prepared to swap it for a bucket.

By 2002 the global pharmaceutical market will be worth $406 billion, and it's growing at a healthy – or should that be unhealthy – 8% a year. Europe will see about $100 billion in sales, the US $170 billion, Africa $5.3 billion. About 1%. Just so you completely understand, that's what the pharmaceutical industry spent on advertising last year. Just so you never forget, how about this? Prozac sales in the US are equivalent to half of Africa's entire drugs bill.

Feeling a little hot under the collar yet? You see it's not just sleeping sickness, it's all of what is known jauntily as tropical medicine. You don't have to be a graduate of the Boston Medical School to know that most of the illness in the world is in the south world and most of the medicine is in the north world. There is more money spent researching a cure for baldness than all tropical diseases. As with DFMO, the pharmaceutical industry says: "Hold on a minute, we're not the bad guys here, let's keep it rational. We live in a cut-throat commercial world, all that free market and democracy stuff you're so keen to profligatise means that our first call is to shareholders – no shareholders, no research; no research and you're back having your tumour removed with a hacksaw on the kitchen table. You don't go after the motor industry for not making subsidised ambulances, and just think of all the good we do."

They have a point, up to a point. Which is that this is only a free market for the sellers, not the consumers. Nobody chooses to be their customer, the old vet who looks 70 and is in fact younger than me, his rheumy, tobacco-coloured eyes fearful of the daytime nightmares the worms form in his head as he shuffles between two sticks up the ward to get some sunlight. Didn't look at the brochures and think: "Shall I get malaria, or river blindness, or sleeping sickness or heartburn?"

Actually, he'd have been better off with river blindness: there's a very good cure and it's donated free to Africa by the pharmaceutical giant Merck (total revenue, $32,714m). It wasn't actually looking for a cure, it discovered by accident that a treatment for de-worming horses did the tic trick. Merck spends 6.3% of its revenue on research, less than most crisp manufacturers, and just over a third of what it spends on marketing and administration.

The vast majority of pharmaceutical research is spent on what they charmingly call "me-too drugs", commercially tweaked copies of other people's best-sellers, usually for the relief of western excess, vanity pseudo-sickness and repeat prescriptions, while three-quarters of the world with an average life expectancy under 50 screams: "Me too, me too."

Over the past decade there has been a consolidating merger frenzy in the pharmaceutical industry. DFMO was originally invented by a company called Marion Merrill Dow, which became Hoechst, Marion, Roussel, and then Aventis Pharma. I know, they all sound like Andorran advertising agencies. Every merger cuts the overall amount of research and, more importantly, the panorama of research. Less money is spent looking at fewer diseases. Have you ever stopped to think how weird it is that you have to take malaria pills to go to places where the population doesn't take them, or that you get injections for yellow fever, cholera, typhus and hepatitis? None of the locals are immune to these things. They just suffer them. Drug companies can find prophylactics for rich western holiday-makers, but not for people who live with disease the other 50 weeks of the year.

Malaria, for instance, is not a complicated illness, we've understood its pathology for over a century, it's one of the biggest adult killers in the world, a million people, two, ten, who knows? There have been persistent rumours that there is a vaccine for it, but no pharmaceutical company wants to be caught holding it, heaven forbid, they'd have to make it and that would be a disaster for the stockholders. And when cases of West Nile fever were discovered in New York, they gassed the entire city as if it were the Ho Chi Minh trail, and Third World medical workers cheered: if it takes hold in the US, you can bet your advertising budget there will be a cure in months.

As for the drug-eat-drug free market that the pharmaceutical companies have to survive in . . . well, that's not quite what it seems either. In the US, where most research is done, they get feather-bedded preferential tax breaks on research, and extended 17-year government-granted global patents for drugs which they extend indefinitely by upgrading them to new and improved, like soap powder. And they have the clout to make governments act as their enforcers. Aids treatment as paid for by US insurance companies costs $10,000 per patient per annum. They can do it for $200 in Brazil, but daren't.

Thailand produced a cheap AZT clone. To protect the drug companies, the American government threatened to put huge tariffs on the wooden jewellery and goods that account for 30% of Thailand's foreign income. We're not dealing with bootleg CDs here, how dare anyone apply the morality of the market to dying people? Not just one or two people, but millions and millions. The US drug companies aren't short of a buck, their domestic market was worth $107 billion in 1998–99, up 15% on the year before. They don't even consider Africa a market at all, they sell to international charities and agencies. At the recent Durban Aids conference there was a much press-released move to get AZT to Africa. Companies had said they'd see what they could do about cutting costs. They're really trying to, five of the biggest have said they will have a go, but it's going to take time. You know, it's a jungle out there.

But Bill Clinton had a plan. He'd lend Africa money (at a nominal 7%) to buy the drugs at American prices while at the same time trying to do something about the pressing need to write off Africa's debt. The joke of all this, if you're up to a joke, is that AZT wasn't even discovered by Glaxo Wellcome, which markets it. It was discovered by a Dr Jerome Horowitz of the Michigan Cancer Foundation in 1964, using a publicly funded government grant. Enough, enough. This stuff goes on and on until you're numb with the horror, the venality, the sheer breathtaking unfairness of it.

But you must also consider there may be another deeper, nastier reason that Africa gets left in accident and emergency. Nastier because at least greed is a simple naked motivation. It's in that eye-rolling, feigned sorry smile that comes with the explanation: "Oh well, that's Africa for you." It's a beat that runs through all First World talk about Africa's problems. They're somehow qualitatively different, there's misery and then there's African misery. And that somehow they are wilfully or ignorantly complicit in their own troubles – look at the amount they spend on arms. (Uganda's defence budget wouldn't buy you the cockpit of a stealth bomber.) And this is why Africans can't be treated as our medical services treat us, as individuals with needs. They have to be seen as a statistical generic health-care problem. It's as if Africa's problems were so confounded and bleak that they simply couldn't be borne by people like us, so, *ipso facto*, they must be borne by people who aren't quite like us.

It's the same rationale that allowed cultured Christians to trade slaves. Already in the world health community there have been murmurings that the 24.5m Africans infected with HIV will have to be written off, for the good of Africa, of course. Any attempt at individual treatment will inevitably be mere publicity showboating, a waste of resources. And so many resources seem to have been wasted on Africa.

There is an awful, inquisitive fascination at the scope, the depth and the stoically borne horror. Unspoken is the bat-squeak suspicion that they don't feel the same as we do, that a dead child, a mortal illness, a war, a famine, a drought, poverty and loss, mean less in Africa. The currency of mourning has been devalued by glut. Africans seem to have managed to do something that drug companies couldn't manage. They've anaesthetised themselves against Africa.

I went back into the recovery hut where Helen is supposed to be lying flat – lumbar punctures give you a socking migraine – but she's sitting up chatting with her friend. They've had their results and they're like different children, smiling for the photographer.

It's good news, no parasites. And it's indeterminate news. In three months, the men on bicycles will go and find them and bring them back for more tests, they're both still high-risk, and that's bad news, because if Helen does have sleeping sickness, chances are there won't be any drugs to treat her and she will die before she reaches 16. But at the moment all she cares about is that in a couple of hours the white truck will come and take her back up the road home; this time she'll enjoy it and wave at the bicycles.

I hope all this makes you angry. I dearly hope you stay angry, because your sustained anger is the last, best hope for Helen and Africa at the moment. Let me leave you with one last fact. Of the 1,223 new medicines developed between 1975 and 1997, just 13 were for tropical diseases. Only four sprang from the pharmaceutical industry's efforts to cure humans. None were found on purpose.

Selassie come home

Selassie come home

Ethiopia, December 2000

First the good news. The long rains have finished and they were long enough, deep, thick and wet enough. Ethiopia is expecting a beneficent harvest, so that's a relief, or an absence of relief. You won't have to wear the T-shirt, listen to the bald rockers or be distressed by the news this year. Whoever thought you'd read: "No famine in Ethiopia"? Now the bad news. That doesn't mean they're not starving. Hardly anyone's got the cash for a mouldy banana. If you look at early maps of Africa, below the Sahara is a big, dark blank inscribed with just one name: Ethiopia. It floats in ignorance, stretching from the Horn to the Niger. The one African name known to Europe since the Middle Ages; the land of Prester John, the legendary Christian king who stood outside the western world. Ethiopia claims it was the first Christian country. Ethiopians say they have been Christians for 3,000 years, 1,000 with the Old Testament and 2,000 with the new. They also say they are one of the lost tribes of Israel, belonging to neither black nor Arab Africa, existing in Africa but not of it.

The name itself was given by the Greeks and means "sunburnt people". Abyssinia, its other name, is Arabic and means "mixed people". Ethiopia is a loose, conflicting collection of shifting tribes and cities half as old as time. There are Christians who circumcise their children, and animist tribes who castrate other people. In the north there are hermits who spend decades living alone in caves, in the south there are sun worshippers who wear metal wigs and terracotta plates in their lips. It has some of the oldest churches carved out of solid stone and the third holiest city of Islam. It has more than 64m people, 86 distinct languages, and hundreds of dialects. The official lingo is Amharic, one of the earliest written languages and the only phonetic one that reads from left to right, though it started from right to left, then bizarrely went both right and left in a zigzag like a man ploughing a field.

In Ethiopia, nothing is quite what it seems. You only believe half of what you hear and it's usually the other half that's true. Ethiopia is a country that elides fact and myth, where everything seems to come as part of an illusion. It's the alleged home of the Ark of the Covenant and the true cross. There are 13 months in its year, so a lucky few have no star sign. Its 12-hour clock begins at dawn, so world-time seven o'clock is Ethiopian-time one o'clock. When people make appointments they rarely stipulate which watch they're using, so they are regularly six hours late, which is nothing to the rest of us being three years early. Ethiopia still uses the Julian calendar. They haven't even begun to think about building their millennium dome yet. They've barely thought about building the 20th century. Ethiopia is the home of coffee. The Blue Nile rises here. Ethiopia grows *teff*, a grass eaten nowhere else, which makes a soggy, fermented bread that looks like a cross between grey foam rubber and tripe. It is rolled up in the manner of airline face flannels.

But, singularly and importantly, Ethiopia is the only African country that was never a European colony. Its borders were not drawn with a lazy arbitration in the foreign offices of London, Paris or Brussels, but were carved out by fearsome warriors with spear and serpentine sword. Central to Ethiopia's pride, and indeed Africa's, is the fact that it boasts the only African army that ever decisively beat a European one, at the battle of Adwa in 1896. Not quite the only one, but the first since Hannibal. Coincidentally, also against the Italians. Finally, and most opaquely, it has an extraordinary number of people with little wads of tissue paper shoved up one nostril.

Addis Ababa (which means "new flower") lounges like a rotten wreath over a series of hills, in turn surrounded by the impressive curve of the Entoto mountains. It's a relatively modern city, just over 100 years old, built round hot springs. It's also 8,000ft above sea level, so every flight of stairs is a consultation with a breathless amateur cardiologist, and every Ethiopian is a middle-distance runner. The city is generously, panoramically free of any smidgen of beauty, but not without a fearsome charm and noisome excitement. It's a black-rap Dickensian stew. The indigenous juniper forests that once shaded it were cut down for firewood generations ago, and replaced with antipodean eucalyptus trees that drink like Australians and are good for nothing much more than admiring and burning. Every night, straggling lines of folded old ladies carry vast bundles of firewood down from the hills. The women carry them because they're just too big and heavy for the donkeys.

Addis is 70% slum, a lurching, teetering stack of shanties – rusty corrugated iron, slimy plastic sheeting, mud reeking of eucalyptus gum, dung and smoke, rather like a long-haul economy toilet. They creep and elbow amid the crumbling, cheap concrete buildings like live Polyfilla. Addis boasts Africa's largest market, the Mercato, a sprawling dark compost of rickety shops, stalls and livid life. There are streets of tailors sewing rags on ancient Singers, alleys of people weaving sweet-smelling grass, making traditional dining plates with coned covers. There's a labyrinthine spice market with precipitous, bright peaks of turmeric and chilli, cumin, coriander and poppy seeds and ground roots with only indigenous names, whose scents are mysteriously, tantalisingly divorced from any western flavour. There are tiny tables selling handmade newspaper pokes of incense for the elaborate coffee ceremony that all families have once a week; steeples of gauzy wool and cotton shawls with delicate silk borders. Lorries deliver man-sized bound sheafs of chat, the mildly speedy drug that many poor chew as an escape, a solace and a hunger depressant. Addicts roam the streets with bloodshot eyes, wild hair and cupped palms. What you rarely see is anyone buying anything. No bag-laden women arguing over fruit or veg. Just thousands of young men loitering and waiting.

Even by African standards, the bothering and begging are exhaustive and unremitting, and the beggars world-beating in their decrepitude and infirmity. Here are the legless, armless, eyeless and toothless; the polio-crippled, the mine-maimed, the buboed and leprous, the self-mutilated and the plain mad. And the pickpockets. In one morning I was dipped three times, and marvelled at their consummate, prestidigitous professionalism. Addis is potless poor, too poor even for advertising. None of the painted walls flogging Coca-Cola and Sportsman cigarettes that decorate the rest of Africa. You want to know how broke it is? It's too broke to even afford rubbish. The meagrest scrap has a value until it vanishes. But it does have filth, gratis from Dame Nature.

With an unbelievable collective self-restraint, it's safe, probably safer than most European capitals, but there is a prickling sense of tension, a muttered, in-your-face, eyeballing exasperation. Some of the most bellicose tribes who ever lived came from hereabouts. A chap couldn't get married until he was a proven, motiveless murderer. Addis feels like the squall before the storm, like it's waiting for something. A spark, an excuse. What it and I are also waiting for is the funeral of Haile Selassie. Like most things here, it's late – 25 years, two regimes, three wars and a pair of famines late. To finally lay to rest the conquering lion of the tribe of Judah, the king of kings, the direct descendant of Solomon and the Queen of Sheba, the only new god of the modern era, will be to finally tie up one of the last loose ends of the 20th century.

While history is written by western white men, its chief protagonists will always be western white men. Selassie drifts through the convulsive modern age like a small, dark, topied ghost. He was the 20th century's Zelig. Most people only know of him as the faintly ridiculous deity of the Rastafarians, seen in the yellow, red and green of the Ethiopian flag on T-shirts with Bob Marley and a joint. Yet if you shift the eyeline of history from its well-oiled western axis and look up from the hot, ancient south, Selassie is a monumental, titanic figure, a catalyst and central protagonist in the story not just of Africa, but of the entire modern world order. He came to power in a confusing internecine struggle in the century's first decades and was murdered by communist revolutionaries known as the Derg. His 54-year reign descended into a static feudal mire of oligarchic intrigue, corruption and fear. So powerful were his image and aura that they physically, as well as symbolically, had to smother him to death. The king of kings was secretly interred under President Mengistu's personal lavatory. Even as a corpse he could frighten the pants off his subjects. Look at photographs. All his life he seems to have had only one impervious sarcophagal expression, a granite stare that glares at posterity with all the regal confidence of a heritage that disappears back into the mist of fairy tales. He was the head of the only independent African country. He led Ethiopia into the League of Nations, and witnessed its demise. In Geneva he made a speech that echoed round the world in defence of the independence of small countries. It is one of the great pieces of 20th-century oratory and as relevant today as it was then. It could have been said of Kuwait or Kosovo or East Timor.

The Italian invasion turned Ethiopia into the Spain of the Third World. The old colonial powers' shameful self-interest, the demeaning, secret Hoare-Laval pact between French and British foreign ministers, tacitly allowed Mussolini to carve up a new Roman empire, proving that for all its brave words and olive-branch ambitions, the league would never confront a western power. The dates for the start of the second world war tend to be arbitrary, dependent on individual countries' experiences. Actually it began in Ethiopia in 1935, with mustard gas dropped on a lion-maned army armed with spears and leather shields. The appeasement of France and Britain, and Mussolini's trumped-up border incidents, were the green light for Hitler's piecemeal annexations. Selassie's Ethiopia was the first country to fall to fascism and the first to be liberated.

The British intelligence officer Charles Orde Wingate and a messianic collection of repressed homosexuals, tortured explorers, noble-savage worshippers and eccentric misfits, along with guerrilla patriots, brilliantly outmanoeuvred the Italians and restored the emperor to his throne in 1941. Post-war Ethiopia under Selassie was one of the founding countries of the United Nations. He was a prime instigator of the Organisation of African Unity, which still has its headquarters in Addis. At home he was Victorianly enthusiastic for selective modernism, particularly in education, though anyone who had read a book or gained a degree was likely to find themselves a political prisoner. His predecessor Menelik sent his army officers to be trained in imperial Russia. Foolishly, Selassie continued the practice *après* Lenin and found himself a medieval ruler with a nascent, educated middle class frustrated by no prospects, an officer class who were hard-line communists, and a pampered, venal family who intrigued at every opportunity. And a country that was slipping into famine. Selassie was caught on film feeding fresh meat to his Abyssinian lions (now extinct) as his nation starved. It was all bound to end in tears.

Today you can reach the royals on their website, www.ethiopiancrown.org. His Imperial Highness, Prince Ermias Sahle-

Selassie Haile-Selassie, is president of the Crown Council. Through the miracle of e-mail, I have arranged to have dinner with him. Ironically, in Addis's best Italian restaurant (established 1946). It's to be a small, informal briefing, so I've also invited Dr Richard Pankhurst, the grandson of the suffragette and a world expert on Ethiopia. To actually break bread with a direct descendant of Solomon will be quite something. It makes our own dear royal family's lumpen Kraut origins seem rather dowdy. Regally an hour and a half late, Ermias arrives with a train of 20 family members, bodyguards and aides. I suddenly feel that I'm hosting royal Band Aid. It's an embarrassment of seeds of Solomon. So embarrassing that I haven't enough cash to pay for them all and have to make arrangements with the jolly Italian owner, who waves his hands and invites me back for dinner on the house. Ermias is a one-man charm offensive. All Ethiopians have infinite reserves of charm. Talking to them is like having your secret places softly massaged with warm butter. He says he's nervous. Indeed, his weakly handsome eyes look frankly terrified, and with good reason. This is the first time in 26 years that all Selassie's descendants have returned, after fleeing the Derg, with its self-named Red Terror and its Cambodian-style mass murders, including asking schoolchildren where they lived, taking them home, then shooting them in front of their parents. The regime lasted 17 years, until overthrown by the slightly rosier-red Tigré People's Liberation Front, part of the regime that is still in power. Nobody knows why they've allowed this burial to take place, how they will react, or indeed if anyone will turn up. Will it be tens, or tens of thousands? Selassie's name has been expunged from school books and public life for a generation. Will they remember? His grandchildren are dotted around the world – England, Canada, Greece, Italy, the United States. They are Italian businessmen, Midwestern social workers, Greek hairdressers.

Ermias lives in Washington, DC. He does a little bit of this and a bit of that and a lot of philanthropy. The American capital boasts a large Ethiopian refugee community, mostly taxi drivers. In his Italian suit with his seamless small talk, Ermias seems further from Ethiopia than even Washington. Yes, of course, he'll give an interview and pose for a picture, though he must be discreet, you understand. Would he mind if I joined the family the next morning in the church service to mark the start of three days of mourning and celebrate the 70th anniversary of Selassie's coronation? Of course, I'd be very welcome. A waiter leans purposefully across the table. Ermias's eyes blink with fear. The man jabs a finger and talks rapid, emphatic Amharic. He will be at the funeral. The late emperor was a great man. Ermias shows me his best Washington politician's face: "I'm very touched by the reverence of the common people."

Six o'clock in the morning, and there's still a chill in the air as dawn breaks over Selassie's square, domed cathedral. We take off our shoes and carry them with us inside. They are too valuable to be left at the door. Priests, acolytes and choirboys pad round a central tent that represents the holy of holies, the spiritual home of the Ark. Leaning against it are sacred paintings done in the Ethiopian manner, with their pale skin and mournful wide brown eyes. The women stand on one side, men on the other. Young servants in white cassocks and broad shawls pile carpets on top of carpets for our comfort. The priests process round the church, swinging clouds of incense, carrying their elaborate silver Ethiopian crosses and richly bound Bibles. There's much genuflecting and kissing and we are given T-shaped croziers to lean on. The congregation looks like an ethnic heat for *One Man and His Dog*. We are an odd bunch. The royal family confused and nervous in black, some of the granddaughters sobbing behind their veils. A couple of big-haired and elaborately shrouded Rastafarians, including Bob Marley's widow, the very laid-back Rita. And then beside me, a porcine pink gent in a pin-stripe suit with polished socks and a large signet ring, who could only be English and turns out to be Sir Conrad Swann, KCVO, PhD, FSA, Garter Principal, King of Arms Emeritus. What on earth is he doing here? The service is long, over three hours, delivered in monotonous Amharic and an older ecclesiastical language like Latin, called Ge'ez. It makes the hair stand up on your neck and dries the mouth. When they start singing, the bishop intones a Gregorian-style chant that sounds both orthodox and Arab and the choir provides a deep rhythmic descant that is unmistakably African. A sonorous, liquid-black, speechlessly sad rise and fall. This is perhaps the oldest Christian service in the world, largely unchanged for 1,700 years. It's as close as any of us will come this side of the grave to knowing how the apostles prayed. Halfway through, Selassie's throne is produced from behind a screen.

The priests step forward and usher a prince to sit in it. The Abun, the patriarch of the Ethiopian Church, is a kingmaker. A pivotal politician. His blessing is essential to any pretender, and the man he's placed on the throne is not Ermias. It's a tall, bald someone else. My prince is three down the pecking order, looking characteristically worried. Damn, I fed the wrong royal. As the service finishes, the carpets are rolled back and a trap door opened. We all squeeze into the crypt and there, finally, he is. The last of the line of Judah. Behind a glass partition like a sweet shop window. His coffin is draped in a white and silver net curtain with a photograph propped on it. It looks like a small piano. In two days a procession will move him from here to the cathedral, and there lowered into a marble sarcophagus beside the altar. We all stare at the little box, not really knowing what to think.

The Sheraton Hotel rises out of the shanty slum like a huge taupe palace. It is by some way the grandest building in Addis. I wouldn't normally mention it, except it's without doubt also the grandest hotel in Africa. Every capital has its hubristic, tourist-enticing, foreign-built splendido, but none come close to the magnificence of this place. For a start, everything works. The fax in your room, the ranks of fountains, the staff, your own butler, drinks come when you order them. The numerous restaurants serve decent imported food and the clean pool has underwater Muzak. This would be a very grand hotel in Hollywood. In Africa it's unimaginable. I also mention it because for a brief time it becomes the royal court. A huge Gormenghast of intrigue, rumours and factions. The royal family effortlessly pick up where they left off and, as a confused foreign observer, I find myself the recipient of a steady stream of off-the-record briefings, debriefings, unbriefings, points of order and just straightforward lies. The players stalk the bars and lounges, knots of retainers huddle and whisper with slidy eyes. All is not well in the court of Selassie. The first thing that happens is that my blessed prince disappears. I call to confirm my interview and he's gone. Where? His aide, an implausibly smooth chap who probably has a double first in the novels of John Grisham and Raymond Chandler, says he's hiding and asks me to come to his suite. The phones are not safe. He tells me the prince was being followed, they'd had to change cars. The government's putting out aggressive signals (an article in the English-language paper written in 1970s cold-warese; fraternal, peace-loving people, feudal capitalist stooges, etc, accusing Haile Selassie of funnelling wealth abroad, which is unlikely as he was famously ascetic except when it came to uniforms).

While we're talking, another man enters the room and silently loiters. Let's talk in here, says the aide, and opens a door. It's a closet. He ushers me in among the swinging coat hangers, he tells me that if I'm inclined to mention a split in the royal family, I'll just make a fool of myself, and he can tell I'm no fool because I ask such naive questions, pretending to be stupid. I'm obviously a very clever journalist, he chuckles conspiratorially. No, no, I really do know nothing. I really am a very stupid journalist. For instance, I'm pressed up against a svelte Ethiopian whispering in a cupboard. Back in the bar, where the piano player tinkles out golden movie moments, I try to make some sense out of the royal family, but it's like juggling mud. Yet another prince shimmies over and French-polishes my bottom. Then, in an aside, mentions that of course I know there's a man pretending to be me in the Hilton Hotel. "He says he's a reporter from the *Sunday Times*." Oh, good grief. I can't work out who any of you are. Now I have to find out who I am. And here he, or I, is. Across the lobby rolls one plump young Englishman, dressed in thick bird's-eye worsted. To an Ethiopian eye he is the epitome of a Brit gent abroad, but to me he looks utterly fictional. The plummy voice has just a hint of suburban cul-de-sac. The coolness a sheen of cold sweat. He hands me a card. Anthony Bailey, MIPR, MIPRA, managing director, Eligo International Ltd Berlin, Brussels, London, Lugano, Madrid, Milan, Paris, Sofia. "I am," he says, dropping heavily into a chair, "the press secretary to His Majesty, the Crown Prince Zara Yaqov." The man in the throne? "Yes." Can we talk to him? "Ah now, that may be difficult. He's not very well. You could put some questions through me and I'll give you written answers."

"We have just received a letter from Her Majesty the Queen." Of the United Kingdom? "Of course." Sorry, it's just that there are so many monarchs about. "You know you once stitched me up over the King of Greece." No, I didn't. I've never met the King of Greece. "Oh yes you did." I'm pretty sure I didn't. "Maybe it was A N Wilson, then." I'm not him either. It turns out that Crown Prince Zara lives in straitened circumstances in Manchester and is looked after by Rastafarians who are trying to get him interested in breeding another heir (as if there weren't enough already). Among all the subterfuge and rumour I'm pretty sure that's a fact, because frankly you just couldn't make it up. I also discover the reason for Sir Conrad Swann's presence. Ermias and the Crown Council have set up a nice little business in conjunction with Spink's, the medal people, handing out decorations. The Order of Solomon's Seal, second class. That sort of thing. In exchange for philanthropic donations and services to Ethiopia, Washington gala ball matrons pin them to their Dior.

I call the British embassy to see if they're having anything to do with all this. After an age the phone is picked up. "Wrong number," an angry voice shouts. But I haven't said who I'm calling. Is that the British embassy? "Well, yes," comes the grudging reply. "You'd better speak to Deirdre."

"Hello," said Deirdre, in a voice that's pure John Betjeman. "You want to speak to my husband. He's playing tennis at the moment. I'll get him to call you back." He doesn't. The next morning Bailey slips the text of Her Majesty's letter (our one) under my door. She is very pleased "that at long last, Emperor Haile Selassie the First is being accorded a proper burial". Which is nice.

Crown Prince Zara's question and answer is a double dose of Mogadon. With it comes a tart note: "As I have not heard from you as we agreed, I have cancelled today's appointment with Empress Work and the crown prince." But we never agreed. There never was a meeting. And who is this Empress Work?

"You weren't supposed to be told that His Royal Highness was unwell," yet another prince tells me in the corridor. This is getting like a pantomime audition. Why, what's the matter with him? "I can't tell you. But you should find out." Thanks. The closet aide asks me to go to a safe phone in the lobby and dial a number. It's

71

my prince. He's fearful for his life. It's terribly sad. He doesn't want to be the cause of any danger for his people. He's in Rome.

When power and prestige slip down the plughole, this black farce is what you're left with. The conquering lions of Judah are just the scum line left on the bathtub of history. It's funny, but it's not as funny as it's pathetic.

The funeral starts early, at 4am. I get to the cathedral an hour after dawn. It's already hot. It's going to be scorching. The coffin, draped in the Ethiopian flag, rests on the steps, surrounded by a patriotic guard of old warriors in baboon-fur alice bands and long, bright tabards with a lion embroidered on the back. They carry boiled-leather shields and blackened spears. On one side of the bier sits the royal family and on the other the Abun, priests, and monks of the church, dressed in the rich panoply of their calling. Bright togas and robes, coruscating coronets and mitres all thickly encrusted and decorated.

Their croziers and huge silver crosses are garlanded with ribbons; acolytes hold aloft velvet and silk sunshades intricately embroidered with stars and suns and images of Christ, like the serried domes of a visionary city. Stretching along each side are lines of choirboys and girls in bright surplices, holding flags and honey-scented tapers. They sing Latin dirges and sway like a gentle ocean. On a gold throne is the patriarch, swathed in burgundy velvet, barnacled and filigreed with gold, wearing a multistorey crown. This steepling tableau is like something dreamt by a black Velázquez. It beggars anything contrived by the Vatican. Here in scabrous Africa it's truly a vision of unimaginable splendour, dignity and ancient pomp.

Slightly apart stand a line of khaki-clad men, ancients with grizzled beards and yellow, rheumy eyes, dressed in tattered uniforms and battered solar topis. They are survivors of the war against the Italians. Their medals, paid for with the philanthropy of blood, droop on thin chests. Some carry faded photographs of Selassie or themselves in their martial prime. One stands stiffly erect in worn rubber flip-flops.

The coffin is lifted onto a flat-bed truck swathed in the flag. The guards surround it, spears at attention. The procession, slowly and with much confusion, makes its way through the slums, to Revolution Square, a flat, featureless area that recently held a million people to welcome home Ethiopia's Olympic runners. Now the ranks of waiting metal chairs are mostly empty. A few dozen officials and Anthony Bailey sit pucely steaming in the sun. There are perhaps three or four thousand Ethiopians watching with a sullen, nothing-better-to-do interest.

Over a crackling loudspeaker there are ponderous speeches. The sun and the boredom climb. The coffin is manhandled back on the truck and heads off through the otherwise-engaged streets towards the cathedral graveyard, where, three hours later, the crowd has grown dense and patient. Perched on gravestones and monuments, it's mostly old men and women who must remember Selassie and his empire with fondness. For all his stiffness and faults, his people were materially a lot better off then than they are now; it's the price of bread that matters most. But the government can relax. This is not a popular demonstration of dissent. It's all about the past, not the future. There will be no trouble. Another service, more tapers and hymns, more speeches and, in front of the coffin, white-robed choristers chant and rhythmically shake silver rattles. Then the great Ethiopian war drum is banged, beaten to send Selassie to his marble grave. A voice behind me says: "The last time I heard that drum was in 1935." It's Bill Deedes – Lord Deedes – the most venerable of all correspondents, who was here with Evelyn Waugh and is the model for Boot, the hero of *Scoop*, the funniest book ever written about journalism; one I feel I have been unintentionally plagiarising. His presence somehow closes the circle, and he's about to have his pockets picked and his camera nicked.

Surprisingly few Rastafarians have come to bury their god, but then I hear one say: "I-and-I know he still lives." Of course: he's immortal. This is not his funeral. Selassie is alive somewhere in the vastness to the south, preparing a land for his chosen people. In the West we tend to sneer and snigger at the Rastas with their drugs and knitwear and belief that a small black Third World dictator could possibly be a deity. But Jamaicans saw the only black man from Africa who had ever defeated the whites; who stood in solitary, righteous splendour in an otherwise enslaved continent. An emperor obliquely mentioned in the Bible, a black man whose status didn't derive from running faster or punching other black men harder. And who is to say that the conquering lion of the tribe of Judah, the descendant of Solomon, is any sillier an object of worship than a carpenter from Nazareth? Only time can give religion dignity.

The prince who told me to find out about Zara Yaqov sidles up. "Come, I will show you what's wrong with His Highness." We slip through the crowds until I have a good view. He's sitting with a look of benign incomprehension. His weak mouth is slightly open; his eyes dull, unfocused. "You understand now?" he hisses. Indeed I do. From here it looks as if he's two Christmas singles short of a telethon.

The heir has retreated into a quiet, safe, simpler nursery in his own head where voices talk of cabbages and kings. Ethiopia's salvation isn't going to be found in the house of Selassie. He's pulled to his feet and stands vacantly and unhelpfully behind the coffin as it seesaws up the steps, carried by the royal family, in a confusion of priests and cameramen. Slowly it makes its way from the sunlight into the cool, dark shadows; the heavy iron doors clang shut. The last emperor has made his final journey from lavatory to cathedral.

Later I ask yet another royal how he liked the service. "It was terrible, the family was distraught. The crowd should have been prostrate, the women ululating. It wasn't fitting. It was so sad." Perhaps, but nothing like as profoundly sad as the lives eked out on every street corner. I'm told, in strict confidence, naturally, that the coffin didn't fit its grave, but is propped up in a corner. In death as in life, Haile Selassie was a bigger man than he appeared.

EAST

My boy Alasdair must have been about four when he asked me where England was. In return, I asked him what country he thought he lived in.

"Kensington."

Where did he think London was?

"Somewhere a long way away, over there."

"Over the sea?"

"Possibly."

I got out an atlas and showed him the world and pointed to where he was. He stared and nodded and said "oh" but I could tell he had no idea what he was looking at. This picture was wholly abstract, it bore no relation to what he knew to be the truth. Where was the fat tobacconist on the corner? Where was his nursery school, the traffic lights? This tiny irregular green blot wasn't where he lived. He lived in a country whose sturdy walls contained his bedroom, the warm kitchen and living room. It had a back door and a cupboard full of cleaning things and it had fraternal relations with other similarly manageable countries: his classroom, his granny's house, the rolling pasture of Kensington Gardens and the great sea of the Round Pond. It was world enough. The intimation that there might be more than this personal topography, that his country might not be secure and complete, that it might not look the way he knew it looked, was a worry and best left alone.

I've always wondered at the huge leap of intellect that allowed the first person to draw a map. It's one of those great turning points in civilisation. How did they ever convince anyone else that this was the story of a possible journey. Maps fascinate me and yet in some small, dark quadrant of my head, I'm with Ali. I don't wholly believe them. They are not how the world looks. I carry round a personal atlas where size and proximity have nothing to do with measurable space. I know, for instance, that New York is just next door, that Cuba is bigger than Germany, and Nice is closer than Normandy. Through the arbitrary silt of prejudice, there are places I'm desperate to see and those I'm not bothered about. Because of Kipling and an uncle who planted tea, I always knew I'd love India but have never had a desire to see China because I don't like those blue and white vases. I've always wanted to go to West Africa because of a collection of carved enema tubes in the British Museum but have no plans to visit Mexico because I can't bear its food (particularly as served in California). This section contains a lot of places that I didn't really fancy visiting. Often I was proved wrong and sometimes right, but for the wrong reasons. Preconception and expectation are an essential part of every journey.

Awayday in a manger

Bethlehem, December 1999

A cold coming we had of it. It started with the Mossad grilling from two 12-year-old immigration girls at Ben Gurion airport. Almost everyone in Israel who exerts any street-level power turns out to be an improbably young woman with a face and figure out of the Song of Solomon and a manner that implies she would happily drive a tent peg through your sleeping philistine head. "Why exactly don't you want an Israeli stamp in your passport?" Well, personally, you know, I'd adore one, but a lot of other countries might not appreciate it. "You are a journalist?" Sorry. "Who are you planning on talking to?" Baby Jesus.

And then there was no room at the inn. Baby Jesus has a sense of humour. You mean you have no rooms at all? "None. We have no confirmation of you. And you know what time of year it is?" Don't tell me, there's a census. It's the perfect start to a story about Bethlehem and the real heart and soul of the millennium. Forget your domes and Ferris wheels and all-inclusive tropical luxury breaks seeing in the sunrise 20 minutes early. Bethlehem is the hub – the *raison d'être* of it all. If this was just another two-camel sheep station in the desert, then all we'd be celebrating on January 1st would be computers that can't count. I'm here to spend one day in the life of God. Sunday. God's day. I finally get a room at the Hyatt. "I'm sorry, you can't check in until 7.30. Sabbath, you know." Of course, God's dad's day. The Hyatt is a tour-guided pilgrim's hotel of irredeemable ghastliness. It's full of money-belted southern Baptists in baseball caps with peaky inspirational messages. At breakfast, I hear a shingled pensioner in complete Christian combat gear ask: "If you see any Jews, can you bring one over to me?" "Sure, honey. What do you want? Orange Jews or grapefruit Jews?"

No corner of the earth has been gilded with as many great expectations as the Holy Land. It is the crucible of the two greatest stories ever told, the Bible and the long homeward journey of the Jewish Diaspora. In terms of tears and blood, and inspiration and hope, nowhere else can begin to compete. What I expected, what I wanted, was some sort of visible exclamation of it all: steeples and spires, gilded domes and Roman pillars, mixed with a pre-war Yiddish sophistication, cafés with chess players, violin music wafting from upper windows, carpets and diamonds, all that old dusty, winey, velvet sentimental richness. I wanted hand-waving and philosophy and cheesecake and chicken soup and Barbra Streisand. It's not here. Not remotely. Not any of it. And it was foolish to imagine it would be.

Israel is a half-century-old Middle Eastern country built in a hurry on the horns of a dilemma. It's low-rise breeze block with limestone cladding. It's dust and rubbish. Cacophonous neon, fraying tempers and suicidal driving, all strung about with barbed wire and observation towers and concrete security chicanes and a sense of extemporary make-do-and-mend. Israel is work in progress where the architects' plans were written after the foundations were laid. The other thing is size. Size shouldn't count, but Israel is very small, and the Bible implies that it's vast, all those journeys, all that old age and those wanderings. Forty days in the wilderness and you could wander round the place twice.

Early on Sunday morning I set out for Bethlehem, which is virtually just a suburb of Jerusalem. "Would you like to go to the Mount of Olives first?" asked my Palestinian driver, who started pounding his horn under the British mandate. Sunrise on the Mount of Olives, that would be wonderful. Up to a point. The Mount of Olives is a car park. More precisely, a bus park and turn-around roundabout. May all your beatitudes be platitudes. But it's not finished yet. Piles of rubble and extruded steel macramé for reinforced concrete fray around its edges. The bulldozers and trucks are already kicking up the dust. An early Arab sits with a sad donkey beside a Portakabin waiting for the stream of photo opportunities, more Kismet-me-quick than hosanna. Beneath us, in the hazy grey morning light, lies unprepossessing Jerusalem. Only the golden Dome of the Rock catches early rays and glitters a counterpoint to the dun city that crawls up the dun, sparse hills. The mosque is the third holiest site in Islam, and it only just avoided being blown to somebody's kingdom come by furious Israeli sappers after the six-day war. Somewhere on the slope beneath us, in the stepped cemetery, Robert Maxwell awaits the day of judgment. Two minutes is more than enough. The garden of Gethsemane is just around the corner. It's also tiny. An amenity area of gnarly olives and municipal scrub planting, about as spiritual and contemplative as a Little Chef playground.

You approach Bethlehem through Israeli security barriers, where nervous, sullen, clean-shaven young soldiers in green fatigues smoke cigarettes and heft their combi rifles-cum-rubber-bullet launchers. A few yards away there's another checkpoint. This time the young men are in black uniforms with moustaches. They smoke and cradle Kalashnikovs and are the Palestinian police. Their shoulder flashes say Tourist Police, which could mean they are there for us, or that they are just visiting themselves.

Bethlehem is an Arab town, part of the disparate segregated ghettos of the proto-Palestinian state. I walk up to Manger Square in the centre of town. This is Bethlehem's moment, and it knows it. Moments like this only come along every thousand years, and they're going to make the best of it. The place is one huge, confused building site, getting ready for the prayed-for influx of millennial tourists. They are building a multistorey car park and bus station, an Arab heritage centre. The streets are being repaved. The gift shops and felafel shops are being scrimmed. Hoardings explain that the money for this development has been given by the Swedes and the Norwegians, the Japanese and the European Union. Palestine is a *Big Issue* state: it only exists on the philanthropy of strangers. But then again, so does Israel.

"O Little Town of Bethlehem, How Still We See Thee Lie" is pounded away in a reggae timpani of hammers and grinding gears. I'll never sing carols again without the ferrous taste of irony and cement dust. The Church of the Nativity, which covers the actual spot where Christ was born, is the oldest place of pilgrimage in Christendom, invested first by the Emperor Constantine's mum, who came here and built the first chapel, which was later shrouded in a second, bigger church. Although most of the religious buildings in this part of the world have been flattened by the ebb and flow of competing dogmas, Bethlehem has remained remarkably untouched. However, the church is not a pretty building, a lumpy block with haphazard additions and three tackily illuminated crosses on the roof. The doorway has been reduced to a serving hatch that a single person has to double up to pass through. How they are going to get a million pilgrims in and out is a mystery, but then so much about this place is a mystery. Inside, I was underwhelmed by the grandeur and venerability of the place – a timeworn barn with fat pillars and coarse tiles, and bituminous eastern votive paintings of boneless, agonised saints daubed onto fraying alligator skin by nameless jobbing artists. Very ornate beaten silver, icon-encrusted altar screen and hundreds of kebab-restaurant lamps, electric and oil, that trail a contradictory confusion of wires and ropes.

The reason for the contradiction in design, and indeed lighting, is that the church is held by three competing sects: the Greek Orthodox, the Armenians and the Roman Catholics. Welcome to God's car-boot sale. They have spent the past 2,000 years tit-for-tatting each other into an uneasy non-speak. At this point, I should admit that I am a believing (as opposed to a practising) Christian, but of the Protestant and low-church variety. We don't go in for this sort of thing, this fixation on lumps of rock and pilgrimage and the argy-bargy of sites. Any smugness on my part, though, must be tempered by the admission that if it were the Bible that you were talking about, then we'd be in there swinging to get hold of Ezekiel before the Methodists or the born-agains.

There is a strict rotation in services, each ancient church's monks waiting in the wings to clear the airwaves to God after the last heretic lot. Each has their own changing room and kit locker. This is made all the more complicated because the real holy of holies is not in the church but in the cellar. Downstairs, in a dank dungeon the size of a coal hole, is the exact spot (honest) where Christ was born, marked by a 14-point star to represent each generation back to King David. Next to it is the place (honest to God) where the manger stood. In this Stygian blackness everyone has their own set of lamps that hang like a 13th-century Transylvanian interior decorator's showroom and have to be blown out and relit for each service. Ah, but that's not all. The Armenians and the Greeks share the altar and its painting. But the Catholics have their own, so the canvas has to be removed and replaced with something equally tatty and glaucous. The Catholics also have the exclusive right to the manger – an area the size of a small lift – where the priest and his helpers all cling together chanting, waiting to be transported. As the Armenian bishop, who actually turned out to be Australian, set up his stall for early communion, I sat on a low stone bench trying to summon up some sense of spiritual peace and awe, a sense of place. A troop of Ukrainian pilgrims shuffled their way downstairs and then crawled between the bishop's skirts to get under the altar and kiss the star. They came up crossing like ticktack men. A scowling cowled monk hissed at me. I looked blank. "Your legs! Uncross your legs! Don't you know you're in church!" Leg crossing is obviously some ancient eastern mortal sin. Defeated, I escaped back up into the crepuscular fug where the Romans were grouping in their 4–2–4 formation, chanting their Tridentine *haka*. The Greek Orthodox priests, big lads with full beards and stiff black chefs' hats, bided their time by barking at tourists, harrying them, keeping them moving. If the Lord's my shepherd, then these blokes are his huge sheepdogs.

The one thing all the chanting prelates are united by is a fierce, barely contained irritation with the pilgrims. There's no congregation for any of these endless rounds of services, and loitering is firmly discouraged, with flapping hands and a shove in the back. Run-of-the-mill vanilla Christians are an irrelevance or a sacrilege, flies in the communion wine. I watched an American pilgrim hold a towel round his waist because he'd come all this way without realising that entering an Orthodox church in shorts was likely to upset people.

Just down the newly paved Norwegian road, but away from the general tourist beat, is the Milk Chapel. I must admit, I'd never heard of it. But then veneration of Mary doesn't come with my lot's hassocks. The Milk Chapel is supposed to be where Mary went to lactate before the flight to Egypt. It's a cave built into chalk. Which came first? The milk or the chalk? Only a Catholic could tell you. Inside is an illuminated case of mum with her *tsitskeh* out for baby Jesus, surrounded by roses and fairy lights. It is of a transcendent level of kitsch, unsurpassed in any votive shrine I've ever seen. The crumbly white walls have been blackened by oil lamps and candles, but holes have been scooped out all over it by desperate women who believe that to eat this holy rock will bring nourishment to their barren breasts. The monk in charge sternly discourages this practice. Of course, that sort of animistic superstition is hardly in keeping with a modern church. Oh, silly me. I've misunderstood. He has a supply of chalk out the back that he'd rather sell to the women. A group of Irish ladies kneel in the pews chanting an endless round of "Hail Mary, full of grace . . . Pray for us sinners now and at the hour of our death," over and over and over, as if God were hard of hearing. I escape again, into the hot, mechanical sunlight. I don't want to piss on anyone's candles, and there's quite enough competitive religion here, but frankly, selling blessed chalk as ex-vitro fertilisation to despairing women is beyond me.

Bethlehem is a place that attracts extremists. The government has just cleared out a number of the more frothing millennial revelationists. But in the desert hereabouts there are still pockets of fundamental Americans in beards and loincloths begging a little honey to go with their locusts, smiley in the knowledge that they only have a couple of weeks to go. And the local overworked psychiatrist specialises in come-again Christs. In fact, there's rumoured to be a special ward for them in the hospital: "I am the second coming." "No, love, you're the thirteenth this month." And John the Baptists waiting in outpatients for their medication: "You think I'm mad, you should see he who comes after me."

Back to Jerusalem, and the Church of the Holy Sepulchre. Birth to death in a single day. The old town of Jerusalem is quite picturesque, huddled behind Suleiman's curtain wall, built to keep Christians out. It has eight gates, from the evocative Dung to the bricked-up Golden Gate that will only open for the true second coming. And the Damascus Gate, famous as a home pitch for Palestinian-Israeli needle matches. Inside, the old town wiggles and winds in on itself, a labyrinth of narrow alleys and high walls, hiding dark courtyards. It's segregated into four quarters: the Jewish, Christian, Arab and Armenian. The Jewish quarter has had a lot of money spent on it. It's neat and rather soulless. A small boy stops me in the street and says: "Welcome to Israel." The Armenian quarter is perhaps the saddest, containing the prettiest church in Jerusalem. The Armenians have had a miserable time of it. They are the oldest Christian church in the world and they've needed to be. Set in a particularly volatile march between East and West, they've been roundly slaughtered by absolutely everyone. A menu in an Armenian restaurant gives a potted history of the troubles they've seen. It's unremitting and quite puts me off dinner, almost as much as dinner puts me off dinner. I really expected it to end up with: "But we had a good day in June 1370. The sun shone and we went on a picnic." The walls of the Armenian quarter are plastered with gruesome photographs and explanatory maps mourning their genocide. It's a measure of their continuing bad luck that they are forced to do this in Jerusalem, not a place to try to elicit sympathy for your pogroms. "Holocaust? Don't talk to us about holocaust."

The Arab quarter is the liveliest; a huggermugger market of fruit and meat and clothes and cupboard shops selling videos and plastic toys and garish sweets, blaring with Arab pop music and dodgy archeological coins, the widow's mite pendant or 30 pieces of silver as a necklace. The little bureaux de change, with a nice biblical turn, call themselves moneychangers. And there's a bric-a-brac of religion. Everyone is catered for here. Crucifixes hang happily with Stars of David and Fatima's Hand. Dimpled pink baby Jesuses lie among the worry beads and rosaries. Fezzes steeple the side piles of yarmulkes, mezuzahs nestle in checked Palestinian headscarves, T-shirts crawl up the wall, Yasser Arafat's face overlapping a picture of a machine pistol with the embarrassing slogan "Uzi Does It". And it strikes me that for all its crassness and exploitation, you can't deny that the free market succeeds where ages of argument and bullets have failed. It makes short work of theological and political differences. You may struggle for a thousand, two thousand years over the minutiae of dogma, but here business makes all religions one big, dollar-friendly, happy family. I toy with the idea of buying a crown of thorns. There are dozens in various sizes at very reasonable prices. But I can't decide who to give it to. Maybe they only seem funnily ironic here.

The Via Dolorosa, Christ's last trip as a mortal, is, like everything else, not what I expected. A narrow, circuitous route, it starts outside the city wall by Golgotha and then traipses past the Arab souvenir shops, with the stations of the cross marked obscurely on the wall, competing with adverts for barbers and pirated videos. There used to be eight stations of the cross, but in the Middle Ages they became so popular in Europe that market forces added a few more. Now there are 14. Christ fell here for the first time, here for the second time, and way over here for the third. You can hire a lightweight, half-size cross from the Holy Sepulchre and do it yourself, like hiring a scooter in Skíathos, or a bicycle in Penrith. It's a novel way to get around, by crucifix. I get caught behind a confused group of Filipino Catholics who swapped over at each station. "I'm No 8, the woman wiping the brow," "No, you're No 9, falling for the third time." Anyway, they were going backwards. I noticed that nobody had volunteered to be the two thieves. That would be real humility.

You come to the Church of the Holy Sepulchre almost by accident. It has no vista. It's almost swallowed up by the Arab warren and, again, it's not a beautiful building. Big and bulbous and cavernous. "In my father's house there are many rooms," has been taken literally. Chapels and altars burrow into the darkness. The fractious bad temper of the Church of the Nativity is multiplied. Here, six, or is it eight, separate pre-Reformation sects vie for supremacy over the holy of holies. A platoon of ancient Egyptian Christians are actually squatting on the roof. Nobody agrees on anything. The brass lamps proliferate like an arms race, spreading ever more gloom. And it's here that I realise what these churches, and indeed Israel, remind me of – it's the way-out-there, end-of-the-universe, lawless, freebooters' planet from *Star Wars*, a votive frontier town mining spiritual gold from dross, a federation of disparate and weird aliens in funny hats and exotic robes, with obscure and ancient ceremonies, tortuous languages and bizarre habits. Here, along with the orthodoxies of Rome and Greece and Russia, Armenia and Serbia, the ancient Copts and Ethiopians, the Falashas, Black Christians from Zanzibar and Angola, there are wimpled Carmelites, cassocked Cistercians, Franciscans, Benedictines and free-range, born-again ecstatics. Outside, there are Ashkenazi Jews, Sephardic Jews, the Chassidim, the Hezbollah,

PLO, and there are migrants from Hungary, Russia and Poland, from Morocco, Alexandria, Slovenia and Slovakia, the Carpathians. There are Baptists from Alabama and Methodists from Michigan. There are Catholics from Macáu and Hyderabad, and everybody, everybody, is drawn to this barren lump of sun-cracked rock that produces nothing more than avocados, miniature machine pistols and olive wood salad servers. But in this dusty rock is the world's largest deposit of crude religion and the natural gas of intolerance. It's in the air. In the dust. You can feel it prickle your skin in the heat.

The first thing you see in the Church of the Holy Sepulchre is Christ's morgue slab, a polished piece of marble on the floor, guarded by the inevitable squadron of hanging lamps. It's kept wet. Pilgrims prostrate themselves like flocks of thirsty sheep to kiss it, dipping their fingers to genuflect. Next to it is Golgotha. The sights in the Holy Sepulchre come like rides in some ethereal Disneyland. Golgotha, the Hill of Skulls, is up a windy staircase, a small room packed with various denominations of professional and amateur pilgrims, gunning their Instamatics at a large cut-out Christ. Like the hero in a Pollock's theatre, it syncopates in the stuttering flash. Again the X that marks the spot of the cross is under the altar, so they crawl between legs to get a snog. And it was here that I saw the only example of real ecstasy. A nun from some exotic denomination, with a pointy hat and a medieval wraparound headscarf affair that looked like a linen wet suit, was transported; her pretty, virginal face a Flemish picture of pity and pain and adoration. It was a fleeting glimpse as the crowd of collected supplicants with their umbrella-waving guides pressed us on to the very heart of the Christian faith – the resurrection.

Without a resurrection, there is no Christianity. Everything else we can and do argue about, but this is the peg on which all the rest hangs, the central, death-defying act of faith. The tomb is housed in yet another marble Wendy chapel. It's falling down and is supported by RSJs as an unfortunate metaphor for the state of organised religion. The room itself can hold perhaps a dozen people, so the pilgrims queue four-deep for hours to get a look in where they can click a shot to ascertain that, phew, indeed, there isn't a body. The line is hot and bothered. It sways and bulges. A lot of people have come from cultures where orderly queuing is not in their natures. There's a babble of bad-tempered muttering. Monks harry and shoo and elbow the crowd. This being Sunday afternoon, it's time for evensong. A flying picket of Roman Catholic brothers, fit lads, start to manhandle the crowd without explanation. The volume of complaint rises in a dozen languages. The queue dissolves into a pushing, shoving throng. Those at the front have been waiting for hours to look in at an empty room, and they're not taking this on the other cheek. They're probably not even Catholic. The brothers get stuck in. Old American women begin spinning into the outer darkness. A Spanish tour group starts shoving back. The monks call up reinforcements. A flying wedge splits the pilgrims in half with some premier-division high-elbow work. In the distant gloom, a choir starts chanting Latin, the monks redouble their efforts and are joined by a Palestinian guard. Everyone's shouting now. The guard gets to the door of the tomb and I notice he is wearing a revolver. I can't imagine any other holy place in the world where it would be acceptable to allow a man with a gun. And certainly not here, where the Prince of Peace passively accepted crucifixion. The choir enter the fray, fronted by a chap swinging a censer like a tear-gas canister. The pilgrims retreat, an angry, confused mob. The monks face them like riot police. A bishop arrives, looks in at the tomb – phew, still no body – and chants evensong. The organ pipes up.

Off stage, another choir starts. That sonorous, sad, dusty descant that is Russian, or perhaps Serb, or Armenian. For a few minutes, the two sects compete in a discordant counterpoint. Then the Romans retreat to a side chapel and the eastern Orthodoxes, led by an imposing bloke in a duvet beard and a hat that looks like Darth Vader's bed cap, takes his place at the tomb and has a look inside – phew. He does his thing. The Catholics may have retreated, but they've regrouped and they're not giving up; they've still got control of the organ. An Orthodox monk produces a mobile phone from his sleeve and has a muttered conversation – probably with the archangel Gabriel. Snatch squads of prelates manhandle stray lambs. This is a schoolboy vision of the Middle Ages, and it makes *Life of Brian* look like a documentary.

The most poignant and distressing thing about all of this is that there's no congregation. Nobody's listening. Visitors are dis-invited. This is between God and the professionals, as opposed to the merely faithful. Faith is a fugitive and difficult thing. One moment you're full of it. The next you can barely find a vestige. If you look for it straight on, it vanishes. You only glimpse it out of the corner of your eye. However annoying and bovine and crass the tour groups of retired American born-agains and Irish single mothers' clubs are, they have been brought here by faith. They haven't come to Israel for the view, or the relaxing luxury, or the food, or that famous Israeli hospitality. They've come to a troubled, dangerous corner of the world because this is where faith began. They've come with their own troubles to allay, with terrible sadnesses, with guilt and with fear and with hope, often at the end of their lives, on pilgrimages they have promised them-selves and saved for over years. They don't have the luxury of a monk's vocation, the glorious lack of responsibility that a life in holy orders gives you. And at the one place where they should find solace and conviction, they are treated like idiotic cattle, as an irrelevance and a nuisance. But still, they leave, not just with their olivewood nativity sets and their rosaries, but with their faith. And that's nothing short of miraculous. God works in mysterious ways.

Here at the spiritual meridian of the millennium, like every-thing else, nobody can agree what day of the month it is. There's the Roman calendar, the Julian and the Gregorian. The Muslims think it's the 15th century. So the great irony is there's going to be hardly anyone here celebrating the millennium anyway, and oh, January 1st is a Saturday, so the Jews can't make it either.

The fatal shore

The fatal shore

The Aral Sea, July 2000

The man behind the desk has a bandaged ear. Perhaps a previous guest let him keep the rest of his head as a tip. He holds my passport and press accreditation as if they are fortune cookies containing death threats. He licks his fingers, then his lips, then the ballpoint and begins very slowly copying out the letters and numbers in triplicate on three ancient, moth-winged ledgers. He has no idea what he is writing, it's all English to him, awkward for his Cyrillic-conditioned fingers.

Finally, he writes US$40 on a scrap of paper and rubs his thumb and forefinger together. Forty dollars. That's more than a month's wages for a middle-class man here – if they had anything as outré and modern as a middle class. He hands me a receipt on a square of brown lavatory paper, which is useful because it's the only lavatory paper in the place. This is only a hotel because they charge you $40 to stay. There's no furniture and no soap. The water comes in a prostated, rusty dribble. The bath has been used to interrogate sheep. The towel is a bar mat. There's a blanket, a chipped tin teapot and a carpet that looks like tar applied with a comb. All night, lost herdsmen bang on my door and stare as if they've seen the ghost of tsars past. Welcome to Nukus, rhymes with mucus, twinned with nowhere. Nukus, no mates.

Nukus is the capital of Kara-Kalpakstan. Don't pretend you've heard of it, a semi-autonomous republic in the far west of Uzbekistan. One of the "stans", shires of the former Soviet Union. A vast area of vast land. Desert, mountain, broken promises and wrecked grand plans once known collectively as Turkistan or where-the-hell's-that-stan. Now cut into five post-meltdown new countries – Tajikistan, Turkmenistan, Kyrgyzstan, Kazakhstan and Uzbekistan – which stretch from the Caspian Sea in the west over Iran, Afghanistan, Pakistan and the Tien Shan mountains of China to Mongolia. This was the Russians' back yard, not open to the public

– a place to dump rubbish, people, embarrassments and five-year plans. Up there somewhere in the desert is Star City and the space programme. Also the glowing half-life of above-ground nuclear test sites and their collateral seeping, cancerous waste. But right here is the big one – the stans' main claim to an entry in the *Guinness Book of Records*. The Kara-Kalpaks can boast the Biggest Ecological Disaster in the World, Ever. Nothing else, no smoking rainforest, no solitary carnivore, no home-county ring road, comes close to the majesty of this disaster. Not just the biggest, but the fastest. Organised and executed with the precipitate callousness, greed and sheer eye-bulging stupidity that only hands-on communism can muster. They've managed to drain the Aral Sea, the fourth biggest inland lump of water on the globe, and they've done it in 20 years. The southern Aral was created and maintained by the Oxus river (now known as the Amu Darya), which rises in the frozen attic of the Pamir mountains and meanders across grassland in search of a coast, finally giving up and creating its own terminus. The Oxus is/was one of the great rivers – the ancient Persians thought it the greatest. Along its banks the towns of the silk route flourished. The orchards and spice gardens, the mulberry trees and roses of Samarkand and Bukhara and Khiva.

Cotton has always been grown here, mixed with silk into a bright material that made Bukhara famous. Then in 1861, across the Pacific, something apparently utterly unconnected with central Asia caused the flutter of chiffon that grew into a wind that became a dust storm that changed everything: the American civil war. Russia was one of the few supporters of the South (we were another). Russia bought its cotton from the South – to make up the deficit they increased production in the stans. When the communists took over, they decided to bury capitalism in a generation, and turned the whole of this vast area into a mono-crop culture of the stuff. In 1932, they started the Fergana valley canal, one of the huge, murderous, wasteful engineering achievements of Stalinism. It was only the beginning. Soon the apparently inexhaustible Oxus was gashed and slashed with thousands of miles of arbitrary irrigation, canals and dams, hydroelectric plants and repetitive ditches. They did the unthinkable, the unimaginable: they bled the river dry. Now it does not even reach the Aral Sea.

Oh, but that's not the half of it. Cotton is one of the thirstiest crops, and all mono-crops are prone to disease and infestation. Cotton naturally is particularly weedy. The haemorrhaging river leached salt that should have gone to the sea into the earth. The water came on and off the field up to 15 times in its course and sucked more salt to the surface, salinating the water table. Now a crystal layer sits on the exhausted earth and the tea tastes like a practical joke (oddly, it improves the coffee). Here, the drinking water is three or four times more saline than is considered healthy or palatable. To salt the land is a biblical horror, the final murderous curse of a place. Kara-Kalpakstan has become the largest cruet set in the world. Ah, but we are not finished: terrified managers facing falling yields sprayed tonnes of phosphates, nitrogen and, worst, DDT indiscriminately over the fields, and it's still all here, blowing in the wind.

Step out onto the wide, grim, grey streets of Nukus, and in one slow pan you can see all you will ever need to know about communism. It is not so much that this place of hateful, cheap Soviet architecture fills the soul with gloom: it's that it sucks everything remotely beautiful or sensitive from the soul, leaving a vacuum of low-grade depression and the tinnitus of despair. Seventy years of communism, all that hardship, terror, death. All that effort and hope and promises, the forced migrations, the cruelty, exhaustion, misery and rationing, the starvation and privation, the mechanical, imperative certainty of it all, ended up with this baking, grim bleakness.

A few bronchitic, gaseous Ladas career along its broadly potted and rotted roads, every one a taxi. An old woman squats beside an upturned box, selling individual cigarettes, sunflower seeds and sluggish, dusty cola. She is the summit of independent Uzbek private enterprise. A man in a traditional skullcap pulls a reluctant goat on a rope. The goats bleats piteously – it knows this is not a good day. Soviet-style posters of happy storm troopers and peasant girls fondling potent sheaves fade and curl in the hot wind. Bits of folk-painted hardboard clap against iron and cement like early drafts for BA tail fins. This is a bad place, a sick place. The damage to the land is as nothing compared with the damage to these people.

Here is a brief and incomplete list of what the Kara-Kalpaks can expect in return for their cheap cotton and blasted land: bronchial asthma, allergic rhinitis, infantile cerebral palsy, chronic lung disease, kidney disease, endocrine disease, urogenital disease, diseases of the nervous system, all of them way, way beyond what would be considered acceptable in a normal, moderately developed world, and chronic anaemia. Even before they're born, Kara-Kalpaks are cursed by their habitat: 97% of pregnant women are anaemic, 30% of births may have defects, 1 in 10 babies may already be dead. These figures, as with all statistics in this piece, are educated, conservative guesses by outside agencies. The Uzbeks don't make a habit of washing their salty linen in public or letting their citizens know what's sitting at the end of their bed. But there are special wards just for birth defects here that no outsider has ever seen, the consequence of DDT and salt and malnutrition – thin bread and tea is the daily diet of most Kara-Kalpaks. What makes all this more ironic is that these exhausted women were the original Amazons, the warrior caste Alexander supposedly would not fight. If a child makes it past birth and the 30% infant mortality rate, then it had better pack its experiences and fun tight, because life expectancy is probably only 38 choked, grim years.

The microscope I'm looking through is a gift from Médecins Sans Frontières (MSF). Through the mist of blue, stained lung gunk on the slide swims a bright red spot. That's it. Yes, that's definitely it. The red spot that marks your card for life: tuberculosis. TB is the number one top-of-the-pops killer in Kara-Kalpakstan. New cases in Nukus come in at a hacking 167.9 per 100,000 of the population (50 is considered an epidemic elsewhere). The microscope is the only piece of equipment in Nukus's TB hospital that couldn't have been made by a carpenter or farrier. This rambling institution, like the hotel, is only a hospital because someone says it is. There is no equipment, nothing that plugs in, just iron beds and broken tables and Cyrillic posters warning against Aids, which hasn't got here yet. The distempered walls flake and sag.

There's an overwhelming smell of sick, hot sewage. A truck pumps out the open latrines. Most patients sit outside in the baking dust, catching what passes for fresh air. The hot wind gusts with thick, poisonous lungs. The stoic sick hawk and spit. Spitting is a national sport. When I suggested, all things considered, they might be asked to stop, I'm told it's delicate, it's a cultural thing. Yeah, and Genghis Khan thought kicking people to death in sacks was a cultural thing. TB is very, very infectious. We walk around wearing paper Donald Duck masks.

As ever, the children's ward is the most depressing: little girls wheezing on beds, watching the motes dance in the sun; the hospital cannot even feed them properly – a little yogurt if they are lucky; mothers in bright headscarves hover in corners, desperately grateful for even this, not wanting to draw attention or make a fuss; infants as young as nine months are brought in with TB. In children, it's likely not just to be pulmonary: it affects the other organs, the bone, the spine, as meningitis.

A small lad tags along with us, pretty, pallid, central Asian features with a mop of black hair. Whenever I look rough, he's there, sneaking with a tyke's smile and a slight squint. His name sounds like Gary. Gary's bright as a button, except he's not: he's got TB and the complications of pleurisy, and he's brain-damaged; and he's an orphan; he's seven.

Today, by chance, is my son's seventh birthday. Thousands of miles from here, his healthy lungs are blowing out candles. I should be there but I'm not; I'm here with Gary, who puts his face close to mine and laughs – the first laugh I've heard in days, a tinkling, rippling noise, an echo from another place. I smile back but realise he can't see it, because I'm wearing this antiseptic muzzle to protect me from his breath.

Being dealt TB, pleurisy, brain damage and a family of one in Nukus is about as low a hand as God can offer a seven-year-old. We walk on through the wards, the little hand fits into mine and breaks my heart. TB is not an illness like cancer or malaria or cholera. It's not the result of bad luck or bad drains or genes or insects. It's a consequence, an indicator of something else, something we've got loads of – money. More exactly, the absence of it. TB hitches a ride on the back of extreme poverty. Only the poor and malnourished, the weak, are susceptible. It's as if they read the instructions on the box the West comes in wrong, and went and got inconspicuous consumption. That it should have returned so violently and comprehensively in what was, until a decade ago, part of a superpower, is a symbol of how precipitous the collapse in central Asia has been.

MSF is treating TB with some success, and for every patient, of course, that's a miracle. But in the general walk of life in Uzbekistan, it means little or nothing. MSF is here because someone should be here to show that someone out there noticed and cared. They can't tell how many of their failures have the terrifying new variant of drug-resistant TB. Oh, it's out there. Prisons have about 40% TB, one in five of those drug-resistant. The only laboratories that could do the tests are in the West. Incidentally, my local Chelsea & Westminster Hospital had a rare case last year: an immigrant who was kept in locked isolation. He escaped, and the health officer ordered a police search. Here it could be anyone: the waiter, the man who spits at your feet, the policeman who leans in the window to check your papers. The treatment for drug-resistant TB costs £8,000, has side effects of kidney failure and blindness, lasts five months and then it's only 50-50, a toss-up.

Don't stop reading yet. The best bit is still to come. We haven't got to Muynak yet, the destination of this piece, the real reason I came here. Someone said to me in passing, apropos of nothing, over lunch in the Ivy: "Hey, why don't you go to the worst place in the world?" The worst place in the world has an emphatic ring to it.

We leave Nukus in an ancient Volga. The driver loves it. A fine car. A good car. It's a deathtrap heap: the safety belt is attached to the chassis with gaffer tape. On the outskirts of town, a bridge crosses the Oxus. The river is a brown, turgid worm as broad as a peaty salmon-spawn stream. "There are the old banks where it used to run," points the driver. Where? I look and can't see. And then, pulling back for focus, the width and depths of the once-upon-a-time river are revealed in the distance. It was huge, wider than the Nile – a dozen motorways across. Awesome, appalling. The road traces the crippled stream north, through the horizon-shoving flatness of semi-desert and large, vacant fields with a frosting of salt. We pass plunky, unstable three-wheeled tractors, sand-matted camels, men in traditional long coats and boots with galoshes riding dusty, ballet-toed donkeys, and patient families with small, plastic bundles waiting for lifts. Every tree in Uzbekistan is painted white. It's the literalism of communism. Someone once wrote an after-lunch memo, and the next day they started painting all the trees. We stop in a village to visit the hospital. The doctor in his white coat, boiled thin and translucent, and the tall chef's hat that medical folk wear here, stands in the dust. A cleaning woman is tearing a strip off him; the patients stare at him. For a moment, he looks at the ants and silently turns back to his barren, distempered office. His one medical assistant has just got TB. He hasn't been paid his pittance of a salary for seven months. The health ministry has fined his under-resourced hospital for not disposing of its rubbish properly. He hasn't got an incinerator, a tin can belches greasy sputum smoke. He drinks. All day, every day, hopelessly.

When the Soviet Union finally collapsed with exhaustion and horror, the stans were the only constituent part that didn't want independence. They actually asked to stay – better the devil . . . Russia had to push them out like reluctant teenagers, so they waited till they had half a dozen Aeroflot planes on their provincial runways and declared independence and a national airline. Nothing else changed much – it just got smaller and meaner. Uzbekistan is still a one-party command economy. It recently came top of a business magazine's list of the world's most corrupt countries (when that was reprinted in the local press, Uzbekistan's name had miraculously vanished, that's how corrupt it is). Every cotton harvest, schools, universities and offices are emptied into the fields. Everyone must pick and sleep in freezing barns, beg food and drink salty ditchwater. It gets harder: every year the fields are scoured for every wisp of cotton. Yet the people don't yearn for democracy. Democracy is an indecipherable foreign language. Since before the birth of Christ, this swathe of earth has suffered under waves of light-cavalry dictators: Macedonians, Persians, Arabs, Scythians, Mongols, Russians. A word was invented for them: horde.

This place is antidemocracy, the opposite of democracy. What people yearn for is a new, better, stronger megalomaniac. There are rumblings of infectious, fundamental Islam coming from out of the desert, and the government is keen to associate itself with the personality cult of Tamerlane, or Timur, as they call him, erecting hideous, *über*-realist statues, gaining strength by retrospective association. Timur was Uzbekistan's home-grown 10th-century monster, creator and desecrator of the biggest land-base empire ever seen. A man who made Stalin look Swiss.

Muynak quivers out of the dust. It looks like solidifying dust, shimmering in the heat haze. It's a seaside town, a spa town, a summer holiday place with a promenade that's also a fishing port with a flotilla of big trawlers and cargo barges in a harbour. There's a huge fish cannery that's won international awards. You can tell instinctively it's a seaside town. It has that sense, that rather tatty, low-rise feeling; light and air, bracing.

We walk up a dune to the edge of a beach and look out to sea. It's desert, as far as the eye can stretch – flat, scrub desert with shells. Muynak is now 100 kilometres from the water. It's as if you stood on Brighton pier and the sea started at Paris – truly unbelievable, shocking. In the distance, dust storms twist, a family walks across the sea bed, the father's angry: "Wolves," he shouts. Wolves took his cow in the night. His son carries its head in a congealing sack. Sea wolves, sea cow. Muynak is a town in shock. It feels the sea like an amputated limb. Still aches for it. Men sit and look out at the waves of sand and hear the surf. The Aral Sea, with its thick deposits of salt and chemicals, is now the biggest single collection of dust in the world. It's the equivalent of a friable, airborne, choking Holland. Every year, suffocating toxic clouds blow into town. Man-killer dust. And I forgot to mention, out there, just over the curl of the earth, is an island that, in the way of this country's negative absolutes, has the biggest chemical weapons plant in the world, that contains the largest dump of anthrax on the planet – abandoned, waiting for the wind.

Of all the ills that have been dumped on Kara-Kalpakstan, it seems invidious, unnecessary, to mention unhappiness, but Muynak feels grief-stricken to the point of madness. The people move with a slow, pointless lethargy. All around, there are signs of psychotic, repetitive comfort: men sit rocking like caged bears, women with short reed brooms sweep their doorsteps maniacally for hours. I watch a man wash an ancient green van from sunrise to sunset, the corrosive dust falling as fast as he can wipe. Early one morning, I notice an old chap sitting on a bench staring at the absent coast, legs crossed, arms folded in his lap. At dusk, he's still there, hasn't moved a muscle.

The town itself is worn out, all its constituent parts loose and sagging; hinges rasp, the edges of things are darkly rounded with abrasion. It's coming to the end, the factories and canneries slowly sink into the grit. The darkly empty fish fridges are slumped saunas in the heat. Steel hawsers and bits of black metal grow out of the rising earth like hardy plants or drowning hands. Even imagining the effort that once invigorated them is exhausting. Stunted cattle plod the street, cudding dust and mud, so scrawny that at first I wondered why they were all calves. Large, hard-boned dogs crack their skulls on the smoky rubbish wasteland on the edge of town, hanks of gory sheepskin lie in the turgid filth and multi-species dung. Only the children run and shriek and throw stones and wrestle like children everywhere, making balls out of rags. The three, parallel Tarmac streets are their playground. The road is covered in chalk drawings: hopscotch and football pitches, pictograms of dolls and soldiers, houses, cars and ships. Ships they'll never sail in. It's a long, black wish-list letter to Father Christmas, the one dictator who never visited these parts.

They're still here, the ships – huge ships, blackened and callused. They lie askew in their dry beds, at anchor for ever, their plates wrenched off to make defensive stockades for houses. Their ribs are like the bones of extinct animals; brave and boastful names peel off their hulls. I lie in the dunes and listen to them, the wind plays them like a sad band: hatches boom, metal keens for the lost sea. A hawk hunts the sparse grass where seagulls should call, runty cattle move silently in line astern. You can still hear it, the echo of the surf hissing on the hot shore. It is the strangest, most maudlin place I've ever been. There's something particularly awful about dead ships. All other discarded man-engineered metal is eyesore rubbish, but not ships. They retain a sense of what they were: a majesty, a memory of the lightness under their keels. Of all the things sailors dread, carry superstitious talismans against, weather and wave, snapped hawser and hidden shoal, none, even in his wildest dreams, imagined that the sea would leave him, would get up and steal away.

This town thought many things, worried and dreaded plenty, but it could not conceive that it would one day be abandoned to dust. Up on a dune overlooking the mirage of water is the Russian sailors' graveyard. The crosses made out of welded iron pipe have, in the Orthodox way, three crossbars. Unkempt and crooked, they look like the spars of tall ships ferrying the dead. All the Russians that could go have gone now, leaving the Kara-Kalpaks. But the old Russian harbour master is still here, living in a dark hovel of memories and smells with his babushka wife, a painting of Stalin and a map of remembrance with fathom markings that are thin air. He has his uniform and grows garrulous about the good days when there were 40,000 people here. Holiday-makers, work and play. "It took a day, a whole day, to sail across the Aral. We knew it was shrinking; we built canals out to it; we chased after the sea." And then, one day in 1986, all the fishing boats went out, cast their nets in a circle, and when they pulled them in, there was nothing. "We knew it was the end."

A story like this, a story of such unremitting misery, ought to end with a candle of hope. There should be something to be done. Well, I'm sorry, there isn't. Plenty of better men with clipboards and white Land Cruisers have been here to put it back together again, but they've retreated, dumbfounded and defeated. The World Bank has just spent $40m on a feasibility study and come up with a big idea. The big idea is a wetland bird reserve. Thanks, that would do nicely. You can't cry over spilt water: it just adds more salt. The sea will never come back to Muynak. The river will never repair its banks to meet it. The people of Muynak have nothing to do and nowhere to go; surrounded by thousands of miles of dust, without money or health or expectations, they'll just wait to die. The children will stop drawing in the street, grow up and give up, and the town will give up with them.

I said at the beginning that it was an ecological disaster, but that's not right. That puts it at a remove, makes the Oxus and the Aral Sea a piece of cowboy exterior design, a cockup with fish and minerals. It's not that. It's a human disaster of titanic proportions.

This hard earth of ours doesn't care if it's a sea or a desert, a river or a dune. It has no game plan, no aesthetic. Eagles will replace the gulls, and there are plenty of salt-loving succulents that see this as a golden opportunity. Rivers and seas come and go, there's just no space for people here. For them, for us.

In the hospital a young lad sits on the edge of his bed. He is frightened, his eyes are like saucers. His breath is as quick and shallow as a trapped bird's. He's right to be frightened. He's very, very sick. His bones incubate a mortal malevolence. His mother has pinned a little cloth triangle to his shirt. I ask what it is. "A protection against the evil eye, for good luck." It holds salt – cotton and salt. Boy, was she ever misinformed.

The city that russia forgot

The city that Russia forgot

Kaliningrad, June 2001

"Hello, I'm Victor, Special Forces frogman, I'm your driver for today." Victor is a poppet. He coaxes his hyperventilating Volkswagen, with its flag of the Baltic fleet hanging from the rear-view mirror as a warning to thieves, into the belching traffic.

"Welcome to Kaliningrad."

Underestimate the Russian at your peril. In particular never underestimate his capacity for corporate ugliness. It is boundless, bottomless, fathomless. It stretches in concrete waves over the horizon and Kaliningrad is its greatest monumental evocation.

Only a very big idea and a steely will could have so relentlessly removed every scintilla of aesthetic pleasure from the vista. Kaliningrad boasts the most stratospherically ghastly building ever conceived: "the people's palace". Huge square towers linked by thick walkways, it stands on a slight eminence and is emphatically hellish. This is communism's Taj Mahal or St Peter's: the 20th century's anti-Sydney Opera House. It was built in the 1960s by Khrushchev, who ordered that a 14th-century castle be dynamited to give it space. The castle had the posthumous last laugh, though. Its dungeons and subterranean tunnels made the monster unsafe. It has never opened, and stands today as a symbolic crumbling ruin to everything Soviet. Russians like symbols, they love this one with a thin, grim humour, as they adore the motorway flyover that hangs behind it, going from nowhere to no place bereft of motorway. There's something rather restful about Kaliningrad's unremitting hideousness. If you're used to living among things picked with care and taste, if your eye is constantly snagged by decoration and proportion, then their absence is somehow soothing. You know you'll never have to arrange your face into a look of cultured interest, you're excused cooing. You have to gasp a lot, though.

Kaliningrad, ugly old fishwife of the Baltic until a decade and a half ago, the secret, closed home port of the Soviet Baltic fleet. An enclave the size of Northern Ireland, wedged between Poland and Lithuania, home to a million-and-a-half Russian souls. Today it's a naval scrapyard with a wallowing, oxidising fishing fleet cut off by 1,000 kilometres from the seedy bulk of Mother Russia. A place that was spat out of perestroika as a stunned, suddenly pointless anomaly. It boasts the highest proportion of drug addicts and associated Aids sufferers in the Russian Federation, and 40% of the population exist below the poverty line – that's the Russian poverty line, which is as low as you can draw a line without falling over. Kaliningrad is gristled with corruption, drugs, smuggling, sex slavery, endemic theft and thuggery. There's also spiralling TB and the associated diseases of pollution. Nobody really knows what military slurry is buried here, how many toxins rust and seep in the earth and air.

Two pulp mills spew chemicals into the river that is the only source of the city's water. What everyone does know is that the emetic, heavily chlorinated and worryingly green stuff that splutters from the tap is undrinkable. Kaliningrad is also the lifelong home and resting place of the philosopher Kant, and digs up 90% of the world's amber. But it wasn't always thus. Kaliningrad, named after Mikhail Ivanovich Kalinin, the first chairman of the central executive committee of the USSR, was once Königsberg.

Named as the birthplace of Prussian kings, a city founded by the Teutonic knights who were to become so politically eroticised by Hitler, Königsberg was the capital of Ost Prussia, a sort of Kraut Kosovo, the spiritual home of Germanic chivalry and bellicosity. It's also one of those historically buried fault lines, the scars that criss-cross old Europe and occasionally ache with ancient, half-remembered resentment. This is where the Teuton West met the Slav East, the furthest point of the Russian Federation.

In 1945, the great, patriotic Soviet Belarussian Army bloodily stormed Königsberg after four days of incendiary carpet-bombing by the RAF that reduced 90% of the huddled German city to its constituent parts and 60,000 civilians into nameless graves. At Potsdam, Churchill, Roosevelt and Stalin carved up a new cold war, and it was agreed that Stalin could keep Königsberg as a year-round, ice-free port. He expelled all the Germans who hadn't already departed westward in starving refugee columns, and moved in Russians from 28 republics. All remembrance of Aryans past would be expunged.

Landing at Kaliningrad airport is like stepping back into an early Len Deighton novel. The hammer and sickle and two very groovy 1950s jets are picked out in wrought iron on the terminal roof. The formalities are old-style Soviet. The current geopolitical scenario for Kaliningrad: in the euphoria of the collapse of the eastern bloc, among the scramble for booty and investment and the sprouting of perky little republics, nobody remembered disengaged Kaliningrad stuck up here on the cold-war coast. So it held its breath and settled into a stasis of residual authoritarianism and new corruption, governed by the Baltic fleet's admiral and Russian mafia. As the EU sets about expanding, they've suddenly looked at the map and, oh my God, noticed that if and when Poland and the Baltic States join up there will be an anomaly, a little bit of old Russia stuck in the middle of our happy-clappy, free-trade kibbutz. So now, belatedly democratic, caring folk with rimless spectacles and concerned frowns are starting to think about Kaliningrad quite hard. The scenarios that slide to mind are disturbing. Already this is called the corridor of crime, and it could become an effluent conduit, pumping illegal immigrants, smuggled goods, prostitutes, drugs, pornography and arms into fortress, market-garden Europe. This is Russia's Gibraltar. Europe's Hong Kong. Twenty years after a tearful "Ode to Joy" was sung over the deconstruction of the Berlin Wall, will the West have to build another one further east to keep the Russkies and the filth out? And wouldn't that be an irony? What's to become of Kaliningrad?

Chris Patten, Europe's foreign minister, recently spent a scant day here asking tricky questions like, could we buy it as scrap? Or would they tow it away as a headache eyesore? A stream of questing Eurocrats would come to wring hands, drink vodka and negotiate possible aid packages with prostitutes. If you're looking for a plot for a post-cold-war thriller, you couldn't do better than to start in the Kaliningrad hotel bar, where the startlingly beautiful, semiprofessional hookers from the technical college smile with a sleek knowing and cadge cigarettes (you have to pay a steep bribe to get into university these days). The barmaid picks up my passport with the reverence of a holy relic, opens it at my gawky photo, then, putting it to her nose like a bouquet, inhales and whispers: "Ahh, Angerlish." Passport-sniffing for a whiff of foreign travel is pretty desperate. But then Kaliningrad is the physical embodiment of desperation.

Outside, the sulphurous sky hangs like grey laundry 100ft overhead. On the broad streets where the German cobbles are patchworked with crusty commie asphalt and potholes, hundreds of nicked western BMWs, Mercedes and Fiats lurch and belch around ancient trams and trolleybuses. On top of the bile-green, slurry-taupe and mortician-grey tenement blocks, the slogans of communism – "bread and motherland", "victory to heroic Soviet workers" – cling on, but are being elbowed aside by the United Colors of Benetton, Panasonic and Coca-Cola. Kaliningrad doesn't know if it's coming or going. In fact, it's doing both. This is one of the last places in Russia that still boast public statues of Lenin. There are a lot of old Soviet memorials: a wonderful, huge and decidedly camp cosmonaut (Kaliningrad produced three), tanks and torpedo boats on concrete plinths. But it's not all ugly. The girls are beautiful, with sickle cheekbones and hammering breasts. They favour tiny miniskirts and opaquely opalescent tights, and have the ice-eyed look of Natashas and Laras who might at the drop of a dollar give a man more trouble than he could conceivably imagine. They also have the worse dye jobs in the history of hairdressing. I can only imagine they go to salons with bits of liver, cement and broken Barbie dolls and say: "I want it this colour." There's a weird vogue for flesh-coloured bobs.

The men have those pinched Slavic or Mr Potato faces, and they universally lurk in black leather jackets that come with unpleasant design features, multiple pockets and emphatic stitching. Everyone seems to move in a world of their own, surrounded by a personal insulation of depression. Occasionally they try to walk right through you. This is a place of sliding eyes and sideways glances, blankly hostile faces that give away nothing and take in everything. Nobody wants to be photographed. This is a society ingrained with suspicion, which reads the tiniest instruction or warning in a gesture, a shoe, a watch or a pair of sunglasses. Only a culture cold-pressed into uniform sameness could produce so many whisper-thin layers of hierarchy and fear. There are a spectacular number of drunks, not laughing or fighting drunks, but dribbling, stoic drunks. Wasteland and parks are crunchy with broken bottles. On every bench and wall sit silent, hunched figures with thousand-yard stares. Men crouch over fishing rods dunked in stinking, turgid canals and other men crouch and watch them. How despairing does a place have to be before worm-drowning becomes a spectator attraction? And over the bronchitic hum of traffic, it's strangely silent. In all the time I was here, I never heard anyone laugh. And I hardly found anyone who spoke English, though I did manage to get a guide from Intourist, the government agency. Now normally, guides are quiet facilitators, useful lexicons who hide unnoticed in the background of stories. But Natasha elbowed herself to the fore, an annoying and winning cross between Sally Bowles and Dick Emery. "I used to work for KGB. I was spy Mata Hari," she said unconvincingly from beneath a kidney-coloured fizz of curls. "We had ships that picked up rubbish from western boats. I translated documents, now I teach English and have small agency where my nice Russian ladies try to meet foreign men. There are no real men left in Kaliningrad. They drink and take drugs. They're gangsters or have been killed by the bloody Chechens. Are you married?"

In many ways Natasha is emblematic, or maybe symptomatic, of Kaliningrad. She grew up in the 1960s and remembers the city as a bombed-out wasteland. Her parents were directed here from the Volga region. She flourished after a fashion through closed, cold communism and now lives in a grim apartment block with her aged father and 11-year-old daughter who inexplicably begs for rap music and e-mail. Natasha's trying to make sense of the new, rudderless Russia. She's gone back to the church – "The Blessed Virgin Mary will protect us" – and has mixed it with the dregs of imported new-ageism: "Always wear amber on your chakras."

She is an uncomfortable collection of contradictions. I learn that Russians can keep pairs of mutually exclusive thoughts in their heads at the same time. (Drunkenness is a social evil, but it's impossible to have a good time or indeed be Russian without consuming heroic amounts of vodka.) She despises the old order, but equally fears and loathes the new lack of order. "Look at those new Russians." She spits the name the way Ann Widdecombe refers to New Labour. New Russian is a euphemism for black-market pimp, smuggler, gangster, any tough young man with capitalist cash, and there are lots of them. Big blokes in slightly softer leather jackets, crew cuts and fat necks, chewing gum and holding mobile phones. They most resemble a Ross Kemp appreciation society. "This is what has become of Russian men." In a very Russian way she wants certainty and a sense of order. "It's common knowledge that Gorbachev was a Freemason . . . perestroika was a plot by international Jewish bankers. This is common knowledge." In a society where all information has always been rumour, propaganda or wish fulfilment, this sort of nonsense is par for the course.

Victor the frogman drives us to the holy bunker where the Germans surrendered in 1945. If you think we have trouble getting the war out of our systems, go and talk to a Russian. Everything comes back to the great patriotic war sooner or later, generally sooner. "Russia has saved the world three times," says Natasha. "Once from the Tartars and twice from the Germans." It's best not to argue or point out that perhaps they've only saved us once by proving so categorically and catastrophically that international communism doesn't work.

The bunker and the city museum boast gory but fascinating dioramas of Russian boys going in with the bayonet – Slav Disneyland. Natasha contradictively points out that while the RAF bombing was an act of barbarous desecration of a beautiful city – revenge for Coventry, a peaceful little village – the Russian storming was an act of heroic liberation. We pass by the people's wedding palace, a place of eye-bulgingly vile kitsch. Inside, a pretty young couple plan their nuptials. She in jeans with borscht-coloured hair, he in uniform, though not the valedictory kit of the navy but the brown overalls of a United Parcel Service driver. A sign that the times are changing and can be delivered overnight. It used to be a tradition that brides placed their wedding bouquets on a war memorial tank, now only kids spray "Punk isn't dead" on the eternal memories of the fallen. And the girls chuck their flowers on Kant's grave.

Kant is Kaliningrad's one great western hero. Alive, he may have been the bloke who said that the objects of the material world were fundamentally unknowable, so empirically they didn't exist – in short, that's not an empty bottle of vodka in front of you, you just think it's an empty bottle of vodka – but dead he makes sense. He brings in dollars and marks from tourists. He's been dug up and reburied three times, so he might say this isn't his grave, we only think it's his grave. There is a further move to rename Kaliningrad Kant's Town, and given the Russian inflection of pronouncing all As as Us, this is a fantastically Kantish idea, so they'll probably do it.

Amber is Kaliningrad's other tourist draw. Intrinsically, 35 million-year-old pine gum is mildly fascinating, it's just that as yet nobody has found anything remotely attractive to do with it. Natasha is tessellated with yards of it, pockets and bags clanking with it. "We must go and see some great guys who polish amber. They were all in KGB. The director is a general."

Looking for flies caught in resin alongside a cold-war military intelligence officer is my best bit of symbolism yet. Later that evening Natasha introduces me to her star pupil. A 17-going-on-30-year-old who smells strongly of shampoo and hasn't quite lost her puppy fat. Her father runs shrimp boats out of Mombasa, so she's relatively rich and as perkily flirtatious as a Pushkin.

After dinner she slips her hand into my pocket and offers to show me Kaliningrad's nightlife, so we troop off to a club where the security is enthusiastically El Al. In all dealings with service-industry Russians, the word that springs appropriately to mind is "bolshie". The new Russian men hang about in groups practising their tough looks and gum-chewing. The girls dance self-consciously in cliques around piles of knock-off designer handbags. It's quaintly reminiscent of a Dundee youth club dance run by the SAS. The restrained, physically ungrammatical dancing makes the young look like they're doing a vocational course in how to be western. Indeed, most Russians have that frustrated look of people learning a new way of life as a second language. The nightclub badly upsets Natasha. "Listen to this American music. It's just noise. American, American, what's so great about America?" It's a resentful loser's rhetorical question. "Look at those girls, where are their men?" Indeed, the ratio is about 10 to 1, but this might have something to do with girls getting in free and the average wage in Kaliningrad for professional adults being $40 a month. Miss Too Pretty By Half asks me to sum up Russia in one word. I say "soul", because it's what she wants to hear, but think "suffering". Suffering is the Slavic cross and their vaunting pride. The ability of Russians to suffer longer, deeper and more stoically than anyone else comes up again and again, invariably with the PS: "But we survive." This is a nation of chronic masochists.

Victor drives us out to Svetlogorsk, a resort town on the coast. Squatting spookily in the slow strobe of silver birchwoods are gaunt sanatoriums for tubercular children and recuperating naval officers. And here are the country houses of generals, general secretaries and import-export new Russians, built in a cupolaed, clapboarded, pitched, German-Russian vernacular hybrid that looks like nothing so much as vampires' holiday cottages.

We walk down the wooded dunes, and there, finally, is the gunmetal Baltic Kaliningrad's point, symbolically shrouded in an undulating, enigmatic fog. Through the opaque air, shadowy figures emerge like characters from Russian epics. Old ladies mummified in shawls searching for amber, a statuesque girl, head held high, tears rolling down her cheeks. Through the whiteness, the muffled drawl of a foghorn repeats. In halting English, Victor the frogman asks me what I think will happen to Kaliningrad, then proceeds to tell me what he thinks. This is the doomsday scenario: once Brussels and Moscow go through their diplomatic gavotte of veiled bribe and implied threat to gain some leverage from this lost city, Kaliningrad itself may take matters into its own hands.

The population falls in half. Almost everyone over 40 served in the military and feels cheated by the Russian Federation. Their respect and pensions dwindle to worthless, but still there's an emotional link to the suffering of the past and the absent mother country. But the young, the sneery thugs, with their rip-off

Rolexes and BMWs with popped locks, or dirty addictions and no hope, only want western things, and out, via the chimera of fast, easy money. They have no work ethic, no stoicism, no appetite for suffering and precious little reason to defer to old ethics or corrupt politics. There is a murmuring groundswell towards unilateral independence. Kaliningrad might declare itself as the fourth Baltic state and throw itself on the charity and self-interest of the EU and Nato. Maybe there'll be a Balkan-style civil war. Christ knows, there's enough military knowledge and kit about. Moscow – so Victor's prediction goes – sees this as a humiliation too far and blames the West for imperial interfering. Moscow tries to intervene across 1,000 kilometres of capitalist Europe.

If you ever wondered what we needed a European army for, maybe it's Kaliningrad. If you wanted a scenario for a third great European war, maybe you should beware Kaliningrad. Who could have foreseen what a shot in Sarajevo first time, or the Italian invasion of Ethiopia second, would lead to? If we don't want to wrest Armageddon from the jaws of a cosy decimal market, maybe we should think very, very hard about how to deal with this far, distant boil of which we know little. Well, that's the hypothesis for apocalypse tomorrow.

Victor smiles and shrugs, digs his hands into his leather pockets and trudges on across the damp sand. He's planning on surviving. Kaliningrad is two hours away – meet the neighbours. Its real curse is that it is caught in the middle, not just between Poland and Lithuania, two countries with long memories and no reason or inclination to love the ugly Russian. It is also caught between the worst of two political systems: a corrupt, crippled and haltingly reactive Russian Federation and carpet-bagging capitalism. Having promised that the free market would be the answer to all communism's ills, we've dumped the worst of it. Bribed and squandered all over them, patronised their struggles and diminished their most precious commodity – their revered stock of collective suffering – as stupid and worthless. The department stores on Kaliningrad's Lenin Street, under the shadow of the monumental bronze Mother Russia, sell cheap tat. There are display cabinets with nothing except Korean paper handkerchiefs. Russians, of course, are used to ersatz tat in their shops. But now it's not home-grown or home-made dross: it's dross from Korea, China, Poland and Turkey (I particularly yearned for a spectacle case emblazoned "Chris Dior").

The large, fêted, grey free-enterprise food market sells lumps of pig fat from Poland, boiled sweets from China, and plastic bags advertising Scotch whisky. There are bruised, callused apples from Poland and dried apricots from Uzbekistan. The mountains of potatoes – eternal staple – are proudly Russian.

Russians are many things, but they're not fools. They know they've been ripped off. There is no love left for communism, but neither do they see in capitalism's big hello anything trustworthy or lovable. Conspicuous capitalism has conspicuously failed to earn the respect it needs as a socio-political foundation. What they have learnt, what we've cynically shown them, is short-term exploitation: the wasteful, careless market forces of the never-never merchant.

In search of more symbolism I wander into Kaliningrad's zoo. In the kiosk an ancient Russian lady wrapped in glutinous rags writes out the tickets on brown tissue paper and tears them against a ruler. Kaliningrad is still garrisoned by a shadowy regiment of these babushkas, left over from a time when it was illegal not to work. They sit in solitary huddles of stupefied, pointless boredom at the end of hotel landings, in dank, crepuscular corners, eternal keepers of the lavatory key. The zoo is a good symbol, the best yet. Half German gothic, half Soviet space-age brutalism, a stinking, thick canal slobs through its middle; the ornamental ponds are filled with rubbish, the jaunty mosaics peel like psoriasis, and there are no animals. This is Kant's zoo. It's only a zoo because the ancient at the door is selling tickets for a zoo she remembers. The animals have been given away. Virtually all that's left are some bears.

All on his own in a concrete ditch, a scabrous, balding, old dirtbag Russian brown bear has obviously grown transcendentally mad with despair. He rocks, shuffles and chews a plastic bottle, then sits in that distressingly human way bears have with his back to the wall and lifts his face to a glimmer of watery sunshine. A troika of small boys, cocky and nervous proto-new-Russians, lean over the rusting barbed wire and drool gobbets of spit onto his head. For a moment he stares straight at me, and I can see in his rheumy, tea-coloured eyes, all the sorrow, all the struggle, the suffering and pity. Through everything, in a dark place all his own, the bear has survived. Then it does the damnedest thing, I promise. It slowly lifts one cack-caked, scimitar-taloned paw and salutes.

A short walk in the Hindu crush

A short walk in the Hindu crush

India, January 1999

Here is my one traveller's tip for those of you considering going to India: don't tell anyone. Pretend you're spending a fortnight with your decaying mother in Torbay, really. Announcing you're going to India is like saying you've got a bad back: everyone has an address, has a cure. The very mention of India turns half your friends into travel moonies. "You are going to Dhinki Dhoobre, aren't you?" they say, with barely contained missionary zeal. "Well, you simply must rearrange everything." I jest not. I had 20-page faxes of handwritten itineraries, imploring phone calls in the middle of the night, notes from strangers, the itinerant yogis of subcontinental tourism. And they all end with the same damning phrase: "If you're not going to see the palace at Mollycoddle, then you're not going to see the real India, and you might as well not bother."

As if all India seen through western eyes isn't sensationally unreal. I tried to imagine Indians saying to each other, "Well, of course, if you're not going to Sheffield and the Arndale Centre then you're not going to see the real England." The rest of your friends, those who aren't born-again sahibs, will say, "Oh, India, how wonderful, I'd love to go, but I don't think I could face it, the beggars you know, how do you handle the poverty?"

India has an unassailable position at the head of the world's poverty league. It is a perceived truth, an unarguable rubric, that this is the poorest country in the world. In the rich West, the implication is that to confront it, you need to have had a caring gland removed. It will be too much for sensitive, charitable folk, so best not go, best not look. How do you cope with poverty is the most asked question about India – the best answer comes from Mark Tully, the veteran foreign correspondent, who lives in Delhi: "I don't have to cope with the poverty; the poor have to cope with the poverty." To which I would add that actually the poverty is what you and I go to see. Poverty is what formed India, made India what it is. If Indira Gandhi's dream of a modern, thrusting, industrial tiger economy had been realised, and it had become a bigger Malaysia or Singapore, you wouldn't be that interested. It's the grinding lot of the vast majority that makes the opulence, the splendour, the architecture, the decoration, and the trappings of the princes and history so awesome. Always in India you're confronted with these juxtapositions of wealth and poverty; power and hopelessness; of sublime beauty and shocking ugliness. Everywhere you look there is binary metaphor, an encyclopedia of contradiction, dichotomy and counterpoint. Indians, all Indians, are the cleanest people in the world; you see them washing in the morning and evening, like obsessive surgeons scrubbing up, and then they work all day in streets that are no more than baked open drains, with rooting pigs and mange-crippled dogs. It's a contradiction, it's India.

Go to Agra – Agra is the one place the born-again sahibs back home will never recommend. "Oh well, of course, there's the Taj Mahal," they'll say, "I suppose you want to see it. It's wonderful, of course (they sigh), but quite spoiled." Don't believe it. Agra is an industrial military town, noisy and dirty, a real place where soldiers inhabit the old colonial officers' quarters and the town is modern, in the sense that in India even things that were built yesterday have a look of ancient exhaustion. But it is also a place that has more bona fide world heritage sites than anywhere else on the globe: it was the capital of Mughal India. And sitting in the middle of it is the Taj Mahal, Shahjahan's tomb for his beloved wife, but like everything in India, it's not that simple. She was his second wife and she died in childbirth, and then one of her sons killed all his brothers, and locked old Shahjahan up in a castle till he died. From his terrace he got perhaps the best, most heart-rending view of his wonderful white tomb. Everyone should see the Taj once. It is an absolute, there are few absolutes in this world, it is absolutely beautiful, absolutely stunning. Set in the corner of a garden laid out in Arab fashion, but – with Victorian confidence and hubris – replanted by the Victorians like an English country garden, the Taj sits against the sky on the middle banks of a river. Its absolute symmetry, the maths of perfection, is almost painful to contemplate. It is the most complete thing ever built by man and nothing can diminish it: not the queues; not the crowds; not the kitsch of endless reproduction and familiarity; not the sneers of Noël Coward or the epicurean India snobs; not the clicking lines of newlyweds waiting to be photographed on Princess Diana's bench. Nothing can touch it and nothing adds to it; not moonlight, or dawn, or dusk, that's just weather and light. If you go to India for just one thing, if you go to just one place abroad in your life, it should be the Taj.

The other place born-again sahibs will never recommend is New Delhi. Nobody does, even if they live there. Like Pretoria, Canberra and Washington, it's a capital without a soul, only a name, because civil servants and embassies were dumped there, but, if for nothing else, Delhi is memorable for the finest example of English architecture. You'll see Lutyens's viceregal palace and its approach from India Gate, a red stone Arc de Triomphe which beggars the Champs Elysées, or the Mall, or any other street built by swagger and power. A mile away is Chowpatti Street in Old Delhi, where traders from all over India buy and sell wholesale. It's a frantic stasis. The last word in free-market economics and capitalist chaos, it makes Cecil B De Mille look like Ingmar Bergman; to see the impossibility of organising India, coping with India, imposing a logic on India, Chowpatti Street is the answer.

Simla is a hill station – it was the summer residence of the viceroys – and it scampers up the nursery slopes of the Himalayas, surrounded by pine forests and vertiginous views. The town is like a cross between Godalming and Alice Springs, Tudorbethan home counties with corrugated tin roofs. A big billboard welcomes you to India's Switzerland; well, Switzerland should be so lucky. Simla is now where the new Indian middle class comes to relax; we didn't see another white face. Families who've done well out of foreign trade and old-fashioned metal bashing industry, avaricious for the West. The men don Pringle sweaters and Sta-Prest slacks, but again the contradiction; the women wear *kurta pyjamas* and saris. They make odd couples: the men look like dowdy, Sunday afternoon Milwaukee plumbers and the women splendidly, riotously Asian, and they promenade, as the Englishmen sahibs used to, to Scandal Point, where tough, bigoted, disappointed paragons of empire had collected in covens to pass vicious gossip. The Indians are too polite, they smile and laugh and pass exaggerated compliments.

I came here in search of Kipling's India. It's here that Kipling's father built an amateur theatre, and here, in the splendid Cecil Hotel, that Kipling wrote. It's been lovingly restored to an imperial grandeur and comfort. I found a second-hand bookshop and curio dealer in a dark nook that could have been straight out of *Kim*, but the more you look, the further the stories and the ghosts slip away. Kipling's India, I realised, only ever existed in the slow, damp afternoons of home counties vicarages. To search India for it is as pointless as looking for Graham Greene's France. Kipling, after all, wasn't looking for Kipling's India, but I bear the literary baggage of empire and my family's clubbable mythology of tea planting and pith helmets. India infected our souls far more than the Raj ever infected theirs. A polite and kindly people, Indians will say what they know you want to hear, that they are terribly grateful for the railways, and the post office, and the civil service – but how often do you think about your post office, or your railways, or your civil service? The Raj hasn't been wiped away on purpose with anger or resentment, it's just sunk beneath the seething surface, beneath the daily grind for dhal and a few rupees. India's poverty absorbs everything and uniquely reinvents it. Reincarnates it and decorates it. The vaunted babus and the civil service that we left behind have become an intricate, impossible filigree of forms, carbon paper, rubber stamps and towers of files. It's as impossible to conceive constructing India's civil service as it is building their temples.

Leaving Bombay airport, I collected nine separate rubber stamps, the last one applied with a grinning shrug to my hotel baggage label because there was nowhere left for it to go.

Walking around the pine-scented streets of Simla, I thought with what quite good manners the Indians had buried our lauded shared two centuries. How little was left – and then, from a parade ground somewhere below, a military band struck up a hymn, the sun was setting, catching the spire of the Surrey church, and the gables of the officers' club, Gurkhas stood on starched guard, "rock of ages cleft for me" words, and the years rolled back, and I was awash in a remembrance of things past, a reverie for a time and a life that I'd never actually lived, that existed only in print and celluloid, of burra pegs and punka wallahs, sepoys and redans. The ghostly echo of our finest hour – but only I felt it and that's another thing about India: everything you can or want to dream is here, everything anyone tells you is true. It's a place that accepts all visions, all interpretations, all are true, but none is the whole truth, like Hinduism, that most beguiling and infuriating of religions. It's endlessly accommodating but rigidly fatalistic. It starts with a simple trinity and then there are 30 million, or 300 million, or 3,000 million lesser gods; I was told all three figures with absolute authority. India has a civil servant's religion of numbing complexity and awful simplicity; no other country in the world believes this, or could afford it. You can't convert to be a Hindu, you can't join the reincarnation train halfway through its endlessly slow, circular journey. Plenty of westerners come, though, to pick through its jumble for something off the peg that fits; they do yoga as exercise, which is a bit like walking the stations of the cross as aerobics.

This is not an empirical, rational place. Here a spade is not a spade, it's a two-man spade, it's a two-man tool. One man holds the handle, the other pulls a rope tied to the blade. In 40° heat, I watched a pair of men, one with a small chisel, the other with a lump hammer, chip away at a rock the size of the Taj Mahal's dome. They were planning on flattening it. It was a Sisyphean task of epic proportions that defied a normal life expectancy. But they worked with a slow rhythm of men who know that all life is just an illusion, there is only karma, only rhythmic chipping away at this existence in preparation for the next, when perhaps they'll come back as a JCB.

Everybody agrees you must see Rajasthan, although again, born-again sahibs will recommend spectacularly inaccessible places. Travelling on Indian roads has a funfair-like, heart-in-the-mouth excitement. The gaily decorated lorries swerve across the rutted roads and all have the imperative "horn please" painted on the back. Eight or nine hours on the Asian equivalent of the wall of death, where you know that every other driver has the ethereal air bag of reincarnation for added confidence, is a little more nerve-jangling than most of us want on holiday. Rajasthan is palaces and forts. In a remarkably short space of time they fuse together into a rummage of blinding opulence. You don't lose the ability to be awed, just the ability to rise to the awesomeness. I'm sorry, my jaw has dropped as far as it will go and my eyes have reached the ends of their stalks. The guides' mantra of impossible facts come round for the second, third, fourth time: "all from a single piece of marble, all laid by hand, all real gold, real silver, the biggest, longest, highest, most expensive". It rolls over you like the blindingly reflected light, and the cumulative effect is of slowly being drowned in decadence. But there is none of the bated, reverential, national trussed-up preciousness of English country houses. One place stood out for its contrapuntal oddness. A man in a hotel said we should see the largest gun on wheels in the world. Now, you know, I'd thought I'd give it a miss. The biggest gun on wheels in the world is not what I'd come to India for, but, somehow, we found ourselves there in front of it, a vast, ornate sewerage pipe on bossed wheels with a soldier asleep in its shadow. As uninspiring and unmemorable as anything you care to forget. But it was set in a place called Jagger Fort, a dilapidated 17th-century barracks on the crest of a mountain, home to nesting pigeons, green parrots and langur monkeys. Scattered in its ru-ined, crumbling courtyards were mouldering Victorian barouches and state sedans, a fading theatre, an overgrown garden, a wall of curling, bleached photographs from durbars and forgotten polo games, all dozing in the heat. From the battlements you could see across Jaipur and out over the dun-coloured desert, kites and eagles hanging in the thermals and wild figs and banyans slowly, slowly pulling apart the teetering walls. It was a moment heavy with reverie.

The first time I came to India, 25 years ago, the rule was eat first. Public food was either poisonous or disgusting, often both. The biggest change in India is that you can eat Indian. The food in hotels is universally adequate, often good and frequently exceptional. Food on the street, though it looks enticing and smells better, is still just too risky to consider, not because the cooks are dirty, but because the vegetables by necessity are grown in human manure. Our soft western guts are just too vulnerable. Gastric liquidity is the second most commonly asked question about India, and indeed you should only travel with people who you feel comfortable talking stools to. Personally I will happily indulge in toilet talk for six or seven hours at a stretch. Indian food tends to be gassy – slow-cooked vegetables and pulses – so you see lines of Dutch tourists who at every step sound like an RAF motorbike display. They wear expressions of pained concentration: farting in India is playing Raj roulette with the linen. I came away with the rarest of all tropical afflictions: constipation.

I finally found my Kipling connection in Bombay. I adore Bombay, a cross between New York and Gomorrah, the most exciting and walkable city in the world. I love the Mutton Street junk market and the red-light district with its filthy streets and brightly saried eunuchs and the chaos of Victoria station and the dhobi ghats, the biggest launderette in the world. The monsoon still lingered and in the afternoon there was a downpour. I'd been taken to see the house Kipling was born in, now an art school. Outside, in the teeming gutter, a small, naked child crouched and washed itself, its black hair cut roughly to the shoulder, the little body wriggled like an eel, and I was transported back to my grandmother's house with its Benares brass, worn leopard skins and Turkey rugs and my favourite bedtime story with its wonderful pen-and-ink drawings: this little child just was Mowgli, the little frog, fishing in the Wainganga river, with taxis and scooters rushing past.

One last word on the poverty. There are more beggars in Soho than there are in Bombay. They're not as good at it, they don't have as much reason, but there are more. And you will be bothered by more peripatetic salesmen in Morocco or Naples than in India. And if you're really worried by poverty here, then allow yourself to be ripped off. Don't argue with taxi drivers or curio sellers – you don't start from an even bargaining position. The most cynically embarrassing thing to hear from born-again memsahibs is that the poverty is terrible but "do you like my shawl? I managed to beat him to half the price". India is a poor place but only in economic terms. On any other scale you care to think of, it's rich beyond the dreams of avarice. Any fool country can have democracy and freedom of speech and a rudimentary social security system when they've got the cash, but to achieve these things when you don't is humbling. India is that most miraculous of all modern states, a secular, democratic theocracy. And if we measure wealth in terms of any of the things that really matter – family, spirituality, manners, inquisitiveness, inventiveness, dexterity, culture, history and food – then India would be hosting the next G7 conference and sending charity workers to California. Of all the places you'll never get to because of squeamishness, trepidation, laziness and a dodgy bowel, India is by far and away your greatest loss.

In the frantic scurry and crush of Bombay's railway, where there is a fatality every day, a man bumped into me. I mention this because it's rare. Indians are dexterous in crowds. As our shoulders jarred, he touched his heart with his fingers. It's a silent apology and a prayer. There is a spark of God in all of us. He was saying sorry to his bit of the deity for bumping into mine. We may have given them the iron of the railways, but they filled it with 3,000 million gods.

Mad in Japan

Mad in Japan

On the face of it, the Japanese are very like us. We are both island nations, about the same size, both mongrel populations with constitutional monarchies; it rains a lot, they drink tea, we drink tea. We're both obscurely addicted to odd sports (cricket, sumo), both had empires, are bellicose, mistrustful of foreigners, and are passionate gardeners. Neither of us are particularly good-looking, we are both repressed, both suffer a class system, drive on the left, and only in Britain or Japan is having a stiff upper lip explicable as a compliment. But that's just on the face of it. Underneath, we're chalk and tofu.

You don't have to go to Japan to have an inkling that the Japanese are not as the rest of us are. In fact, they're decidedly weird. If you take the conventional gamut of human possibility as running, say, from Canadians to Brazilians, after ten minutes in the land of the rising sun, you realise the Japs are off the map, out of the game, on another planet. It's not that they're aliens, but they are the people that aliens might be if they'd learnt Human by correspondence course and wanted to slip in unnoticed. It's the little things, like the food. They make the most elegant, delicate food in the world and then make it in plastic for every restaurant window. Only a Japanese person could see a plate of propylene curry and say: "Yum, I'll have that." And the loos. Heated loo seats are slightly worrying the first time you encounter them, but after that they're a comfy idea; and there are buttons for jets of variable power, warm water, one for back bottom, one for front, with pictures to tell you which is which and hot air to help you drip-dry. All of which is strangely addictive and makes you question your sexual orientation, or at least wish for diarrhoea.

But it's not that which gets the canary of weird coughing, it's the lavatory paper: it's like rice paper. They have 21st-century bogs and 13th-century bog roll. Your bum's clean enough to eat sushi off, but you need to scrub your fingernails with a boot scraper. This is a country where the men pee in the street but it's the height of bad manners to blow your nose, and they wear woolly gloves on their feet.

Hiroshima is shockingly empty of grave resonance. You feel next to nothing. There's a memorial garden in the bland civic style, a hectoring museum and the peace dome – one of the few brick and concrete buildings in old Hiroshima whose skeletal rubble has been preserved as a symbol. It was built by a Swede.

The atomic bomb that wiped out Hiroshima, killing 140,000 people and reducing a wooden city to ash and black rain, was, if you ask me, with the benefit of hindsight, all things considered, a good thing. As a direct result of Hiroshima, the war ended. The emperor overrode his military, who wanted a banzai suicide last battle, and broadcast their unconditional surrender.

The only vibration left in the place is a saccharine sentimentality and a trite, injured morality. Hiroshima wears its unique, nuclear-age victimhood with the simpering pride of a geisha's wig. The quiescent kids in quasi-naval uniforms line up for peace studies and group shots; all make peace signs, or maybe they're victory signs, because if anyone won the peace, Japan did. Any sense of sympathy for this place is snuffed out by the petition I'm asked to sign insisting that the Americans apologise for dropping the bomb.

Well, hold on, Tojo. When it comes to apologies, Japan's silence is cacophonous. What about your treatment of prisoners of war? "Oh, they were soldiers," I'm told with a quiet, slow patronage. What about the Chinese massacres? "Exaggerated." The Korean comfort women, don't they deserve apologies? "Oh, they're just making a fuss because Japan is rich and they want money. And 20,000 Koreans were killed in Hiroshima." True, they were slaves, and when they asked if there could be a memorial for Koreans in this peace garden, the Japanese said no.

Let's get the Japanese as victims into perspective. During the war in the East, half a million allied soldiers died. Three million Japanese died and 20 million other Asians perished under Japan's brief expansion into an empire. That's 20 million we in the West rarely remember. As I stand here, the newspapers are full of

Koreans and Chinese bitterly denouncing Japan's new school history books, which deny any culpability. The Japanese don't think they're worth a sorry. The detonation of an atomic bomb above Hiroshima was the starting gun for modern Japan. It blew away not just the most deeply cruel military government but a thousand-year-old political and social system – the most inhuman and exploitative ever designed. The violent burst of the nuclear age was the best thing that ever happened to Japan. It didn't destroy anything like as much as it created.

What's extraordinary about Hiroshima is how fast it has grown back into a huge neon and concrete city that looks as if it's been here for ever. Before the war, Japan had an economy that was a small fraction of America's. A wood-and-rice peasant place, its main exports were textiles and soldiers. Today, even in the slough of a prolonged depression, it's still the second biggest economy in the world, with a GDP as large as Britain's, France's and Germany's combined. That's astonishing, not least because Japan is about one-and-a-half times the size of the UK with twice as many people and only a third of its land habitable, yet it has no natural resources to speak of. So, where did it all go wrong? How come Japan has such commercial success but still manages to be a socially weird disaster? Because, have no doubts, they're not happy.

Kyoto is Japan's old imperial capital, and escaped being Hiroshima by the whim of an American diplomat who once visited it. Kyoto boasts more heritage sites than you can shake a fan at. And you get there by a bullet train that looks like God's suppository and is twice as fast. The bullet trains run like clockwork, as if there were anything as techno-regressive as clockwork in Japan. The ticket collectors bow when they enter carriages, and there are little girls in pink cheerleader's uniforms who collect rubbish. It's the symbol of modern, efficient Japan. But, and I'm not obsessed, the lavatories are pee-in-your-socks squat jobs. It's very odd.

Kyoto is a disappointment: an ugly sprawl of low-rise confusion. The streets are a tangle of stunted electricity pylons and cat's-cradle power lines. Hidden among it are thousands of shrines and temples, which are beautiful, up to a point. There's an anaemic, minutely obsessive quality to them and they're very repetitive. I did rather love the gardens, though: vegetative taxidermy. Everything is tied down, wired up, splinted, truncated and pruned. In the pools, albino carp slip and twist with a ghostly boredom.

Religion is one of the reasons Japan is so socially crippled. In the beginning they had Shinto. Now, if religions were cars, Shinto would be a wheelbarrow. It's your basic animism: ancestor worship, goblins and ghosts, tree and rock spirits. It lacks the most rudimentary theology. It made the emperor into a god descended from the sun. Onto that was grafted Buddhism – the wrong sort. Not the happy Dalai Lama stuff, but Zen Buddhism via China. Zen is so desiccatedly aesthetic that nobody knows what it means. On top of all that, the Japanese chose to add Confucianism. Now, it has been said there's no such thing as bad philosophy and that below a certain level it simply stops being philosophy at all. Confucianism is the exception that proves the rule. It's unpleasant and lowbrow. Confucius and Taoism were the excuse-all, get-out-of-work-and-responsibility for the samurai. Modern Japanese people get born Shinto, married Christian, buried Buddhist and work Mazda. Consequently they believe everything and nothing. There is no solace in Japanese religion, no salvation or redemption, hope, encouragement, and most importantly, no concept of individuality, which is why you always see them mob-handed. A Japanese man on his own doesn't think he exists. It's just a static, miserable round of corporate responsibility and filial duty. I've never come across a place whose spiritual options were so barren. This pick-and-mix theology has stunted Japan like a tonsured, root-bound pine tree.

Kyoto has the most famous rock garden in the world: the ultimate Zen experience, 15 stones set in raked white gravel. You're supposed to sit and ponder. Nobody knows who made it or why, but it's deeply aesthetic, and fundamentally risible. Look, I'm sorry, but this is the emperor's new garden, an impractical joke. It's medieval builders' rubbish. Oh, but then, silly me, of course I don't understand. I'm constantly being patronised for my coarse sensibilities and told that naturally I couldn't comprehend the subtlety, the aesthetic bat-squeak of Japanese culture. No country hides itself behind the paper screen of cultural elitism like Japan, which, considering they've bought their entire civilisation from other people's hand-me-downs, is a bit of a liberty. When it comes to Japanese civilisation, it's mostly eyewash. Kabuki theatre is only just preferable to amateur root-canal work. The three-stringed guitar is a sad waste of cat. Japanese flower-arranging is just arranging flowers. Their architecture is Chinese, as are their clothes, chopsticks, writing, etc. The samurai were thugs in frocks with stupid haircuts, and haiku poems are limericks that don't make you laugh. Indeed, they are so aesthetically difficult, one haiku master managed to compose only 23,000 in 24 hours, including gems like: "The ancient pond, A frog leaps, The sound of the water." Marvellous.

And then there are geishas. In Kyoto's wooden old town, hundreds of Japanese tourists loiter, cameras at the ready. Nothing happens in Japan unless it happens at 400 ASA. Kyoto has seven million tourists a year, 90% of them indigenous. It's a pleasure to see that even at home they travel in gawky, bovine groups. They're waiting for a glimpse of a geisha slipping into a teahouse. There used to be 20,000 geishas in Kyoto; now there are fewer than 200. They hobble out of their limousines, bowing in all their pristine, extravagant absurdity. Geishas are trained to devote their lives to rich, drunk men.

Only the very, very rich can afford geishas. The salarymen dream of them. The trainee geishas, the backs of whose heads are dressed to represent vaginas, clip-clop down the road, their smiling white faces making their teeth look like little yellow cherry stones. A geisha's *raison d'être* is to pour drinks, giggle behind her hand, tell men they are handsome, strong and amusing, listen to boastful lies, and never show any emotion except bliss. Occasionally, for a great deal of cash, some will allow men to copulate with them. We, of course, have geishas back in Blighty: we call them barmaids.

Then there's the traffic, the fabled stasis of millions of drivers Zenishly not going anywhere. Naturally the cars are all Japanese, though not models you'll ever see in the West. Strange, clunky, misshapen things in tinny, bright colours, with antimacassars. Dozens of men lurk around car parks in white gloves and the uniforms of Ruritanian admirals, waving batons. They look like retired chief executives, and many of them are. Japan has a bonsai social security system, relying on businesses to over-employ on minuscule wages as a way of hiding unemployment. After school-kids, retired men have the highest hara-kiri rate. In a country with no sense of individual value, belonging to a job is their only source of self-worth. A Japanese man tells me that the key to understanding Japan is to grasp that it is a shame-based culture. In the West, success is the carrot. In Japan, fear of failure and ostracism is the stick. This isn't merely a semantic difference, it's a basic mindset. Westerners trying to do business here complain that it's impossible to get decisions made. The Japanese negotiate for months without saying yes or no. Nobody wants to lay their face on the line; there is no comeback from failure. Decisions emerge out of group inertia. Japan manages to be both rigidly hierarchical and enigmatically lateral. It's no accident that alcoholism is endemic; drunkenness is not a social problem, it's social cohesion for a depressed and confused male society.

The thing westerners worry about before getting to Tokyo is that all the signs are pictograms. Well, being constantly lost is as close as you're going to get to knowing what it's like to be Japanese. Most of the shop signs, though, are in English, but written by people who don't speak or understand it. So they're a continual source of amusement. Japan has actually two written languages: borrowed Chinese characters and a phonetic squiggle alphabet. Usefully, there is no word for claustrophobia and, more disturbingly, I'm told, no indigenous one for the female orgasm.

Sex is where the weirdness of the Japanese peaks. I should start by saying that the widely held belief that you can buy soiled schoolgirls' knickers from vending machines is apocryphal, but it certainly could be true. It would hardly be out of character.

The area around Shinjuku station is the Japanese red-light district. There is the better-known Roppongi, which is distressingly reminiscent of Bangkok, but Shinjuku is the real local thing, and foreigners are not encouraged. I was told that the station has more people going through it in a day than go through Grand Central in a month, and it's only the second largest in Tokyo. Salarymen stop off at one of the many bars, get tanked on beer and sake and perhaps slurp a bowl of noodles before staggering off to a girlie bar. In the streets, girls ply their wares and gangs of lost boys, all sporting the same long-fringed peroxide hair and mod suits, try to recruit schoolgirls for Tokyo's latest sex craze, telephone dating. Men go to booths, pick up a phone and chat up a girl. If they hit it off, they go to a bar and reach an arrangement. This is not seen as prostitution because the girls audition the men and they do it on a part-time basis. The latest, hottest variation is bored married women, called literally "someone else's wife".

Yakuza gangsters slip past in blacked-out BMWs or saunter round the streets, conspicuous in shiny suits, permed hair and laughable socks and sandals. Japan's mafia, they invest every facet of life with a dull, unsophisticated violence. They're universally seen as modern samurai and folk heroes.

Every street has seven or eight storeys of girlie bars and sex clubs. What do you get inside? Well, what do you want? If you're Japanese, you probably want pole-dancing crossed with amateur gynaecology. You can rip the knickers off a teenager and, for a bit extra, keep the knickers and a souvenir photograph. Underpants do seem to loom large in Japanese sexual fantasies. You could catch a massage with a happy ending, or go to a fetid little room, stick your willy through a hole in the wall and be manually relieved by an old lady sitting knee-deep in Kleenex, wearing a cyclist's anti-pollution mask.

And then there's the weird stuff.

If you do pull a prostitute, there are the "love hotels": themed, by-the-hour rooms, where you get sex toys in the minibar. Although used mainly by the sex industry, their original purpose was more prosaic. Traditionally, the Japanese live with their in-laws, and, in a cramped apartment with paper walls, marital harmony can be strained. So harassed couples, carrying the shopping, sidle in for half an hour's conjugal bliss. It takes the spontaneity out of sex, but then if you asked a Japanese man to do something spontaneous, he'd have to check his PalmPilot first. To say that they appear dysfunctional when it comes to fun is missing the point.

Japanese men must be the vainest, with the least justification, on the planet. Hairdressing, waxing, face-packing, ear-grouting and general pandering and pampering to aesthetic hypochondria are multi-million-yen businesses. My favourite bit of male kit was an electric razor specifically for thinning body hair. The reason for their *X Files* sexuality is again said to be down to religion. They don't consider sex as something that demands a system of morals. This is a country where eating etiquette is more complex than the instruction manual for a Sony video, but with your clothes off, anything goes. There are no rules, not even handy hints on sex. Anyone who thinks that ethics are best kept out of sexual politics ought to go to Japan and see where it ends up. And there's another reason for male sexual dysfunction: Japanese boys' relationships with their mothers. Worshipped is not too strong a word. Mothers are adoring handmaidens to their sons, often literally.

Worst of all – by far, far and away worst of all – is the Japanese males' view of women. Historically, women were next to worthless: peasant daughters were regularly sold into prostitution. In the 19th century, most of the brothels of the East were staffed by Japanese girls, or they were sold to factories as indentured textile workers. Today, women rarely make it above the non-commissioned ranks of business, which is still the preserve of very, very old men. In offices they are ornamental secretaries, encouraged to wear short skirts and have harassing lunches and drinks with their bosses.

Women are either silent housework drudges or sex toys. You see this dehumanising view of women in *manga*. *Manga* are those ubiquitous pornographic comic books. Men read them openly on the trains and buses. You can buy them anywhere. But the motherlode of *manga* is a massive basement bookshop in Tokyo with staff dressed like fantasy cartoon characters. Pick up almost any book at random and be prepared for a sharp intake of breath. The stories, such as they are, generally involve schoolgirls being attacked and raped; the scenarios are inventive in their nastiness. Children are abducted, gagged in their beds, dragged up dark alleys. The victims are small and defenceless, with unfeasibly large breasts and round, tearful eyes. They are regularly killed or commit suicide. I kept thinking that the last pages must be missing, the ones with the comeuppance, but there's none. And, to add a peculiarly Japanese weirdness, the drawings are delicately censored. Minute slivers of genitalia are Tipp-Exed out. Nothing is as unnervingly sordid as *manga*, and nothing would so distress the

European parents of a daughter. And the Japanese think less than nothing of it.

How young girls react to the violent sexualising of their youth is equally depressing. They consume; they shop with a myopic concentration. You stand at a crossroads in the shopping district of Tokyo, with video screens flashing out western ads and pop videos, and when the traffic lights go green, which they do to the sound of cuckoos, 1,500 people cross the road. That's 1,500 every three minutes, all day, every day; and most of them are little girls.

For a nation that puts such a high premium on elegance, Japanese girls walk incredibly badly. They slouch and yaw on foot-high platforms, dye their hair a sort of gingery blonde and look as sullen as 4ft-high Japanese teenagers can, which isn't very. Their parents despair of this generation, calling them bean-sprout children because they lack the backbone and single-mindedness that forged Japan's economic ascendancy. They're giving up on the exam-passing, company-cog work ethic and exchanging it for a western girl-band fanzine mindlessness. This teenage rebellion isn't political or social or even sexual, it's a plastic copy. It's not even active, it's passive and pouting and decorative. These kids are turning themselves into the living embodiment of the *manga* comic victims: pigeon-toed, mini-kilted, white-socked sex dolls. They are a generation of social anorexics who want to remain provocatively pre-pubescent.

This was a culture that forged a minimal aesthetic of tatami mats and single twigs in vases. But now it's drowning in puerile, syrupy decoration. Even police notices come with cartoons of Disney coppers. These teenagers are running from the heartless culture of guilt and blame, to hide in a fairy-tale nursery.

I started off this journey by saying the Japanese were weird. Well, weird is an observation, not an explanation. By the end, I was absolutely convinced that the explanation is that they are not eccentric, not just different, but certifiably bonkers. Japan is a lunatic asylum built on a hideous history, vile philosophy and straitjacket culture.

If Freud had lived in Tokyo, we'd never have got analysis. He wouldn't have known where to start. It's not that we can't understand the subtlety of Japan. It's that we've been looking at it from the wrong angle. When you stop reading the signs as cultural and see them as symptoms, it all makes a sad, shuddery sense; the national depression, the social Tourette's, the vanity with its twisted, eye-enlarging, nose-straightening, blonde-adoring self-loathing. The psychopathic sexuality and the obsessive, repressing etiquette.

For 300 years, Japan committed itself to an isolation ward. It tried to self-medicate by uninventing and forgetting things. When it finally let in the rest of the world, its fragile arrogance couldn't cope with the deluge of information from a far more robust western civilisation. Their plan had been to take the technology and medicine and turn their backs on the rest, but it can't be done; you can't put on the suit and not the beliefs that went into tailoring it.

Japan has become the West's stalker, a country of Elvis imitators. To walk among them is like being in a voyeur's bedroom. They loathe the objects of their obsession. An English banker who has lived there for over a decade, speaks the language, married a Japanese girl and takes his shoes off in his own home, told me: "You have no idea how much, how deeply, they despise us. Don't be fooled by the politeness; it's mockery. They are very good at passive aggression; it's the only type they're allowed."

He went on: "You must have noticed they're obsessed with perfection: a perfect blossom, an ideally harmonious landscape. They can't abide a chipped cup. We're imperfect, coarse, smelly, loud." Japan has taken the worst of the West and discarded the best. So it has a democracy without individualism. It has freedom of speech but is too frightened to say anything. It makes without creating. And, saddest and most telling, it has emotion without love. You never feel love here. They have obsession, yearning and cold observation – even beauty and devotion – but nothing is done or said with the spontaneous exuberance of love, and I have never been anywhere else in the whole wide world where you could say that.

I want to finish back in Hiroshima. After the war, the survivors of the atomic bomb were ostracised. People would hire private detectives to ensure that prospective spouses weren't from Hiroshima. So the survivors lied and hid their guilty secret and trauma.

Imperfect, embarrassing and tainted, they should have died. It's the absence of the western idea of love – of brotherly, charitable love or sensual love, that finally explains Japan's appalling, lunatic cruelty.

In the market of Kyoto I saw something that was so madly bizarre, yet so unremarkably mundane, it summed up something of Japan. A very old woman, bent in half and tottering on crippled legs, slowly and painfully pushed her own empty wheelchair.

WEST

WEST

One of the culs-de-sac that a travel writer has to continually watch out for is the pervasive assumption that poor people are intrinsically nicer than rich ones. It looks silly in print but on the ground, in the dust, it's more seductive. A fond belief that poverty is synonymous with dignity, that kindness, politeness and humour are shown by the less privileged is somehow quantitatively more valuable because it comes tempered by hardship. And there's the balancing assumption that all those things that come from rich people are consequently worth less because they're bought and paid for with such ease, that their happiness is less real because it's sullied with money and possessions. What we end up with is a cartoon version of the Sermon on the Mount. An unhealthy belief that poverty is of itself ennobling because riches are demeaning.

Economically and spiritually, this is a eugenic nastiness yet I've noticed it curling up in my own writing from time to time. Indeed, the people I've collectively liked the most often do have lives I couldn't suffer for a day but I think you can love the poor without loving their poverty. This unhealthy dichotomy arises through the natural guilt of being a First World visitor with a return ticket. And because the stuff of travel writing is so often a consequence of poverty. Those street markets and shanty towns, the hand-woven basket and the exaggerated care for meagre things. After a time it's an inescapable conclusion that the rich eat the poor. And the richest, most powerful and wasteful country in the world – America – takes, like so much else, the lion's share of loathing.

For many habitual travellers, hating America is a given. Not just America at home, but the detritus of America abroad. The States are the font of all ignorant interference, all destabilising of delicate cultures and economies. America is the cause and the symptom of what's going wrong. Of course the people on whose behalf travel writers feel this righteous ire adore America. They may not care for its alternatively tentative and strident foreign policy, its splashing about in the rest of the world like an excited toddler – but they love its baggage. Its films, its music, its clothes, the cigarettes and soft drinks: its sheer profligacy. If you're poor, the most joyous thing in the world is waste. Well, it would be wouldn't it? When it comes to America, I'm with the poor. I just love it.

In my father's study there's a framed photograph of a group of cowboys posed in that way cowboys always seemed to adjust themselves for formal portraits. Straight backs and languorous limbs, guns fingered with a pre-Freudian ostentation. They're my cousins four generations back. Three Yorkshire brothers who left the farm and went to Wyoming to raise cattle and horses next to Buffalo Bill. They prospered and their children went on to raise motorcars in Detroit.

It was through my grandmother that I first learnt to admire America. Her brother had emigrated, and after the war when England seemed a shabby exhausted place he would send food parcels and luxuries. He even lent my grandfather (a chief clerk in a Canterbury bank) a dashing saloon with a chauffeur. My grandmother's love for her brother and everything American never wavered. I remember coming home to find her crying – the only time I ever saw her cry – when President Kennedy had just been shot. And we had American neighbours: a Service family from the nearby USAF base (it now seems strange and another facet of ration deprivation how few foreigners there were in England in the Fifties). My mother used to shop at the American PX store. All the goods were so self-assured, so confident, so new, compared to ours. Even the washing-up powder had a Doris Day glamour. It was there I got my first pair of blue jeans – as hard as an indigo pasteboard.

For Europe, America has always been about things. Stuff. You can hate or love stuff. You can even love and hate it simultaneously. It's been easy to patronise the States as a capitalist bran-tub of childish newness and obsolescence. But this misses the point. The "things" are symptoms of a remarkable and enviable energy and freedom. In Europe freedom has always meant saying and thinking things. In America it means doing things and making stuff. Which is just as profound and a whole lot more useful.

In my early twenties I spent a year living in America. Half in New York with a girlfriend, where I worked as a painter and decorator, and the other half in the coal mining Appalachian mountains of Kentucky. This was an America that few Americans ever saw: dirt poor, semi-literate, inward-looking, suspicious and proud. A population made up mostly of Scots immigrants deported after Culloden. This is where Country music was born and where a type of depression, self-sufficiency and mutual dependence still lingered up smoky hollows. They are a remarkable people and it is a place that, once experienced, never leaves you.

I lived with my cousin Wendy – the granddaughter of the food parcel man. I painted and drank moonshine and she took photographs. We both grew and cut sugar cane, made molasses, rescued stray dogs and listened to stories. Storytelling was a big part of mountain life. One spring we drove from Cincinnati north across the flat cornfields of Ohio to Detroit and on to Chicago. I caught a glimpse of the vast middle of America – those square-edged states that are so unlike the coastal America most Europeans are familiar with – and I grew a great admiration for its small-town values of community and civic responsibility, hard work and decency. In this culturally remedial, geographically taciturn place you still find the hope and enterprise that originally attracted millions of Europeans. The great heart of America is a place that's obsessive about individuality but chooses relentless conformity. It's ardent for freedom but is fundamentally prescriptive. It's aesthetically bereft but venerates the merest scrap of civilisation and out of this vast sprawl of contradictions emerges the most imaginative, challenging and talented people of the last 150 years. They invariably leave middle America of course; it's like a huge nursery school that grows greatness out of a thin earth.

There is a universally dismissive belief in the old European world that America and Americans lack irony. As if an ability to discern irony, polish it and use it decoratively were the secret heart of an epicurean culture. That lives spent without a marbling of irony were essentially banal. Well, leaving aside the fact that you could travel through provincial Germany with a regiment of irony detectors without ever getting a twitch, it's simply not true about the States. How could anyone watch Woody Allen, read Norman Mailer or Tom Wolfe, stand in a room full of Andy Warhols or listen to the blues and believe that America lacked irony? What America does lack – is indeed joyously free of – is cynicism: the polluting, corrosive effluent of an old civilisation.

What I love about America is that it still has a glut of optimism. It still believes in new dawns, distant horizons, happy tomorrows and the triumph of dreams. All the stuff my culture can't mention without the tell-tale inflection of irony. Or should that be cynicism?

Born to be riled

California, October 1999

Looking over the balcony of my hotel room, directly beneath me, 12 floors down, is the swimming pool, a patent medicinal blue, not quite kidney-shaped, more spleen with attached gall bladder. There's a man swimming slow, curvy lengths; it's 6.30am, around him Los Angeles fades grey and smogged into the distant hill. This little figure is the only sign of life. Nothing stirs, the gridded streets blink silently. I'd been told LA is a city that rises early. It obviously doesn't get out much; only a few birds called their agents.

The man's breaststroke has become unsynchronised, his arms and legs contradict. He is disproportionately, fantastically annoying – I have a barely containable desire to drop the television over the railings. George Bush is being courageous and advertising erectile dysfunction from a flaccid leather armchair in the middle of a programme on power aerobics from Hawaii. It would be a good opening shot, follow the box down in slow motion, LA skyline spinning fast, George promising his fellow Americans sustained growth, then crashing into the water pinning the get-fit-get-ahead spaz to the Mexican-style tiles down the deep end. I flick a cigarette instead. Breakfast is on a trolley; the milk jug has a little cardboard sign beside it that says simply, unequivocally, unarguably "milk", just in case you thought it might be toothpaste or root beer, or the elixir of life. Or maybe the milk's just got more clout and can demand top billing. The tea and coffee don't get a mention and it's far harder to tell what they are. The Danish has a website – everything here has a website. Cyberspace hangs over us like digital thunder.

LA is not what you expect. Personally I didn't expect a northern hemisphere version of Johannesburg without the barbed wire. Low, creeping *faux* family-friendly, built in a vernacular of amateur whim and sentimental detail, patched onto functional boxes with occasional timid touches of eccentricity. Like Johannesburg, the major architectural direction is lent by God and gardeners. In the steady retirement climate, almost any herbage can be trained up a wall to obscure a building. Very little here has the energy to grow above two storeys, and the overall sense is of a hasty impermanence, a city thrown up on a whim while they thought of something serious to put in its place.

LA is a suburb in search of a city, a ramble of stupid, gullible bricks and plaster that got misdirected. Extraordinarily, there is not a single man-made thing that is a recognisable icon of the place, no Eiffel Tower, no Big Ben, no Empire State Building. It is the only major city in the world that doesn't have a postcard image, except for that cheap billboard saying "HOLLYWOOD", like a name tape sewn into a pair of school knickers, as if Los Angelenos might from time to time look up to remind themselves where they are.

Nobody could ever conceivably miss LA, think with pleasure about returning here, want their grandchildren to grow up here, but this is arguably the most important non-capital in the world. Even if you have never been here, this place has touched you – more than that, it has run its smoggy, soft hands all over you. This is where up to 90% of the world's culture comes from: movies, television, recorded music, pornography, and all their myriad spin-off industries. We may not like to think it, but it is the 20th century's incarnation of classical Athens, of Rome, Constantinople or Renaissance Florence. For our moment this is the hub of civilisation, and we think so little of it, it thinks so little of itself, it can't even build a decent fountain.

LA is empty and quiet – not a calm, at-ease quiet but a holding-your-breath-something-bad's-about-to-happen quiet. You walk about the broad, low-rise streets and feel uncomfortably as if you've stepped into an episode of *The Twilight Zone*, occasionally finding collections of daytime shoppers, valley girls thumbing racks, going "Whatever" to each other like dowdy budgerigars. Rodeo Drive is one of the most famous shopping streets in the world and it's a big disappointment. Gaggles of seriously confused Japanese and out-of-town Americans wander around with the bored, neurotic wives of studio accountants and florists to the stars, who shop in the distracted, therapeutic way of women who have reached a precarious chemical balance and need a mantra of familiar labels to stop them exploding at the psychic seams.

Walking in Hollywood is an unnatural occupation and immediately marks you out as a non-player, one of the little people, a bum in search of a seat. Actually it's like being on safari, because as a result of begetting the Lion King share of our culture, this is also the Serengeti of celebrity. We all keep a weather eye out for big-game stars. I catch sight of my first in a shopping mall early one morning. There she is, shyly stepping through the shadows, poised as if for flight, Audrey Hepburn. Unmistakable, razor-thin in a Givenchy evening dress, hair in the characteristic chignon, a discreet little tiara and the big black *Roman Holiday* glasses. In her evening-gloved hands she's clasping a small blue box from Tiffany's, of course. I tick her off in my I-Spy book and walk round the corner and, would you credit it, there's another Audrey Hepburn, identical down to the blue box. And then another, and another – I can barely believe my luck. I've come across the annual migration of Audreys. Very few people have ever seen these shy, utterly beguiling creatures on their immemorial trek. I know that the more literal of you will want to point out that Audrey Hepburn is, in fact, dead. Well, I knew that. But I also know that (as the deific biopics say) stars never die: they glitter for ever in the celluloid hearts of their fans. I've seen a dozen Mickey Mice, and on Sunset Boulevard a lone Charlie Chaplin shouting into a mobile phone. In Hollywood it comes as no surprise to see the dead walk, because frankly none of the natives look 100% alive anyway, not life as we know it, Jim.

Perhaps the point of LA is that it isn't a real place: it's a cowboy-town frontage, a back lot, a sound stage waiting for a Leonardo da Spielberg to apply the SFX and the soundtrack. Perhaps the big, bland, blue sky is really a mat on which the computer graphics will be masked in post-production. It's a place that's not supposed to be visited, it's supposed to visit you. This is, as they endlessly say, a dream factory, and like most dreams it's better if you're not awake and you forget it once you are.

As well as rising early, LA goes to bed early. By 9pm the restaurants are emptying, by 10pm they've stopped serving. The streets are deserted again; only the visiting rap stars' stretch limos circle slowly, like great nocturnal beetles, their variegated fairy lights winking a secret amorous semaphore. I expect to find a couple mating in a parking lot. Ask anyone who lives here what the best thing about LA is and the answer is invariably valet parking. And that tells you just about everything you need to know about LA.

Never was it so true of a place that the best thing to come out of it was the road north. But then the road north of LA would be the best thing to come out of almost anywhere, and I've wanted to travel it since I sat in the dormitory at school and listened to the Grateful Dead and read *On the Road*. Route 1 is one of the great journeys in the world, a winding highway that hugs the Pacific coast up to San Francisco. The other great thing about this journey is that you're allowed to smoke. The main reason I haven't been to California before is their impertinent, nannyish tobacco fatwa. This is the only place on earth where smoking can kill you stone dead in seconds: you get so frothingly angry at the temperate health fascists, your head might explode. Cigarettes in California should carry warnings saying: "Prohibiting smoking can cause fatal heart attacks, strokes and spontaneous miscarriages." Everywhere else in the world, smoking is done inside; in California you do it in the street. All the coolest people are posing on street corners looking like Humphrey Bogart and Lauren Bacall. Restaurants will let you smoke if they have a garden or open area, and they just love it if you do: it adds a rakish, bohemian, devil-may-care atmosphere that the locals are too fearfully self-obsessed to provide. I asked in one place if they had somewhere I could light up, and the waiter beamed, "Hold on a moment, sir," pushed a button, and the roof slid off.

Back on the road in the open Mustang, we sashay out of LA through Santa Monica towards the sea, along Venice Beach, a Blackpool-like stretch of oscillating buttocks being leered at by gang-bangers in risibly baggy shorts. Muscle Beach is a lounge of thick-necked men with blurred blue prison tattoos, looking bored, all in stark contrast to the surburban-lawned Santa Monica. This place is noticeably ethnic, black and Hispanic. A group of radical Muslims dressed up in uniforms, like extras from a silent version of

The Lives of a Bengal Lancer with Ray-Ban product placement, shout separatism to a rubbish-strewn strip of grass.

We slowly leave the LA 'burbs behind and hit Route 1 proper. Apart from anything else, this road is an impressive feat of engineering, cutting through the cliffs that mark the end of the continental United States. This is the boundary road of the great itchy trek west, the 200-year journey that was Europe's last great adventure, which started with the precipitous, dour landing on Plymouth Rock and finished with the migration of Okies to pick oranges and lettuce. It's a cliché that the story of America is a journey, or a series of journeys, but like a surprising number of clichés it's surprisingly true. Migration is at the heart of America. On average, Americans move every three years.

Route 1 was built when America's journey had stalled, become a desperate shuffling queue for a hand-out. It was one of the monumental engineering projects instigated by Roosevelt to turn the Depression, built at a cost that made it mile for mile about as expensive as getting to the moon, and it was essentially unnecessary. There is no great need to connect LA to San Francisco: they've never had much to say to each other. This road was an act of faith, and a perfect example of the hope that the trek is more important than the destination.

Our first stop is Santa Barbara, a Spanish-ish residential town of quaint prettiness. Santa Barbara is very nice indeed, they're nice people here, and so they should be: they've spent a lot of money making themselves nice. There's a sense that the whole place has been constructed as a perfect, smug example of small-town America, a heart-warming show town. There's no industry here except service industry and slothful self-love. The shops are twee and cute and sell a million varieties of soap; you could browse for a lifetime upgrading your T-shirt collection. In a dozen little cafés they sit under a rich man's sun and read the *New York Times'* literary review.

If California claimed independence it would immediately be one of the half-dozen richest countries in the world, and Santa Barbara is one of its richest spots. Here you can see what the collected dreams and collated wishes of uncountable wealth come up with as a nice place to live: an intellectually undemanding, cinnamon-flavoured, provincial, lethargic Pleasantville that's both strangely alluring and creepily repellent. Is this really what's at the top of the pyramid? Is this really the last square on the Monopoly board?

I suppose it is. Santa Barbara with its brain in neutral, comfy-fit, easy listening, easy eating, easy streets. Even the beggars here have a laid-back insouciance. A healthy, semi-comatose young man sits in the shade with a tin cup and a cardboard sign that reads: "Why lie, I'll spend it on beer." I badly want to kick his head in.

In the big bookshop with a café, naturally, there's a master class on how to become a writer, and I take a seat with four aspiring would-be romantic novelists and a man who I'm sure has a penchant for bondage erotica. The lecturer is a professional writing teacher who spends the first 20 minutes telling us how well qualified he is to teach us how to write. His CV seems to be strangely bereft of any published work except the book he's now selling on how to write books, called *Let the Crazy Child Write*. "You're three people," he enthuses, "a head editor, a heart writer and a crazy child, like in Freud, the unconscious. Crazy Child says, imagine a three-legged dog, okay? Now imagine a three-legged dog running!" He beams a smug Freudian beam. "You can't. Isn't that great? You can't imagine a three-legged dog running, can you?" Well, yes, actually, I can. Thank God I never learnt how to write. There is some great metaphor or symbol in this but for the life of me I can't imagine it – this man talking about how everything that ever happened to you is inscribed in every atom of your body, and you have to tune out to tune in, and that he'd once met Allen Ginsberg so he knows about feelings.

But I walk out of the bookshop with an armful of things to read, some of the most disciplined, technically brilliant, head and heart literature of the 20th century: Fitzgerald, West, Chandler, Kerouac and Steinbeck, who produced the greatest Californian story of all, *The Grapes of Wrath*. This stretch of coast has given us some of the best books of the century, and they go some way to mitigating for *Baywatch* and *Star Wars*.

Next door is a chaotic record shop. Every journey needs its soundtrack, and among the CDs I buy for the car is *The Best of the Byrds*, which I haven't heard since school. The old knit-yourself-into-a-gonk bloke at the till says: "If you're interested in Roger McGuinn, he's playing here tomorrow."

In a nice Spanish hacienda-style theatre, McGuinn walks onto the stage dressed in black. He looks like a good-natured liberal studies lecturer with a 12-string guitar, unrecognisable from the helmet-haired, trippy-spectacled dude on the record cover. He does a little light chat: "So Dylan wrote this line on a napkin and said, sing this, and I did, and this is how it goes." He did all the old ones, "Mr Tambourine Man"; "Turn! Turn! Turn!"; "All I Really Want to Do", and when he started "The Ballad of Easy Rider", the damnedest thing happened: I began to cry. For a moment I couldn't think why, but then of course I did know why. I was just unprepared. Nothing, but nothing – no image, no taste, no scent of cabbage and floor polish – can whisk you back like the popular music from the time when popular music was written just for you. The 1960s were my formative years, and I was back on the iron bed in boarding school in flat, grey, clagged-clay Hertfordshire, turning the volume up on the Dansette, pictures of Don McCullin's war and Martin Luther King sellotaped to the wall behind me, with everything else before me and this image of California in bright Day-Glo hippie colour, the coolest, most energising place in the world.

California was the filament in the light bulb whose hot, bright ideas lit up the darkness of post-war, post-empire, short-back-and-sides Britain. Whatever I have become, those years between 14 and 19 made me; I was a sponge for ideas and beliefs and hope, I'm marked indelibly as a child of the 1960s, tattooed by peaceful protest and women's lib and civil rights and ban the bomb. Being here, finally, in this laid-back, reverential hall felt like a secret reunion of ex-heretics. All around were men and women of about my age, their hair now faded grey to bald, dressed in paunchy jeans and Gap T-shirts, still wearing secret talismans of an earlier, wilder life. The string of love-beads, a turquoise and silver bracelet, the Joan Baez hair framing faces that no longer looked like Ali MacGraw. It was touching and it was sad and more than a bit pathetic. What had we all become? Computer programmers, muffin shop tycoons, writers, parents, mortgage holders, decaf-latte drinkers, ex-smokers, early risers, neighbourhood watch co-ordinators.

We got stiffly to our feet and clapped the encores, applauded and cheered the memory of what we once believed and wanted to be. And then he ruined it all by inviting us back to the folk den on his website. On every face I saw a *frisson* of regret and guilt – it wasn't supposed to be like this.

Next day I saw a matinée of the new Austin Powers movie and it annoyed me; I didn't laugh. Current America has ridiculed and buried the 1960s, and everything it stood for, so deeply. The rational Right has broken the butterfly on the wheel so comprehensively that now, to most American kids, the 1960s is something that happened only in England, all dolly birds and moptops and funny old David Bailey types, Carnaby Street and innocent sex. It's easy to dismiss with a sneer, but at the time, for us, the energy and the momentum of the 1960s were not in Liverpool or London but here in America, and it was much harder, more political, more purposeful. The names come back: Mayor Daley, Lieutenant Calley, the Minutemen, the Soledad brothers, Abbie Hoffman and Kent State. How come we swapped the Whole Earth catalogue for LL Bean's catalogue, and when did Ralph Nader morph into Bill Gates?

Of course my morbid reverie could have something to do with the fact that it would be my birthday in two days and I'd be 45, closer to being a pensioner than a teenager. I have never regretted getting a year older, experience has always seemed to be a fair swap for youth, but I do regret some of the things I left behind. And I wanted to see if this road that once seemed as impossibly romantic as Xanadu or Shangri-La was where I had left them.

Out of Santa Barbara, with its gated residential ghetto, Hope Ranch, so exclusive it's invisible behind walls of greenery, past the golf courses where you can catch sight of the staggeringly rich children of the 1960s who've swapped Harleys for electric golf buggies. One of the odd things about California is that everyone over the age of 40 seems to have retired or at least is starting out on a relaxed, home-bound second career. The day-to-day business of the state is left entirely in the hands of children. Everyone you come across doing a job is still at school, and they go about business with an exaggerated politeness and prematurely furrowed brows. I bought some chewing gum, the chewing gum had a website. What could there possibly be on a chewing gum's home page? When you've finished with it, does it stick to the bottom of your screen?

Lompoc, ugly name, ugly place, another dull, sprawling municipality with fantastically wide streets. American towns that can't be bothered to build anything over three storeys often do this, as if calling them boulevards is going to fool anyone into thinking they're the Vienna of the Wild West. There are millions of towns like Lompoc, spread from California to Maine, with the same concession shops and fast-food restaurants and illuminated signs on poles. They are where the vast majority of Americans exist and they're a reminder that, on the whole, despite the money and the power and the glory, you'd rather live in a tent than in provincial USA.

Lompoc is a service town: there's a huge air base here and rusting nuclear silos. Just to the east is Los Alamos, where they discovered what you can do with a well-split atom. Even though California has irredeemably dumbed down the world's culture, it could have been worse – they could have dumbed it off altogether. We stopped here because they promised a flower festival. Intercontinental ballistic missiles and cut flowers are the town's two industries, that and the wearing of bellicose baseball caps. The festival is a ragged parade of high-school bands, firemen, the Asian Immigrants' Association, and hairy rednecks in an army-surplus Jeep with a heavy machine gun mounted on it calling for a holy war against drugs through a megaphone: "Do you love Jesus?" Nobody replies, because they're so far away from the sidewalk they can't hear.

On up the coast. Every other building seems to be a U-Lock storage warehouse or an animal hospital. The number of vets and pet parlours gets disturbing; either Californians are the worst, most dysfunctional animal lovers in the world or all the lhasa apsos are screaming neurotic hypochondriacs. Probably both.

San Luis Obispo is the home of the barbecue. Well, I suppose somewhere has to be. Barbecuing here, says the guidebook, is a religion. Don't so many religions end up as barbecues? Every restaurant advertises special old-time barbecues. How can a barbecue be anything but ancient old-time? Chucking meat onto an open fire is prehistoric. I see a fleeting sign for a Museum of Barbecuing. Well, I think, we just have to go – but then I change my mind. It will never be as good as I can imagine it. Some things are best left tantalisingly unexplored. I can fondly fantasise about rooms of barbecuing memorabilia, the ashes from Christopher Columbus's Sunday barbecue, a briquette from Custer's last barbecue, a Ku Klux Klan hot cross barbecue, the tongs Buzz Aldrin took to the moon, the John F Kennedy memorial barbecue flame . . . Barbecues are to cooking what Stonehenge is to architecture: a start.

We went to what was billed as the best in town and, by implication, the whole damn world. It was a hellish *auto-da-fé* in a car park, stoked by a greasy, sweating yob who poked seared carcasses with the malevolence of a Hades work experience student. Everything for 20 yards was treacly with gritty black fat. We got given two ribs on a paper plate and a Styrofoam cup of mushy baked beans and a side of slaw (Side of Slaw ought to be a minor character from *Beowulf*). In the shade of a pick-up truck, the ribs tasted of cow dung and creosote, shards of flesh had been welded to the vast hacked bone and had to be gnawed until they resembled oily sacking. It was one of the foulest and most dentally challenging eating experiences I can remember. This doesn't taste remotely like beef, I said. "No, it wouldn't, it's pork." Christ, the pig must have been the size of a rhino. Entertaining and energetic though barbecue culture was, it wasn't the real point of San Luis Obispo: that is the Madonna Inn. Set right on the motorway, the Madonna Inn is one of the wonders of California – no, it's one of the great wonders of the world. If you stay in only one hotel in the whole of your life, it just has to be the Madonna Inn. The rooms are all unique and called things like Romance, Hearts and Flowers, and Caveman. It is a huge rambling jumble of gaudy decoration and riotous colour. Let the Crazy Child cater. Nothing to do with the singer or indeed the mother of Jesus. It was conceived 30 years ago by a road builder called Madonna and his wife, Mrs Madonna, one of the great surnames of history. The Madonna Inn is the Vatican of kitsch: it has an obsessive, slavering attention to doll's-house detail with an equally complete disregard for form or structure, which is the true mark of great kitsch.

You could sneer at the Madonna Inn but it wouldn't care, it would be like spitting at Niagara. It's constructed on such a clichéd sensual scale that the sneers just bounce off, irony sidles away defeated. The Madonna Inn is as close as I'll probably ever get to seeing heaven, because in heaven if we are relieved of earthly burdens and physical desires, so surely we must also finally be able to lay down the handbag of good taste.

On up Route 1 to San Simeon, we pass a truck bearing the sign "Culver City Meat, you can't beat our meat". San Simeon is famous for one thing, Hearst Castle, a gloomy robber press baron's palace on top of a hill. Americans often say they don't have any history – they say it to us as a sort of polite apology, because we obviously have so much and because they think we don't have any hot water or dentists, and so history is a consolation. It's nonsense, of course, America has as much history as anywhere else. What Americans mean is they don't build history, their past is nomadic. Only a very few have taken the time and effort to plant bricks and mortar for posterity, and even if they have, someone else will come along and rip it all up. America is addicted to new deals and starting afresh. So when they do come across something like San Simeon they don't really know what to do with it. In Europe you buy a ticket from an old lady in a kiosk and a catalogue written in 1962 and wander round. Here you have to book in advance, check into a sort of airport lounge, take a bus from a specially designed terminal, and then be herded by a guide through a quarter of it. You'd need to go four times to see all of San Simeon, which, frankly, is not much more than a gross memorial to a man who was comprehensively ripped off by every sharp art dealer in New York. His favourite period of heavy European gothic is particularly unsuited to the Californian coast.

Hearst Castle is the Madonna Inn with pretensions and nothing like as much fun or honesty. Its pretensions still posthumously rankle; *Citizen Kane* the movie is what made Hearst and his joyless mausoleum famous, but it hates Orson Welles with a passion. "You've seen the film?" says the guide, like a teacher asking the guilty party to confess or we'll all be kept behind. "Good movie, bad history," he says sternly, but incorrectly. Kane is a good movie but Hearst Castle is still bad history.

There's something about coasts that inspires flights of tasteless-ness. Everywhere in the world, seaside towns are tacky, jolly places that don't seem to care, and so it is here. Strands of trailer parks and cheaply cheerful motels and gift shops selling nude women made out of shells, and restaurants with carved sharks on the roofs. But there is also the shore and the huge Pacific's chilly fists beating on the white sand, with the pale dune grass bent into the prevailing wind. This is not a coast for paddling and lilos. It's the point where the immovable object of the richest continent in the world meets the unstoppable force of the biggest ocean in the world. These are beaches for walking and composing, for deep breaths and thoughts of God. Only the elephant seals can insouciantly sunbathe like visiting Germans.

The road twists and turns through the cliffs, occasionally reveal-ing vistas of heart-stopping beauty. Parts remind you of the western Highlands, their steep passes covered in wild flowers and gale-contorted pines. It's a landscape that seems to accommodate, even welcome, the curling man-made ribbon of Tarmac as a natural part of itself. The great American journey is also part of this nature's story. It's easy to imagine the staggering awe of Núñez de Balboa and Lewis and Clark and the refugee Okies in the Model T Fords when they finally saw it, journey's end.

On north, and Big Sur. I'm not entirely sure what I was expect-ing from Big Sur but I expected something. Actually there's nothing, or as close to nothing as makes no difference. You see the sign, go, "Oh, hey, Big Sur," and it's all over. A roadside shop, a couple of clapboard buildings, the Henry Miller Library, and that's it. A population of under a thousand, hidden away up winding tracks and down secret gullies. Big Sur was a name that you conjured with in the 1960s. It embodied all the *Easy Rider* alternative magic, and actually I know what I was expecting here: ridiculously, preposterously, I was expecting Kate Healy.

I remember the term she came to school as a boarder, tall and rangy and blonde with blue eyes and freckled high cheekbones, that smiley white American look that seemed to belong to the next rung of natural selection to us scrawny, dark, whey-faced, woollen-flannel English boys. She was Californian. Californian from Big Sur. She wore Indian jewellery and had a plaited hippie headband and Day-Glo felt-tip pens that she used to make psychedelic native rune patterns on all her exercise books and the back of my hand. Most of all I remember her breasts. Very white and very exciting, lying on a chilly Hertfordshire golf course. For one night, we shared a bottle of cider and a lot of saliva. I've never forgotten it, it was my brief taste of Big Sur and the big picture out there, the revolution that was happening to young people and the world that I could only hear between bells and bedtime on a tinny record player and in magazines. A part of me expected to see her just standing on the side of the road, still sixteen, those fabulous breasts in a flower-power vest, her hair tied back with a plaited band, bare feet and bell-bottom jeans.

I'm pleased there was nothing here, no strip of taco restaurants and pet parlours. Big Sur remains a place that geographically is a spot high in the pine forest of the Californian coast but really, actually, exists in a moonlit bunker on the outskirts of Letchworth.

On to Carmel, another morbidly cute seaside town with a manicured main street. We stop for lunch. On the table of the café is a little paper sachet that a teabag came in: "Tazo, a calm herbal infusion. Ingredients: camomile blossom, hibiscus flowers, spearmint, rose petals, blackberry leaves, peppermint, safflower, lemon balm, lemon grass, natural flavours and the mumbled chantings of a certified tea shaman". And a website. Time to move on. On through Monterey, and the final leg to San Francisco.

I love San Francisco. We drove in on an uncharacteristically bright, hot day; the endemic mist that rolls in across the Golden Gate Bridge was absent. This is a real city with a heart and a soul and a story. Pretty architecture trundles up the vertiginous hills, which are the only reason I couldn't live here (well, I could live here, but I wouldn't live for long). San Francisco has a liberal, humane feel, a diverse population and good food. I particularly wanted to see Haight-Ashbury, another name that's heady and exciting with vibrations from my youth. It's just a crossroads, but here at last I found the 1960s that I'd left behind, that I'd so ardently yearned after for 30 years, and pretty sad it was. Haight Street is Carnaby Street, where tourists can buy Grateful Dead posters and bongs and hippie-dippy paraphernalia. I got a tie-dyed T-shirt that I shan't ever wear, because in one of the monumental rows I had with my father as a teenager he shouted in wholly justified exasperation that if I didn't get out of bloody bed I'd end up selling tie-dyed T-shirts in Haight-Ashbury.

Unlike Carnaby Street, which is now populated by Scandinavian tourists and crocodiles of underage French shoplifters, Haight Street still has real hippies, looking completely authentic. Bearded men playing guitars, kids selling dope, teenage runaways with bedrolls looking for enlightenment and sex. It's a pitiful, muted place, a colonial Williamsburg experience, drop-out culture that dropped off. It doesn't want to grasp the future, just endlessly rewind the past.

The 1960s were a crossroads – we had the moment and we chose to go by another route, all of us. This trip stirred a lot of things: beliefs, hope, optimism and innocence, stuff that I'd chosen to pack away because time and experience told me they wouldn't be needed on the journey. But I miss them. I regret their gaucheness and their passing. And it also seems to me that the restless journey of America has stalled in another depression – of wealth. There is an apocryphal story of a monk who's a counsellor here in California. "Which would you rather talk to," asks a reporter, "rich miserable people or poor miserable ones?"

"Oh, no question," says the monk, "rich ones. The rich already know that money isn't going to fix them."

In California the rich are still trying to buy a homespun humility. They've exchanged the childlike for the childish. The *faux* hippie geeks of the microchip revolution would like us to believe that they've got another electric new deal, built another Route 1, an information highway that's moved into the ether, and that the great adventure is still out there on the Web with Gandalf and herbal tea and bubblegum, an armchair nirvana. But it isn't so, it's just a toy, a babbled diversion, it's instead of, not as well as, real life. At the heart of the ridiculed 1960s was the fundamental belief that money couldn't, wouldn't, buy what was really worthwhile, but that the pursuit of wealth would prevent us gaining what we really desperately needed, but we all more or less chose the pursuit anyway.

We can't go back to the 1960s, but we need to find another crossroads, another way through the woods, and at 45 one of the Byrds' lyrics still runs round and round my head. "I was so much older then, I'm younger than that now."

When DD met AA

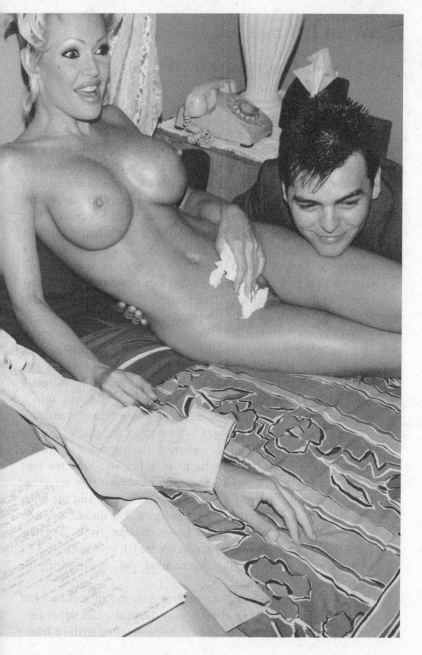

When DD met AA

US Pornography, November 1999

"Dead puppies," shouts a barely controlled voice from the dark. Dead puppies. I'm laughing so hard I think I'm going to strain something. We're all laughing that whooping, rip-roaring laughter that comes along all too rarely after you're old enough to have your own overdraft. Back-of-the-school-bus, infectious hysteria. We're all laughing here in the dark. Five feet away in a bright pool of light, a man wearing only a chef's hat at a rakish angle is manipulating the end of a vast penis as if it had a childproof cap. A naked woman with breasts the size and texture of pink bowling balls is lying, legs akimbo, in a wedding cake. They're not laughing. "Dead puppies" is the technical term for "shut the fuck up and concentrate."

"Sex, please," shouts another voice from the hot blackness. "Rolling, speed, action," and the chef heaves the penis like a sock of billiard balls at the girl's frosted sphincter. It nuzzles the puckered blind eye like a physics problem – how do you get a quart into a shot glass? How do you get an elephant into a telephone box? How in God's name do you get that monstrous willy up a bum? The chef spreads his feet on the sticky floor for purchase, places a hand on his own muscular buttock for leverage, and pushes. A single marine raising the flag on Iwo Jima, the staff bends then takes the strain. The girl's dead-tarantula eyelashes flutter, her pink-taloned fingers grip her own hock and the knob begins to disappear. Inch by truncheon-inch. The breasts, two true troopers, never move – they don't even shudder. In the darkness there is a faint drawing-in of breath. Let me tell you, nothing Paul Daniels ever made vanish was remotely as awe-inspiring or captivatingly magic as this.

It's halfway through the second and final day of shooting *Hot House Tales*, my debut as a director – my debut as a film writer also, actually – and I've spent most of it helpless with mirth or transfixed with admiration. I'm in Hollywood, well, Hollywood Lite, and I'm an author. I'm a player. I'm a name. I'm a call-back. I'm a table-hopping destination. I'm in movies. This is the dream, my dream, that I've had since my mother took me to see my first porn movie, *The Devil In Miss Jones*, in Times Square when I was 19. The idea that you could realise your hot, sweaty-fisted fantasies and make them happen, show them in Technicolor, is the ultimate boys' fantasy. All my adult life I've wanted to have a pneumatic woman buggered on a wedding cake by a cartoonishly hung black man. Who hasn't? It was surprisingly easy to make it happen. This is America, after all. A country addicted to making dreams come true and pneumatic breasts.

Metro, one of the biggest adult entertainment companies, with a multimillion-pound turnover and a listing on the Nasdaq, was only too happy to have an unknown hack write and direct a movie and do a feature on it. In fact they had a free slot in a month. Could they possibly have an 80-minute script by Monday? (It was Friday.) For the next two days I asked everyone I knew what they wanted to see in a porn movie. Is there a consensus as to what's sexy? I particularly wanted to know what women found erotic. Men's fantasies are all either desperately predictable – naughty underwater nurses, surprised maids, bored housewives – or solitary-user specific, as in: "I've always wanted to see really elegant girls in evening gowns scrabbling through piles of manure for diamonds." I'd imagined that women would want a story, a context and, above all, romance. In fact, all the women I spoke to had the same fantasy: anonymous sex. Fucking a stranger. Just eye-contact and then down to it. Well I never, I must have brushed past a million women since I was 16 and never once have I been propositioned. I thought you had to make them laugh first, at least.

I started off with a list of things that didn't turn me on – spotty bums; socks (porn stars wear them because they think dirty feet are even less sexy); clichéd, aggressive swearing of the "you know you want it, you dirty bitch" type; snarling; cheap jewellery; stick-on nails, and most of all, the violent domination and humiliation that's so often a feature in pornography. Metro had its own requirements. It faxed a list of movie must-haves: six to eight females and four to six males. One female will be the star, be featured on the video box and do two scenes. There should be seven scenes in total, of the following types: boy-girl; girl-girl; girl-girl-boy; girl-boy-boy; girl-anal; boy-girl oral; and solo girl masturbation. However, girls wanking is something else that doesn't do it for me, so I ditched that and started typing with my other hand. The plot had to be simple, the dialogue simpler. "They don't do talking," Susan Yanetti, Metro's sardonic and amused PR, told me. "Really. They won't read the script and they can't act. It's not what they do."

After some thought, I decided to set my vignettes in the rooms of a cheap boarding house, and have them all link up, like *La Ronde*. Some would be funny, some deeply erotic. In all of them, the power would be with the women. Initially, I wanted each scene to be surprising – something I hadn't seen before. But as I started writing, I realised that many of my fantasies were second-hand, formed by erotic films I'd seen or books I'd read. And much eroticism is in a nuance – the sway of a hip, the look in an eye – something intangible that fires a spark between the screen and the viewer. Still, the plot came fast and I started to have a ball. (It's impossible to talk about pornography in anything but *double entendres*. Just ignore them.) I plagiarised the *Decameron,* the *Canterbury Tales* and Greek myths for storylines. I'm telling you – writing a porn film is the best fun.

At 4am on Sunday, I faxed the script to Metro and waited for the call. Susan Yanetti called me back within a few hours. "I reckon we've got a porno movie here," she said. "It's very good. Really, you have a talent for this. It's much better than the stuff we normally get."

Let me tell you, I have won more than my fair share of press awards. I have been paid disgusting amounts of money to write for prestigious magazines. I have had fan mail from Elizabeth Hurley, and been kissed by Michael Winner. But nothing – no gong or compliment – had ever filled me with such pride.

However, Susan had some changes. "A lot of this is way over the customers' heads, let alone the actors'. And this boy-on-boy scene has got to go or they won't stock it in the shops. The merest hint of homosexuality and the poor dears lose their erections. Remember, what we're making is a masturbation aid; the wankers can't handle a hint of gayness. And I think we have to drop the scene where the Chinese girl smokes a joint in her vagina and says, 'My pussy's got the munchies for you.'"

"Why?" I asked. "Can't you find a girl who can do pelvic floor-exercises?"

"It's not that – it's drugs. They're real strict about that."

"So you can have a girl gang-banged by twenty strangers in ways which are illegal in eighteen states, but smoking grass is immoral?"

"Adrian, this is America."

This is Van Nuys. It is 40 minutes outside Beverly Hills and 20° hotter. It has a baked-on, low-level grimness which should make it illegal to buy razor blades here without a prescription. The Metro office is situated in a prefab hangar in a street of hangars beside a military airport. The Tomcats howl orgasmically up the runway, but everything else is eerily silent. You'd never know what they did here.

Inside the offices, there is a matter-of-fact air. There is not an inflated breast in sight – the pictures on the walls are, bizarrely, Disney animation drawings. Susan greets us and gives me my rewritten script. To say that it had been emasculated wouldn't be entirely accurate. Everything that isn't masculation has been filleted; a plot and dialogue that I'd thought *Sesame Street*-simple is now Care In The Community-remedial.

But never mind. It's a movie script, it's got my name on it, and we're in production. We have our first production meeting with the producer and cameraman – two young dudes in shorts and band T-shirts with futuristic facial hair, both called Michael (though the cameraman calls himself "Quasar Man"). They are a team. They make 20-odd movies a year and they talk like a double-act, finishing each other's sentences, sliding into pop-song riffs, and making each other snigger. Quasar Man is Canadian and has a Tourette's-like obsession with talking in an Austin Powers accent and clicking the air with inverted commas. Ironically, of course. They are like the Valley version of Beavis and Butt-head and I like them immediately. The production meeting is brief.

"Have you got any questions?"

"No."

"Good. We'll see you on the set."

Before we begin filming, Susan shows me round the warehouse at the back of the hangar. Racks of VCRs are continuously making copies, while thousands of videos lie waiting to be packed and shipped. The films are arranged by subject: black men; white girls; gang-bangs; nurses; gay men; transsexuals; and anal (or "A", as it's known). There is also a section devoted to double-A – two penises in one bottom – a thought which makes the mind boggle and the cheeks clench.

Porn is one of the biggest businesses in the world. In America alone it turns over $7–10bn a year – that's more than Hollywood. Worldwide, it grosses half a trillion. The cosy, liberal assumption that pornography is a sad, solitary, under-the-mattress toss-aid for socially inept, underclass old men, is patently untrue. A few low-rent, dirty old wankers and some hairy-palmed students simply don't generate that sort of money. But then, no one does know actually who's watching this stuff – although we all assume we know why.

"Nobody has ever done any real market research," says Susan. "There is no demographic picture because people just lie about sex. It's stiff with hypocrisy, guilt and shame. But, essentially, pornography is bought by men. Women may watch it and enjoy it, but no woman rents a video to watch on her own with her hand down her knickers."

I asked how many films Metro had in its catalogue. "No one's counting," says Susan, "but it must be 25,000 at least. They get re-edited and made into compilations." That's just one company and it's all been made in the last 15 years.

Porn's boom came with video. It is said that it was the porn industry that killed Betamax by choosing VHS. Certainly, it is the porn industry that is driving DVD – for every mainstream video title there are 12 porn titles available. An American computer company wanted to advertise the power of the Internet by listing the top ten most popular sites. It gave up, because all of them were porn. In fact, the top 20 sites are porn with the singular exception of the Mormons' Doomsday Census.

*

The studio is low-rent and decrepit, but fantastically exciting to me because my boarding house has finally come to life. Each room has been built and dressed with remarkable care and authenticity. They all look deeply seedy.

Among the collateral pleasures of porn are the stunningly hideous bedspreads, coffee tables and pictures in the backgrounds. If you ever wondered where they come from, I can tell you there's a props room in the Valley that is the British Museum of solitary ejaculation. Hundreds of horrendous beds, sofas, lamps, statues, rhinestone-covered telephones, soft toys, kitchens and operating theatres. It's an X-rated style obscenity all of its own.

Upstairs in make-up, Clarissa is being plastered for the first scene. My story called for a Vietnamese girl. Clarissa is half-Mexican – close – and also very young and exceedingly nervous. I try to talk to her about motivation and the Method.

"Have you actually read the script?"

"Yes." She's such a bad actress she can't even lie in a single affirmative believably. This is only her second movie and she's terrified of being recognised, so has insisted on a wig. Unfortunately, the wig is exactly the same colour, cut and length as her own hair (she's not bright). "It'll be fine," I say. "You look wonderful." She smiles gratefully, proving I'm a better actor than she is. She has every reason to be nervous. Her scene is with Ron Jeremy and she's never seen him.

Ron Jeremy is a god, there's no two ways about it. He is the most famous male porn star in America and he's hideous. Truly, madly, deeply hideous. Fat, short, balding – he is a soft, dank, hairy fast-food bin with a greasy Village People moustache. Ron is the Mickey Rooney of porn: he's been around since naughty postcards and has had everyone. They all love Ron. He's funny and he can act. Trouble is, no one wants to fuck him any more. Clarissa is getting a $200 premium to do it with Ron.

When Ron arrives, he's wearing a filthy red T-shirt and shorts that do nothing for him. "Hey," he yells, "great script!"

"Don't take any notice," whispers Mike the producer. "He says that every time."

Ron wants to talk about motivation. He knows his lines and he takes it all very seriously. "Hey, I've done legit work, you know.

I've done England. I've been on Ruby Wax twice." (My, there aren't a lot of men who can say that.) "Look, I brought some costumes along. See what you think." He produces a plastic bag containing three T-shirts and three pairs of shorts – all grubby, identical variations on the vile things he's already wearing.

I get my first bad set of giggles.

The scene doesn't go well. Clarissa sees Ron and goes as stiff as a board. She's the only thing that does. Ron, once famous for being able to auto-fellate, come on cue and hit a nostril at five paces, can't get it up. He has to use what is technically known as the "kung fu death grip" – pinching the base of his penis so hard the blood can't get out. Clarissa is horrified.

"Just a minute," Ron pants. Gunther, the video tech, groans. "The three words you never want to hear on a set are: 'Just a minute.' It means the talent can't get wood." In the end, the scene is cut down to a facial. That is, Ron wanks on to Clarissa's cheek. It's not pretty, it's not erotic and it's not a good start. I follow her out into the sunlight. "Are you all right?" I ask. She says she's fine – she's grateful for the money but isn't sure she's going to do it again.

Being able to achieve and sustain an erection to order is the great improbable at the heart of porn movies. Very few men can do it. Lots think they can, but in the business there are only about 25 men who work regularly. Viagra is changing that, but no one with an ounce of professional pride will admit they use it.

The next scene – boy-girl-girl – has the best, most sought-after erection in the business. It's British and (wouldn't you know?) it's from Essex. Stephen Scott – whose stage name is, incomprehensibly, Mark Davies – has been voted Best Male Porn Star three times at Cannes. The crew love him. "Woody" is his middle name. He gets it up, goes grinding on and on like the good ship *Venus* and then ejaculates in a blur of fist. Most importantly, the girls love doing it with him. One of the many myths about porn films is that they exploit women. Philosophically, we can argue about it but, practically, it's quite the reverse. The girls get paid up to three times more than the men, can choose their male partners and their positions. Mark is in demand, sometimes making two films a day. He's been in the sex business since he was 17, first as a stripper and then as a Chippendale. He's also easy-going and charming. As we chat about England and California, I quite forget that I'm making small-talk with a naked man who's licking his fingers and manipulating the bell-end of a very big penis. He's also the proud owner of a "convertible" – he's got a foreskin, most Americans don't – though he's fucked so much that he has torn it twice. Stress fractures in a cavalier's bonnet – you couldn't make it up.

Mark does everything. "What about double-A?" I ask him.

"Sure. Some guys won't do it, they think it's sort of gay. You know, touching another guy's cock. It doesn't bother me."

"But what about the girls?"

"Well, they're big, you know? You could drop a golf ball down them and it wouldn't touch the sides. There's one girl who can stick a pineapple up her ass."

It's not just being able to do it, it's considering it in the first place. Anal sex used to be rare in porn movies but now it's *de rigueur*. Every show has to have it. Susan thinks it is because punters want to see what they can't get at home. Mostly, the male actors don't like it – it's not as nice or as well-appointed as a vagina – but the women do. Johnny Black, a female ex-paratrooper captain who's starring in a later scene, asks specifically if she can do A. (I tell her that if she feels it's in keeping with the motivation of her character to go for it by all means.)

In the make-up room, naked bodies are being primped and patted and plucked. The producer comes in and shouts, "Time to blow the pipes!" The couple for the next scene go off to the loo with vinegar douches and enema pipes. It's a little touch of hygienic good manners – like brushing you teeth before kissing Michelle Pfeiffer.

Mark's scene is with Claudia Chase and Temptress, who begin with girl-on-girl and move on to a boy-girl-girl number. There is a definite frisson on the set; both the girls are truly beautiful and Temptress is doing a man on screen for the first time in ages. Up until now she has mainly been doing lesbian work and stripping (she takes dollar bills from punters' mouths by clasping them between her buttocks). Mark's trick is to turn the girls on for real.

Temptress is a pushover. Between takes they don't stop – his head stays butted between her thighs.

"What makes him so good?" I shout.

"Oh, he's really good at going down on us," giggles Claudia. "He's the best."

Mark comes up for air. "I've got a really short tongue," he smiles.

"Oh, I've got a really short tongue as well," I mutter. "What a coincidence." The crew dissolves into fits.

Real female orgasms aren't as rare as you'd imagine on set. Some girls hold back because they think orgasms should only be with their boyfriends, but most just go with it. Temptress comes at the top of her voice. With great professionalism, Mark gives both girls a simultaneous facial. "I'll come from here to here, and I won't get it in your eyes." He's the Tiger Woods of sperm. As we pack up the scene, Mark asks Temptress if she has a boyfriend. "Not any more," she replies.

"Well, if you'd like some uncomplicated fucking, let's get together." It's rather touching, if a little bizarre. You have troilistic sex, *then* ask the girl for a date. And so it goes on.

That afternoon, a German TV crew turn up, then a Dutch one. There's a seedy little guy making a documentary to go on the backside of the DVD. At any one time there are five cameras on the set all trying to keep out of each others' way. Quasar Man keeps up a steady stream of Austin Powers jokes and teases the naked talent remorselessly. "OK, time to stick the Johnson up the colon."

We're actually shooting two films simultaneously – the hardcore video version and a soft *Playboy* channel one, so every shot has to be duplicated ("Legs together, I'm getting ball sack"). Johnson-touching-sphincter is definitely hardcore.

Quasar Man is terrified of penises touching him. Has he ever been hit?

"Once I got a ricochet on my shoes. This job really puts you off sex." Continuity is also a problem. "Was that duvet cover on the bed?" he shouts.

"Who cares, for Chrissakes?" cries the producer. "If the masturbators are stopping to say, 'Oh look, that duvet cover is a different colour,' they must be gay."

"I know it's just porn, but I want to get it right," replies Quasar Man. "I don't want to be back handing out the lube." The assistant responsible for the condoms, KY and tissues has the lowliest job on the lot.

I quickly learn the language of pornography. The come shot is a "pop"; an FIP is a "faked internal pop" for the soft version. All the positions have names. The "cowgirl" (her on top) is good for bum shots. "Reverse cow" (her on top facing the other way) is good for close-up plumbing shots. "Monkey-fucking" is a position never seen in real life, where the man squats over the girl in a sort of simian doggy fashion. Between takes, a stills photographer known as Creepy Drew takes publicity and magazine shots in quick succession – hard, soft and ultra-light. All day, the most disgusting chef I've ever seen, a man who looks like the wagon-train cook from a John Wayne film, scuttles round the set handing out canapés. Prawns and guacamole on tortilla chips; tuna and onion sandwiches; chicken and mango salsa. As the cameras are moved or videos changed, the girls look after the male talent, helping them keep their erections. They ask them, "What do you need honey?" and kiss or give blow jobs, fondle scrotums or just lie with their legs apart "showing pink". All day there is a masturbating man somewhere in my peripheral vision, until the last pop is shot at 2am. I go back to my Beverly Hills hotel and watch a porn movie, too tired to sleep. It's an 8am start tomorrow.

Houston is currently the hottest thing in porn movies. She became a major star by lying on a turntable and having sex with more men in one day than anyone else in the world, ever – 620. Climbing Mount Everest in a sandpaper bikini would have been an easier route to stardom.

Houston is our featured talent. I meet her in the make-up room (her make-up takes longer than Chewbacca's), where she is trimming what's left of her pubic hair, gingerly circumnavigating a pudendum that looks like a badly made pastrami sandwich. She grabs a clump of clippings. "I should sell this stuff, you know."

Ah, a true diva.

We talk about her role. "I really like this scene with all the cakes," she says. "I do something like this in my act." A lot of the girls make serious money dancing in strip clubs, using the videos to promote themselves. Houston has a body that's built for pornography. Built with care and attention by real craftsmen. She's tough and very professional, going over and over her lines. "I don't think I can say, 'Oh bugger me' here. It doesn't sound right. Can I say, 'Hey, fuck me in the ass' instead?"

Houston's first scene is a blow job. She makes it look incredibly exciting. "The trick is that you've got to really enjoy it." Her second scene is the wedding-cake buggery. It's complicated. She has to talk, eat cake and have sex in a number of camera-pleasing but precarious positions with a man who should have "Not for internal use" tattooed on his cock. Here we hit a glitch. Houston, we have a problem. While the actor is willing to have his equipment varnished and to mime reciprocation for the softcore version, he won't actually go down on Houston. "I've got an allergy to sugar," he mumbles, "and she's covered in cake." Great. We get the only porn star in the world who's allergic to icing. The producer has his own theory, however. "It's a cultural thing. He doesn't want to put his mouth where 619 guys and Ron Jeremy have been." Quite.

Eventually, Quasar Man shoots around the problem with a string of obscene jokes. "Time for Johnson to probe colon. Park the Cadillac in the cul-de-sac . . ." The buggery scene comes to an abrupt end, however, when the Caddie hits creosote. Now, imagine the most embarrassing thing in the world, and then compare it to being covered in cake, having anal sex with a stranger, being filmed up-close by three camera crews, and then shitting yourself. That's top-of-the-range humiliation, but Houston never blinked. She didn't blush or even smile apologetically. She just called the lube guy for a paper towel, cleaned herself up and went for the pop shot. It was the most damnably cool thing I ever saw. Houston is a true, 18-carat star.

The next problem we had was the Catholic girl and the two strangers. This set-up had been utterly mangled from my original. All that was left was an unexplained Catholic shrine and a girl who took the double-pop shot like communion.

She was to start off by praying. Melody Love, a small but perkily formed Hispanic girl, throws a fit. "Oh my God, I can't do that.

I'm Catholic. Not in front of Jesus." I try to reason with her. "You're going to have sex simultaneously with two strange men for money as an aid to masturbation (a sin). Do you think God's going to mind more because you're pretending to pray?" We compromise by removing the picture of Christ. What He can't see won't bother Him. I just hope He doesn't watch the *Playboy* channel.

One of the men, Tyce Bune, comes in for a lot of ribbing from Quasar Man about the size of his penis. "God, here it comes – the smallest dick in movies, cock in a sock. Hey Tyce, you going to get an erection? Oh, that *is* an erection. I'll get in close, then." Frankly, if I had a willy his size, I'd wear it on the outside with a blue rosette saying "Best In Show".

I watch the scene from a redundant sofa. Beside me is the porn-star wife of the other exorbitantly hung man in this threesome. After a couple of minutes, I look round. She's concentrating intently and masturbating. Catching my eye, she smiles politely. "Isn't he great? We've been married for ten years. I wish you'd ask me to do this scene, I'd have been much better." Actually, the producer tries not to cast husbands and wives together – their familiarity transmits to the screen.

"You still find this exciting even though it's work?" I ask her, totally bemused. "Oh yeah, honey, you've got to love sex if you want to survive in this business. If you don't really enjoy it, well, it hurts for a start. You can be rubbed raw. You've got to be into it. Here," she continues, "you want to see the best natural bosoms in the business?" Oh, if you must. She shows me. They would be the best natural bosoms in any business you care to mention.

At 2am, we get to the last set-up. The lesbian scene. Two excessively exuberant girls – one blonde, one dark with thin, parched, recreation area pubic hair – play a cop and an illegal immigrant. The cop pulls on a surgical glove and, in a Texan accent says: "I'm going to have to search you, Maria. Bend over."

"No, no! Not that!" For a moment, I have an image of her as Rod Steiger with implants and think that perhaps we should call the movie *On Heat In The Night*. Though the crew are exhausted and have been watching sex for 16 hours straight, they really like this bit. Outside the pool of light, they squat in the shadows and silently watch the girls slither about on the bed, howling like vixens. But then I notice something odd. The gaffers and grips and runners and sparks and the lube boy have all turned from the action to stare at the monitor. Five feet away from them two live girls are having sex, but they'd rather watch it on the screen. Pornography is something that happens on a screen. This is its familiar, omnipotent voyeurism; its erotic charge comes from being disengaged.

The last-gasp close-up is caught. It's a wrap. The girls roll off the bed giggling, kiss and say, "Thanks, we should do this again." The studio lights go on and the crew divvy up the few remaining cigarettes. Plugs are pulled. The miles of cable are wound round thumb and elbow and that's it. We say goodbye in that intense way you do when you've shared a common task, and exhaustion, with a team. Manly bear hugs. Many a "Hey, keep in touch". Michael the producer says, "You ever want to do this again, just call. We should make one a year."

And that's it. Exit, roll credits. I walk into the cool darkness of the Valley, get into the black limo and sleep, dreamlessly.

No story I have ever covered has elicited such fantastic interest as the making of a porn movie. Not war, pestilence, politics or celebrity. People come up to me in restaurants, at parties. They call me, wanting to know what it's really like. "What are the stars really like?" "Do they really . . . ?" "Is it actually . . . ?" Everyone wants to see it. There is a vast, intense interest in seeing people have sex on screen.

This may be because we live in the only theocratically censorious state in Europe, where hardcore pornography is illegal. The first film was produced in 1896 in this country. The first act of censorship was in 1898 when the British cheesemaking industry had a shot of blue-veined cheese withdrawn. Censoring cheese is no less absurd than censoring an erect penis. All the pseudo-social-scientific arguments about pornography encouraging rape and violence and sexual dysfunction have been made patently bogus by the 15-year experiment of us having no pornography while the rest of Europe has as much as it likes. The sexual-crime rates in Switzerland and Denmark are not notably soaring compared with ours. The things that most of us think should be banned – underage sex, violence – are already covered by the law whether you have a camera there or not.

But although everyone who has spoken to me wants to see the movie and wants to know every sweaty detail, so they have all wanted the sex stars to be dysfunctional, unhappy and exploited. "Well, of course they're all on drugs, aren't they?" "They're pretty sick people, aren't they?" "It's a very sleazy business, isn't it?" There is a need to have received wisdom confirmed. The bottom line is that we want filmed sex to have a riotous comeuppance for the actors because sex is the intimate act that proves the invisible truth of love and love is the most precious and powerful thing our species owns. But again, this doesn't make sense. Why don't we censor or become outraged at actors faking all the other facets of love? Why aren't two strangers who say, "I'll love you for ever" on screen far more wholly immoral? Why isn't *Romeo and Juliet* by common consent the most disgustingly depraved play ever written and only performed in seedy clubs on the Rieperbahn? It doesn't make sense, but then, nothing about sex makes sense. Why should it? The wiring in our heads that connects desires, lust, jealousy, passion, devotion, frustration and biology is so complex and irrational, that to even consider a rational debate about sex and pornography is absurd.

Making *Hot House Tales* I learnt that these are not exploited people. The set is matriarchal with the women choosing what they'll do and with whom. Only the film crew are cynical about the act – but then, all film crews are cynical. The stars are surprisingly innocent. I mean that in a fundamental not a physical sense. They are incredibly kind to each other. Each scene would start with the girl saying, "OK, what are your do's and don'ts? I don't like fingers up my arse or my hair being pulled, but slapping's good. Do you mind me biting your balls?" They would help the guys keep their erections between shots in a fond, almost loving, way. And the sex is real. It's real in the sense that running round a track is as real as running for a bus. I discovered that to compare porn stars with actors is a misinterpretation of what they do. They're much closer to being athletes. They physically perform for public pleasure.

They are an elite. Very few people can do what they do. You may play tennis but you're a million miles away from winning Wimbledon. You have sex but it's not in the same ballpark as these people. They take it seriously. They train, they're focused and they're very, very good. Is a girl with breast implants who'll take two penises up her backside any weirder than a shot-putter who'll take male hormones to throw a cannonball? There's no question which gives the most pleasure to watch. But one is a national hero and the other a seedy pariah. It doesn't make sense.

Are the stars exploited? Well, a lot of the women have what are known as "suitcase pimps" – parasite boyfriends who carry their bags and take their money, and there are some pretty seedy agents on the periphery of the business. Is there a lot of disease? Everyone has to produce a DNA test every 30 days. It's an unbreakable rule. A porn film has safer sex than a lot of you have with your own spouses. Are they happy? Well, that's a piece of string. They have the same run of broken marriages and fractured lives that you'd find anywhere in LA. Certainly they're far less miserably abused, abusive and disposable than their equivalents in Hollywood.

What I found, though, was a sincere sense of awe and envy for their ability to be straightforward about sex and still get pleasure from it. I have never met a group of people who were so relaxed about their bodies and their function. They've shed the strait-jacket of insecurity that the rest of us lug into bed. In the pool of bright light, I watched a remarkable fraternity of nice, attractive and amusing people doing what the rest of us cool libertarian liberals have been talking about since the Sixties. That is, be honest, relaxed and open about sex. I also learnt that we look for truths that will confirm and bolster our own complicated social, political and moral dilemmas about sex. We see and understand what we want, what we need, to see. And if you are reading this with a disbelieving sneer on your face, well, join everyone else I've said it to.

What *Hot House Tales* will look like, heaven only knows. I'm pretty sure it is not going to be the *Citizen Kane* of adult entertainment – probably more like the *Chitty Chitty Bang Bang* of skin flicks. But I do now see what a vaunting piece of hubris and self-delusion it was to ever imagine you could direct sex. I might as well have tried to pole a punt with my penis.

Sex and the city

Sex and the city

Cuba, March 1999

December 31, 1958, the National Hotel: the great stone good-time fortress on a rock overlooking Havana's harbour. A new year's party is in full swing. Cuba's upper crust, rich on sugar and spice and all things vice, and the backs of peasant labour, drink their rum cocktails, wear funny hats and throw streamers. The band is preparing to get its maracas round "Should auld acquaintance be forgot" when in walks the man who made all this possible, General Batista, the island's military dictator and president.

Outside, as usual, his outrider tanks have blocked both ends of the street. He takes the microphone, acknowledges the sycophantic applause and makes an announcement. Sadly, the game's up. He's leaving for good, *que sera sera*. The motorcade streams through the suburbs to a military airport and it's all over. He is followed precipitously by everybody in Cuba who owns anything. Still in dinner jackets and party frocks, the professional class scrambles to hop the 90 miles to Miami. Having lost one Caribbean island, Batista goes on to buy another with money gratefully and unaccountably donated by the feudal Cuban economy.

"My father was a waiter here then," says Carlos, my driver and guide. We are sitting on the National's terrace, one of the most evocative, beautiful bars in the world. He looks out to sea through the colonnade, past the neat palms of formal garden where peacocks strut and fountains splash. "I was seven. I remember my father coming home very excited." And what happened then? Sipping a small espresso that cost the equivalent of two days' pay, he says: "Nobody got any room service." Room service has been problematic ever since.

Next day, Che Guevara rolls into town and proclaims a new socialist republic: happy new year, *muchachos*. A week later Castro swings by, and the regime can well and truly start the way it plans to carry on.

Forty years later, Cuba is famous for failed politics, syncopated music, immoral women and cigars, and if an island could be a person, then Cuba would be Bill Clinton. The first thing you notice about Havana is how terribly 1960s it still feels. I remember the 1960s. So this is where it ended up – not the hippie flower power 1960s that gets revived every two years on the catwalk, but the political, righteous, romantic, didactically impressionable 1960s. There's music and mess and clots of policemen and 1950s cars and posters of Che. It's Che that really does it, really reminds you that this is the last un-tidied student bedroom in the world.

But it is difficult to remember that this is a truly bona fide, grown-up communist state. Communist countries are cold, grey, utilitarian and miserable; Cuba is warm, bright, sophisticated and outwardly happy. There are none of those solidly heroic symbols of universally uniting workers, or the international solidarity of metal and dogma bashers that are such a rustily ironic feature of state socialism elsewhere. There are no fraternal statues of Lenin or Marx, just a few walls with Pink Floydish official graffiti. There are statues, though. Havana is stuffed with memorial bronze but it's of the romantic Spanish type – heroic *hombres* on rearing horses, remembrances of small, hopeless revolts highlighting a municipal truth from all over the world: the more piddling the war, the grander the memorial. Cuba's revolution saw in the decade of left-wing youth and right-on liberation. It is the country that Joni Mitchell, Timothy Leary and Bob Dylan would have designed if anyone had been foolish enough to give them a country to tinker with. It has a fantastic free education system, an enviable free health service, plentiful guilt-free sex and cheap rum. It also has hardly any petrol, food, enterprise, industry or cash.

Although it is the 40th anniversary of the revolution, and communists are generically addicted to anniversary knees-ups, there are no signs of rejoicing, no banners in the streets, no new memorials or exhibitions of international revolutionary art, no callisthenics from schoolchildren. In truth there is little to celebrate. The past 40 years have been tough, the future looks tougher – in fact the future doesn't look like anything at all.

Castro (who is always referred to as Fidel), having been the most famous man in Latin America for so long, having outlasted every Yankee president since Eisenhower, is incapable of confronting his own mortality and appointing a successor. Ask anyone what will happen after Fidel and they just shrug: who knows? The levers of power are kept rigorously in his old but firm grip – anyone in the government who looks even remotely like a contender finds they've been promoted and re-educated in revolutionary lavatory-swabbing.

Havana feels like the town where time stood still. There is an uncanny sense of stasis, as if 1960 had stopped mid-stride, the left foot planted, the right caught in mid-air. The past 40 years in real terms – in human, everyday, quality-of-life terms – have achieved precisely nothing, less than nothing. Cuba just beats time. It nearly wasn't like this. It could have been so different. If Cuba had even been on how-do-you-do terms with its big neighbour, it could so easily have become the Caribbean Switzerland: nonaligned, independent, fat, with sun, salsa and sex instead of snow, yodelling and surface wiping.

Beating time is something Cubans have become very adept at. Music is everywhere. In the hundreds of Hemingway-fell-over-here bars of Old Havana, music syncopates and shimmies across the brindled, crumbly streets, all of it live; it's cheaper to hire the band than buy the CD. Troops of roving musicians stalk public spaces; you're continually mugged and maraca'd by gangs of smiley Desi Arnazes chuntering out "Guantanamera", the original 1960s "Birdie Song", and, of course, salsa.

Cubans have salsa instead of lunch. Salsa is country and western music for happy people. They dance continuously. Even when they're not dancing, you know they're dancing inside. There is a sort of pan-national, hip-grinding, buttock-gyrating infection – people dance in queues, they dance pushing wheelbarrows, they dance behind desks. If dancing is a vertical expression of a horizontal desire, then Cuban salsa is sex in Braille.

These are the most libidinously choreographed people in the world. Above and beyond the beauty of this city, its people are beautiful. Beautiful and nubile and erotically confident and deeply cool. Here is proof that God gives with one hand and takes with the other. The lines of wobbly, pale, plump, clumsy tourists in the ghastly leisure-wear of sloth look like another species, doughy human mistakes compared with the curvy, coffee-coloured, ice-eyed grace of the Cubans. God's joke is that the poor got all the things that the rich so desperately want to buy, and without labouring the point, the Cubans have all the stuff you want in spades. The mixture of Spanish and African blood has produced something close to a middle-aged German's fantasy of perfection. With no money and hand-me-down charity, Cubans still manage to look 100 times more chic and svelte than the rest of us. The look this year, I am happy to say, is Lycra, and Lycra was invented with Cuban bottoms in mind.

The sex, of course, is why most of the tourists come to Havana. Have no doubts about this. They're not here to show solidarity with 40 years of continuous revolution, or to study architecture, and they certainly aren't here for the food. Cuba has a glut of just two things: musical instruments made out of coconuts, and erections. The Teutonic traffic wardens and Nordic civil servants on have-it-away-day hols dribble and ogle like middle-aged Willy Wonkas at a chocolate factory clearance sale. Cuban girls are the Ferraris of prostitution, top-of-the-line Formula One hookers and, boy, are they enthusiastic. But, and this is a big but, a Cuban teenager on the arm of a paunchy, balding pink-eyed Kraut in his holiday socks and sandals says much the same thing about him as his owning a Ferrari would.

In 1492 Havana was invented by Christopher Columbus. Cuba, the island he discovered, was the New World, American before America. The city is built on a natural harbour with commanding forts. Now, it festers in a post-imperial splendour (Spanish colonial is the most elegant of all exported western colonial styles of architecture). The poverty and patina of huggermugger neglect suits Old Havana, the baking balconies decked with pale bleached laundry, the psoriasis stucco and exotic weeds growing out of verandas. There are cool dark patios glimpsed through heavy sun-bleached doors, and a particular washed-out shade called Havana blue.

The grandest dome in the city covers the Museum of the Revolution, full of the cheap tat of desperation and anger, moth-eaten berets and rusty revolvers, and the suit worn by Cuba's only cosmonaut. Weirdly, it appears to be made of denim – perhaps the Russians made him take out the rubbish. On the lawn outside is an installation of decrepit bits of revolutionary kit, skips and bulldozers turned into tanks, a blitzkrieg baker's van and a cabin cruiser incongruously kept in a glass box. This is the *Granma*, the boat that brought Castro to Cuba from Mexico. He is inordinately sentimental about it, naming the only daily paper after it, and presumably it is kept in a box to stop someone nicking it and making for Florida. Everything else that floats has gone west.

There is also a motor museum – old American cars are a feature of Havana, the tourists love them; Cubans would rather have something with air con and windows that work. Americans like to point out that the fact they're still running is a triumph of Yankee engineering, which begs the question, well, why can't they keep a car on the road in Detroit for more than three years? Rather, these Studebakers, Pontiacs, Chevvies and Thunderbirds are a testament to Cuban ingenuity, make-do and tolerance for inanimate objects.

My favourite car in Havana wasn't a western classic: it was the boxy little 1970s Lada that the Russians exchanged for sugar in the 1980s. The Cuban cabbies stretched them – a stretch Lada, that's class. Despite everything, Havana has bundles of class. The traffic cops outside the National Hotel, for instance, posed all day beside the gleaming Motoguzzi that presumably had an empty tank because it never moved. They'd walk up to change shifts looking the business in Ray-Bans, stretched skintight trousers, gleaming helmets and high boots. I was particularly taken by the spurs.

There is a 17th-century square, shady with old trees, that is a market for second-hand books. As I wandered around the exhausting hagiographies of Che and medical-student manuals, a salesman asked if I was looking for anything in particular. "English, ah." He produced two books: *Examining Urine*, and *History will Absolve Me*, Fidel's most famous speech, made to a court before it locked him up for an abortive little attack on a barracks. It is his political defence and his agenda for the next 40 years, and quite succinct by Castro's standards, at only 78 pages long. Taking the piss or a Fidel rant – tough choice.

Cuba's revolution wasn't meant to be communist, at least not communist in the Russian sense. Its guiding light was neither Marx nor Engels but a 19th-century journalist called José Martí, a political, modernist poet who invaded Cuba after almost a lifetime of exile and got shot a month later in one of the final sad, bitter uprisings against the ruling Spaniards. Martí preached a sort of arcadian equality. He also wrote the words for "Guantanamera", so he has more to answer for than your average social-engineering theorist. Cuba ended up as an outpost of the Warsaw Pact not because it wanted to, but because it didn't want to be American. The United States always saw this largest of Caribbean islands as part of its rightful sphere of influence. Not only was Cuba extremely profitable, producing at one time a third of the world's sugar but, straddling the Gulf of Mexico, it strategically commands the southern ports of the US and the mouth of the Mississippi. It tried simply to buy Cuba from Spain, lock, stock and indentured labour, the way it had bought Louisiana from the French, but when that failed, the US settled back into the ripe apple theory of colonialism: it would wait until the Spanish empire collapsed with exhaustion and incompetence, and Cuba would fall naturally into US hands.

But in 1898 the US lost patience, invaded and occupied Havana, leaving only after having rewritten the constitution for its own benefit and taking a military base that still exists. One of the most grotesquely grandiose war memorials in Havana was erected by Americans to commemorate Americans who, in a typically American cock-up, had blown themselves up. For the next 60 years Cuba's economy was owned and run almost entirely by the worst sort of American agri-business, and the mafia. The 30-odd years of economic blockade since has been an act of pointless vindictive bullying, the ugly spite of a powerful country that feels cheated because it hasn't got what it wants.

The blockade, more than anything else, has formed Cuba. For the ten years since the collapse of the Soviet bloc it has served no conceivable geopolitical purpose: it is simply there because it has always been there, and to back down would be to admit that it had failed, and the US, as ever, would rather be unjust than unmanned. In the face of all international law, the Helms Burton

Act pushed for a mandatory international embargo against Cuba. Recently, $6.7m in legitimate telephone payments owed to Cuba by US companies was sequestered by a Florida judge, in part-payment of compensation awarded to the families of four people shot down by Cuban MiGs in 1996. The island has been forced to cut off its phone lines to the US as a result, sending itself even further to Coventry.

The blockade effectively includes large-scale humanitarian and medical equipment so although Cuba has one of the most impressive and successful research complexes outside the West, and has found the only cure for meningitis in the world, and has an internationally renowned centre for neurological surgery, and an infant mortality rate that is lower than in the US, it does so with virtually no American drugs, equipment or a market outlet to sell its own medicine. So while presidents wink and tap their noses at the embargo on imported cigars, the workers who grew and rolled them are kept in a dreary poverty. And if that sounds like the politics of the playground, it's made all the more infantile because in many ways Cuba has plenty of things that America would dearly love and needs.

In a generation it has become a truly racially harmonious place, wiping away centuries of colour bar. It is virtually drug-free, the crime rate would be envied by a Midwestern suburb, families are important, close-knit and respected, religion is becoming more tolerated and widely practised and everybody eats, although they don't eat well and they don't eat much. The ration is pitiful: a bag of rice a month, a handful of beans, two small pieces of pork or fish and all the sugar you can manage. But the poorest here aren't as poor as the poorest across the water, and they're proud of that.

The blockade has managed, in a predictably contrary US way, to produce exactly the opposite of its desired effect. In sealing Cuba from change, it has made impossible any sort of organic liberalisation or transition. Now cut off from the support of Russia, Cuba is a nation in limbo, it can't move forward and it can't go back, it just sits in the sun, slowly falling to bits. The one incontrovertible effect of the US animus has been to keep Castro in power and Cuba locked into a defunct, meaningless, one-sided confrontation.

The Bay of Pigs is about two hours from Havana. Roads in Cuba are surprisingly good, because they don't get used very much. If you want to get about, you stand at an intersection and wait for a lift from a lorry or an asthmatic Chevrolet. Hitchhiking is the official Cuban integrated transport system and neatly encapsulates everything you need to know about Third World communism. The country is mostly flat and quietly beautiful, spiked with royal palms. The sun bleaches the red earth to a pastel dun. It looks all sweetness and light, and that pretty much is what Cuba is. Great swathes of hot sugar cane, stretching away as far as the eye can see. Sugar was always the point of Cuba.

The New World gave Europe something like 30% more new things to chew on, but it was an imported crop that made it worthwhile – sugar brought by the Arabs from India to Spain and then by the Spanish to the new Indies. The world sugar price has always been volatile, boom or bust. To create a market, they invented rum, and sold it to sailors and navvies. Just as an indication of what a serious growth business sugar was in the 19th century, Cuba imported 600,000 slaves between 1800 and 1865. Their descendants still work in ragged lines, hacking their way across the landscape.

You should put cane-cutting right at the top of your list of the worst jobs in the world. They start just after dawn, using a machete that looks like a large Chinese cleaver. There is nothing rhythmic about cane-cutting: it's speed tree-felling. It's clearing a path through dense jungle. They don't sing sad spiritual songs. They don't talk. They just chop and trim and stack at a remarkably unnerving pace until dusk. Two harvests a year. Endless back-breaking piece-rate work. The infant mortality rate may be something to boast of, but death still comes early for Cuban rural workers. Like everything in Cuba, cane-cutting is done by hand. Beside the sugar, oxen tug and buck ploughs over stony earth, men ride high-stepping horses with long stirrups and straw cowboy hats pulled down over their eyes, looking like extras from Hollywood. There are no Russian tractors or pick-ups here to spoil a picturesque scene that has remained unchanged for 150 years.

We stop and watch and listen to the silence and the clopping swish of the machetes and the sighs of the oxen, and suck a cool stalk of sugar and ponder that life-shortening, unremitting poverty and hardship so often have the sharp corollary of a fiercely magnificent aesthetic. Just as long as you're not expected to join in.

On the approach to the Bay of Pigs on the southwest coast, the road becomes dotted with stone slabs, the graves of militia men who defended the way to the heart of their new republic from the CIA-backed invasion by Batista refugees. Incongruously, the bay itself is now a utilitarian holiday resort that looks like a white-washed, breeze-block RAF station. On the ruggedly ugly beach, ruggedly ugly, red, bare-breasted women from the old East German metal-bashing factories do aerobics classes to tinny Tannoyed pop music, avoiding the empty concrete machine-gun bunkers. It's a surreal vision. The resort's logo is a machine pistol. And there is the inevitable small, unvisited museum, with its obsolete heavy American machine guns and twisted bits of aeroplane. Smudged, cracking photographs of dead martyrs hang above their personal effects, a plastic comb, a cheap fountain pen, a dusty packet of cigarettes, a home-made belt, a mother-sewn badge, "Liberty or Death". It is deeply touching and pathetic. The price of admission is $2.

The average Cuban wage is between 200 and 300 pesos a month (between about £5.50 and £8). Wages are pretty even, this being a communist country. A cabinet minister earns perhaps 400 pesos. The accepted unofficial exchange rate is 20 pesos to $1, but the exchange only works one way. Nobody is foolish enough to buy pesos, not even the banks. A peso is actually worthless. You can't buy anything with it except a banana. The currency might as well be bananas. If a Cuban wants a pair of shoes or an ice cream, then the price is dollars. Get into a cab, and the meter is in dollars. Restaurants and shops only quote in dollars. Small boys only beg for dollars. Officially, Cubans aren't allowed dollars, but the country is desperate for them. The peso economy is bought and paid for like an aged relative, 100% by dollars. Trying to gain some control on all this to save some face, Castro invented another peso, a super-improved peso, the tourist peso, that has parity. In practice, it's dollar lite. As far as I can see, it is minted entirely in nickels and dimes to be given as change. Convertible currency comes from the depressed sugar market, Cuba's mono-crop.

And, of course, cigars. It is another irony that the most clichéd symbol of paternalistic capitalism should be made in communist factories. They look exactly like a 19th-century set for *Carmen*. The workers sit at desks in long, Dickensian school rooms listening to novels read aloud from a dais. The women really do spread the leaves over their thighs, and smoke huge hand-rolled *splendidos* knowingly, and wink at you. A skilled roller makes 50 cents a day for perfectly hand-making 200 of the finest cigars in the world that would cost you $17 each in the official shop. A lot make their way onto the black market, as do even more made out of dried banana. Even though Cuba is replete with cigars, as if to prove everything you ever heard about communism, it's virtually impossible to find a cigar cutter.

To attract dollars to this parched economy, Castro is forced to open the country to tourism. He would prefer the organised visitation of international conferences. In a very 1960s put-the-world-to-rights way, Cuba is still big on conferences, and Castro is not averse to a keynote speech himself, regularly coming out to get-togethers of anaesthetists to show them how the job should be done. Most of the conferences are medical, and you could, if the mood took you, come to attend an international get-together or laboratory animal anaesthetists or laser urologists later this month. But it's commercial tourism, sex tourism, that brings in the big bucks. The largest single group of people to visit Cuba are – and you couldn't make this up – Canadians. Presumably because it's one of the few things they can do that's one up on their North American neighbours. Cuba and Canada are the diametrically opposing poles of possible human variation, and unaccountably they love each other, staring across the immense social, cultural, emotional and physical divide with a mutually amused awe.

Making a virtue of necessity, with its woefully basic infrastructure, there have been allowances for tiny outbreaks of private enterprise like the very successful *paladars*, or family-owned restaurants. This usually means eating like a character from a Hispanic Pinter play in someone's kitchen. The food is supposed to be better than the official stuff. It's still utterly appalling.

Cubans can't cook, because there isn't anything to practise cooking on. These little businesses are viciously taxed and continually slapped with punitive, arbitrary regulations. They're not allowed more than 12 seats and they're not allowed to serve lobster, which is the only luxury ingredient Cubans have. Cubans are allowed to catch lobsters, but by law they're not allowed to eat them. They must be sold for dollars to tourists. Having never tasted one, they cook them until they resemble fishy Nike inner soles. It's as if Castro, taking a leaf from America's book, wants these small businesses to fail to spite his craggy face. He'd rather be proved right.

Dictators invariably spend the first half of their lives moving and shaking, and the second defending their reputations against the vibrations of current affairs for some brazen posterity – "history will absolve me". Castro is the exception to the rule that no man is an island. He *is* Cuba. And he's not going to stop being Cuba until they carry him off in a cigar box.

The first officially sanctioned small cracks in revolutionary socialism, the accommodations made for western tourism, point up a truth: capitalism can handle a degree of socially conscious engineering; indeed, it sticks in the throat without it. But communism is wrecked by even the smallest scrape with the free market. Cuba's fragile fabric, based on equitable hardship and a commonly shared isolation, is being ripped apart by dollars. There is a semi-legal, grey middle class emerging – Cubans who have access to tourists: hotel workers, drivers, guides, pimps, prostitutes – and a growing disparity between the rural and urban communities. Although there are no official crime figures, anecdotal evidence suggests that crime is beginning to rise: lost, gauche, innocent Canadians wandering around in the middle of the night, half-drunk from Hemingway karaokes and with two or three years' wages in their pockets, are a temptation. The frustrations of 40 years of hardship are simmering beneath the smiles and gyrating hips. A pretty girl earns more in one night than a consultant surgeon makes in a month. So periodically the police crack down on bars and nightclubs. But the truth is that Cuba needs the vice to pay for its virtue.

In a late-night club in Havana's suburbs, a salsa group frantically rattles out the atmosphere to a half-empty room. At dark tables, couples drink Cuba Libres – the ironic name given to a socialist rum drowned in Yankee Coca-Cola. The price of entry is $10, an impossible amount for a Cuban. The only locals here have been brought by foreigners, and foreigners would only bring a local for one reason. The prostitutes hang around the neon-lit entrance pouting and hissing in their tiny stretch miniskirts and platform heels. Inside they squirm and cling to their meal tickets. Helmut and Günther are drunk, trying to strike a pose of worldly insouciance. They catch each other's eyes and smile, frightened by their good fortune. For a mere $40 they get to use these two impossibly stunning women, who will be the most perfectly beautiful creatures that ever agree to have sex with them. Having exhausted their meagre shared vocabulary, the girls lick hairy ears and stroke clammy thighs, twitching desperately to escape into the music and dance. Finally pulling the two men to their feet, the girls undulate and slide round them, the men jig spastically, faces slack, impassive, trying not to see themselves looking this foolish. The girls are transported. They swim through the music like dolphins. The men flail and drown. Finally, unable to stop themselves, the girls turn to each other and dance with a fabulous synchronicity. In the strobing lights two men risibly, solitarily, jerk.

We take a young chancer, a ducker, a diver, to dinner, to a smart restaurant where "Guantanamera" stalks every table. We found him in the hotel making a dangerous meagre living, selling bootleg salsa tapes to tourists. He orders an incinerated steak and eats tiny slivers with a deep reverence. He doesn't like salsa. He likes American music. He listened to it on the radio until the radio broke. He loves American things. His running shoes, his T-shirt. His best friend escaped to Miami. Everybody in Havana has friends or family in Florida. They talk about them as if they were dead and Florida were heaven.

In Miami, pizza-delivery boys and valet parkers send easy-street dollars back with stories of the opportunities in that great Mall of the Free. "I should have gone," says Raul. "My friend begged me. He built a raft. When everyone was going, when it was allowed." But Raul didn't go. There was this Canadian girl. "I was going legally, man. I was going to get married. Do you know Toronto?"

You wouldn't like it. He speaks good English, with heavy, inappropriate use of disc jockey slang. He stares at his plate. It was just a holiday fling. But, hey, he brightens. "I know all the states in America. I'm not dissing you, man. And their capitals. I study. New York, Albany, California, Sacramento, Kentucky, Frankfurt."

It's a sad, semi-mythological litany, a prayer of impossibly imagined places. It might as well be constellations and planets. Of all the hardships and restrictions that institutional communism expects of its subjects, the most grating, the most frustrating, is the inability to travel, particularly for the young. Almost anything is bearable if there is the faintest hope of escape, of getting away. The possibility of making plans, of a new, better horizon next year, the year after. And Cuba is a young place, bursting, throbbing, humming with youth. They're missing out on everything. Money, clothes, fun, their lives. And they know it. They don't remember what it was like before Fidel. Will they absolve him, venerate him for giving them dignity and equality, instead of Armani and passports? Probably not. They won't thank him for the hot claustrophobia of being stranded on this island, living in the ashes of a picturesque cul-de-sac decade that the rest of the world left behind a generation ago.

Every evening, young lovers meet on the Malecón, a long promenade that curves round the bay. They lie on the sea wall with bottles of rum and snog ravenously. Sex is Cuba's Prozac. As the sun sets, they stare out across the Atlantic, just over the horizon. Temptingly just over the curve of the earth, 90 miles away, is Florida, and the party that the rest of the world is invited to, but not them. To Cubans, this ocean stretches on, measured not in distance but in time; featureless and flat, and endless, for ever. As it was for Columbus 500 years ago.

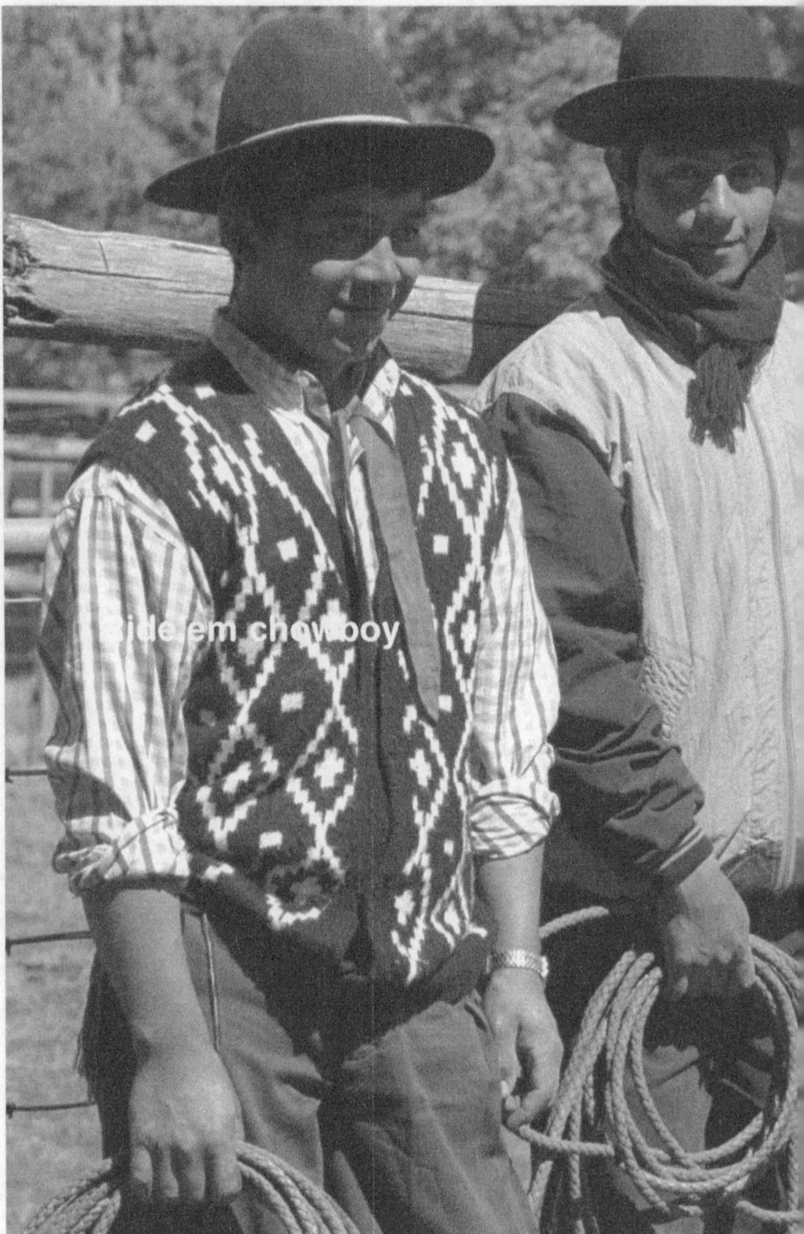
ide em chowboy

Ride 'em chowboy

Argentina, January 2001

A publisher once told me that the best way to absolutely guarantee never to sell a book was to write one about South America. "It's amazing," he said, "it's the great remaindered continent." And you sort of know what he means. In terms of travel and curiosity, our imaginations are still hooked on holidays in history. We tend to revisit the bits of the globe that were once pink and where the natives have second-language English we can patronise and giggle at.

I have a mental picture of South America, but no idea which bits fit into which country. Then, in passing, a psychiatrist mentioned to me that Argentina has more citizens in full-time Freudian analysis than any other on earth, and that did it. Buenos Aires, here I come. When I got there I thought there must have been some mistake, that the plane had been diverted while I slept. BA is utterly familiar: the restaurants, the traffic, the shops, the sounds and smells; it's a European city, and the people hustling off to make their appointments with their shrinks are all European. This, it turns out, is Argentina's little problem. There are Italians who speak Spanish and want to look English. And they can't understand why they're stuck here on the edge of the River Plate. Argentina is a country of postponed promises, it was going to be the great powerhouse of Latin America. It had it all – the brains, the culture, the sophistication, *Come Dancing* – but it never happened. The great expectation collapsed into political sleaze, hyperinflation and an Andrew Lloyd Webber musical.

It's that disappointment, the unfairness of it, that sends them to the couch. To begin with, I minded that Buenos Aires was so European, perversely in a way that I don't mind with New York. You don't go to New York and ask: "Where are all the Mohicans?" But after a bit I just fell into it, fell for it. It's a modernist city that's all of a piece, in a butch, macho, histrionic sort of way, and it has the most wonderful trees. I wouldn't normally mention trees in the city, but BA's are spectacular. Jacarandas, eucalyptus, rubber trees, long, shady avenues in gardens, and it's very Anglophile, which is always a relief.

We have more in common with the Argentina that I knew. We built their railway, tried to invade two or three times in a half-hearted, flirty sort of way, and where would English food be without Fray Bentos (a real place)? Then there's polo. Wherever there are horses, the English will slavishly follow with a broom. Many English have settled here and they all have one thing in common: they're all women. Can there be a horsey girl from Fulham to Cirencester who hasn't shagged an Argy polo player? If there is, could you pass on her phone number to them – they'd be happy to accommodate, mostly because Argentine girls don't. Ever. Certainly not until they're married. This is still a Latin Catholic country, with 19th-century colonial morals and snobbery. The girls are beautiful and bewitching, and they maybe know ways of not having sex that even the Vatican hasn't considered. One of them is the tango. On every street corner and bar there are people being *in flagrante* tangoed. It's a syncopated mime of what you're not gonna get later, sonny.

We left BA for Patagonia, but only just. I'd been warned about South American airlines – never travel with a football team, they said – but this is the first time I've got on a plane where neither the check-in girl, the stewardess nor the captain knew the destination. "Is this where we're going?" I asked, pointing to the name on my ticket. "Who knows?" lisped the hostess with a wiggle, then added: "We'll see." Not going all the way is obviously a female obsession in Argentina, and, as it happened, we didn't. The captain came in to land, but at the last minute decided against it. So we were dropped off somewhere else all together, which in England isn't so bad – being diverted to Stansted is a bore, not a tragedy. Argentina, though, is the size of Jeffrey Archer's self-delusion, and it matters a lot.

We continued in a taxi for a month, through a snowstorm. The snow was a worry, it was meant to be tropically spring-like, not awayday Reykjavik. Finally we arrived at an estancia that was going to be our holiday home, having travelled through a landscape that might have been nice if it hadn't been seen through God's net curtains. The next day I woke with a grim British determination to make the best of things, muttering boy-scoutishly words like "bracing" and "adventure" and "should have packed my thermals". I opened the door, took a deep breath and felt a severe pain in my jaw as it fell to the floor. The sun was out, it was crisp and clear, and there was Patagonia, right there, there and way over there. Patagonia is unfeasibly beautiful and vast. The beauty never lets up, it's like ocular tinnitus, a repetitive deafening of the eye, a visual peal of bells that rings from dawn to dusk. We all have a personal template for nature's wonder, some scale to hold up against a new landscape. Mine is Scotland. Patagonia is Scotland squared, with sagebrush instead of heather. It has all those sense-tingling ingredients that push my personal buttons. It's leggy and fit, a sinuous place with great curves, it's competent and emphatic and it's got a temper, it swears, and, most of all, it doesn't give a damn. It's not one of those landscapes that are arch and secretive, it isn't gentle or flirtatious. It doesn't wear make-up and it's not promiscuous. It's not for everyone.

The best way, indeed, the only way to see Patagonia is from a horse. Which is why we're staying on a working ranch, with a few thousand head of Hereford that need seeing to. Now, I have a problem with horses, I don't like them. Not just that, I actively loathe them unless they come with potatoes. I don't do equestrian. I've ridden twice in my life, once on a malevolent, child-abusing pony, and once to do a story on fox-hunting. It's been enough. So after breakfast (very good bacon and eggs), the English woman who runs the estancia, who has a character and demeanour that has been hewn by the landscape, threw a pair of chaps and a poncho at me and introduced me to a horse whose name I can't recall. I can never remember animals' names, but then they never seem able to remember mine, and I leapt into the saddle just like that. Well, not so much leapt and not so much a saddle. More like a four-year-old trying to get into the top bunk onto a sheepskin. Within half an hour the damnedest thing happened: I was having the time of my life. And I realised that it wasn't horses I hated, it was English horses. These Patagonian jobs are neat, elegant and as sure-footed as cat burglars, and they're automatic. You drive with split reins in one hand, held loose, left to go left, right to go right, tug to stop. This is how riding is meant to be. Not that manual shift, hands-knees-and-bumpsadaisy business they tell you to do in Gloucestershire. Best of all, these beasts don't trot, which is great because neither do I. They go from ambling to 40 in five seconds flat.

Herding cattle is surprisingly good fun, a bit like being a mounted policeman at a Chelsea match – you get to shout "yee-haw" and "yippee kayo" and "horseradish". There is the pain, of course, which is just the other side of extreme. After two days the only place I felt comfortable was in the saddle, which suited me fine, as I didn't want to get off. Apart from herding, corralling, separating, branding and roping, I won a calf first go and the rawhide lasso nearly ripped my hands off. There are other things to do on a horse. You can ride up vertical shale mountains to see condors, which are very big vultures that hang in winds you can lean against, and you can visit Indian burial caves with abstract wall paintings.

This sort of hacking beats mooching around B-roads in Surrey into a ten-gallon hat. When the dog goes off foraging it doesn't come back with a mixy rabbit, but an infuriated armadillo. There are eagles and bright, burrowing parrots, deer and extremely badly designed ginger llama things. From the tops of bluffs, the big sky races, tracing shadow patterns over the country over a panorama of winding rivers, mice, gullies and sloping grassland, all framed by the distant, shimmering white, vertiginous Andes.

Patagonia was a late developer. It wasn't really colonised until the late 19th century; the final, sad Indian war was in 1903. Now it's what the North American West must have been like in the 1920s, it's John Wayne country, thankfully without John Wayne. What they have here instead are gauchos, the last real cowboys. Extraordinary horsemen and even more extraordinary vain show-offs. Their kit is incredible, and I got so deep into the dressing-up box that an Outward Bound group of English holiday-makers thought I was a hired hand, which is the first time I've been mistaken for a small brown Inca on a horse.

Sadly, too soon it was time to fade into the sunset. I badly wanted to go on to see the monkey-puzzle forests at the foot of the Andes, to drive the cattle to high summer pasture. But it was time to kill something.

If you're used to shooting in England, then dove-shooting in northern Argentina seems indecently sybaritic and comfortable. For a start, it's bright and hot, you stand under shade trees with a boy who loads and fetches an endless supply of cold drinks. But what separates it from England most is the number of birds. This isn't your 200 birds a day or even your 2,000 birds a day; this is a never-ending stream of a million birds a day, and it either improves your shooting no end or makes you want to take up stamp collecting. Ubiquity doesn't necessarily lead to competence. These doves are as tricky as anything I've ever fired at, about the size of jays and as fast as partridge, as acrobatic as woodcock and as canny as their pigeon cousins. And they come not so much in coveys as flurries. At the end of three days (as long as the average human shoulder can stand; the estancia had a fabulous masseur) my average after firing a jaw-thumping thousand cartridges a day was 25%. Better than the RAF, but still pathetic.

The country is different from Patagonia, lush and flat, a mixture of water meadow and marsh, with occasional weird ombo trees. In the hot afternoon we took a sackful of doves and motored on a flat-bottomed boat across the maze of vegetable rivers, sticking a breast on a hook and flinging it into the water. We idiot-fished, getting a satisfying bite every ten minutes and hauling in piranhas the size of dustbin lids, then getting all girlie about retrieving the tackle from their psychopathic mouths. They never told me fishing could be like this, and I never imagined Argentina could be like this, which just goes to show you should always pack as few preconceptions as possible. And only once did anyone mention the Falklands, without rancour or looking for a rematch. "A silly war," a man said. Yes, a silly war. We were joined for a moment, *mano a mano*, both coming from continents that had suffered an embarrassment of silly wars. "Of course, afterwards we got rid of the military and Galtieri, became democratic and pegged inflation, it's been boom ever since," he added. Ah well, we got a billion-pound airport in Port Stanley and Margaret

Thatcher for another ten years. There was a moment's silence, then we both laughed. If the subject ever comes up again, I'm on their side.

NORTH

NORTH

Writing travel pieces from your own back yard is difficult. For a start it's a masquerade. You can't look through fresh eyes and nothing much comes as a surprise. I display far more prejudice and a far shorter temper towards the folk over the garden wall than the ones I encounter over the ocean. On the other hand, large expanses of England may as well be overseas: I have travelled very little at home. My generation was the first to be able to fly cheaply and easily – so we always went abroad. I've always been interested in the country, as in countryside, and its relationship with the urban. I'm such a complete city boy. Always lived around traffic lights and been able to walk to the cinema. The benefits of cities seem to so greatly outweigh the grotty, unmade nature of the country, that it never ceases to amaze me why humans want to stay there overnight. The only thing the country has over the city is that once in a summer while it's nice to go and look at it. But if you lived there, you wouldn't even do that.

Some years ago I thought that the conflicting interests of town and mud would be the great political issue of the 21st century and I wrote a novel about it. Now I smugly bore on with "I told you so's". The upside of writing about home is that it's a place that exists as much in our imaginations and characters as it does on the map. And that's really what I try to explore. I went to the Royal Agricultural Show because I wanted to find out how this mythic country rubbed up against the reality. Without much hope of success, I asked if I could have Don McCullin as the photographer. I knew that he was pretty reclusive and nowadays worked mostly on his own, but he'd always been such a hero. When I was a student his images of the wars in Biafra, Vietnam and Lebanon had decorated my bedsit. Amazingly, he agreed and we spent a terribly funny weekend at a surreal County Fair. His pictures were exactly what I wanted to say – just put better and more succinctly. The piece appears here with one of the best of Don's images.

One of the things I like about journalism is the way the writer is just the pointy end of a team. There's a familiar sense of belonging, knowing that the rest of the paper is behind you, that you're part of something big, loud and confident. And they don't come any bigger, louder or more confident than Jeremy Clarkson. We started writing in partnership by chance. I mentioned that I was planning to do a piece on Cheshire and he exploded, "You bastard – I want to do Cheshire. You won't understand it. It's all about cars. You won't get the point." So I said, "Fine – why don't you come and we'll do it together." The piece was a huge success. A lot of people read it. So we went on. And as Cheshire had been my choice, the next one – Iceland – was his. Then we did all the brown signs on the M1. I hope we can go on. These articles are without doubt the most fun I've ever had as a journalist. Though we laugh at the same things, we get serious about utterly different stuff. I think he has all the political and social sensibilities of a radish: hot, one note and windy. He thinks I'm a whingeing, soft, effete southern pouf. We tease each other viciously. He's also cleverer than he'd ever like you to know. Not just a self-evidently brilliant writer, but properly, intuitively, well-informed smart. But he argues like a duck in gumboots.

When we write together we roughly divide the story but never see each other's copy and in that vein, I'm not including his half of the articles in this collection. He's good, but not that good. After Iceland, Julie Burchill wrote a beautifully vicious piece in the *Evening Standard* about us. She called us "The Past It Boys". As ever, Julie was absolutely right, that's exactly what we are. The past it boys.

The thin line

Milan Fashion Week, October 1995

The Galleria Vittorio Emanuele is a shopping arcade. At one end is La Scala and at the other the Milan Duomo, the second largest church in Christendom. The galleria is no ordinary mall. It is to Burlington Arcade in London what Gianni Versace is to Jeff Banks. This is the biggest, most histrionic promenade in Italy. And this week, Milan Fashion Week, the world has come to see and be seen.

The old men of Milan, too, come here to talk, all year round. They move in little gaggles, very slowly with great gravitas. I sat and watched a group outside Prada, the handbag shop where you can on impulse buy a very thin, very discreet crocodile wallet for the price of an airline ticket to Sydney.

This year, ancient Italian men are wearing generously cut worsted suits, either with waistcoat or cardigan, in natural earth colours with muted checks. Ties are carelessly knotted and discreet, and collar sizes are too big for the neck. Hats are in, shoes are brown and highly polished, and elasticated clip-on braces seem to be making a comeback. The whole look is rather like Quasimodo Medici meets Jimmy Hoffa.

The show eddies and shimmers around these little islands of ruminating retired burghers. A crocodile of tiny matt-black Japanese girls files past, questing labels like polite, smiley soldier ants. German fashion editors in short skirts with bulldozer knees and steel-tipped blitzkrieg pumps hurry to their next show. Impossibly tasteful New York editors carrying vast sea-snake Filofaxes try to look European, their hair as glossy as mink, cut in that dramatically understated I've-no-time-for-all-this, working-girl way that needs only two visits to the hairdresser a week. Navigating down the middle of the walk is a woman who looks like an indecisive Ivana Trump who, because she was unable to make up her mind, decided to wear everything in the steamer trunk. She's sweating and glowing because she's pushing her daughter in a wheelchair. The girl is about 16, pretty and embarrassed. She has been dressed in an expensive silk two-piece suit with gold Chanel earrings, and a quilted bag hangs by a chain from the arm-rest. On her feet are black patent leather court shoes with clean soles. Her atrophied legs are swagged in black silk stockings. The skirt is very short. The elaborate lacy tops show against her white thighs. Her mother's having difficulty getting the chair into Prada. The door is heavy and there are steps. The assistants with the Novocaine expressions watch without helping. Milan Fashion Week isn't designed for the disabled. Not the physically disabled, anyway.

You can't pick up a newspaper these days without thinking that the world has gone mad. Well, nothing will more convince you that the whole of western civilisation is utterly, howlingly, stark-staringly, foamingly doolally than the collection will. If they finished the shows with a grand catwalk parade of Naomi, Kate, Helena and Claudia wearing spangly straitjackets, I wouldn't be in the slightest bit surprised, and neither would the fashion editors. They would just go and blow a week's rent on one and tell you to do the same.

I've never been to a fashion show before, but I've seen so many on television and in magazines that I thought I knew what they were like. No image can prepare you for the truly disturbing 3-D reality. First you get to a doorway in a side street that's blocked with crash barriers and riot police and badly parked winking Mercedes with lounging, winking drivers. There's a huge scrum of fashion victims all shouting and waving their hands, breaking off every so often to kiss each other and make foreplay noises. On the door are squads of camp couture Stasi in suits and hatchet-faced girls with long legs and lists. When you've finally shoved your way in past a dozen impeccably rude bouncers there is a dark room with a raised catwalk, a backdrop and ranks of tiny chairs. At the end of the catwalk there is a bank of photographers packed so tightly that their vast lenses mould into one and look like a single huge composite bluebottle eye. The smudgers and the camera crews argue and snap at each other like starlings on a town hall. A Stasi in a suit unceremoniously evicts the Korean gatecrasher who is in my chair. She looks unconcerned and moves down two seats.

In the gloaming I watch the audience scramble in, middle-aged women with puffy legs wearing tiny dresses, and see-through black silk shirts over cretonne bosoms propped up on bony rolling lacy corsets. Fortysomething ladies with leather skin and leopard-fur hair the texture of guinea pigs' beds stumble over the furniture because they're too vain to take off their dark glasses in a room where you really need a torch. An ancient crone sits beside me. She's got hands like carmine-tipped liver-spotted claws and her lips have so much collagen in them that her mouth won't close properly. If the women are bad, then the men are worse. The woman who is dressed ten years younger than her passport is sad but understandable. A balding American fashion editor with a pigtail, a Johnny Depp beard, a paunchy male version of the Elizabeth Hurley dress, all safety pins down the side, and a cravat is beyond pity. Nobody looks normal, nobody here could walk down the aisle at Sainsbury without accompanying laughter. These are professional fashion watchers, men and women whose whole lives are dedicated to knowing what looks good, what is chic; they spend hours dressing models for photographs and then poring over the transparencies. You wonder what happens to their eyes when they look in the mirror. Fashion professionals don't see things like you or I. The whole room is a zebra pelt of black and white and that colour that has been the fashion staple for so long they've invented a dozen names for it – taupe, camel, fawn, buff. Frankly, it's beige. Suzy Menkes hurries in and takes her seat, front and centre. She is the fashion correspondent for the *International Herald Tribune* and by the lights of the arcane pecking order of this bizarre business is accepted as the queen bee. Her hair looks as though she has forgotten to take out one of the curlers, but it's not funny. It's her personal fashion statement. The show can begin. Music, lights, models.

If the fashion writers look odd, they at least have recognisable human shapes. The models are from another planet. No photograph prepares you for the way they look in the absence of flesh. A photograph adds a stone to everybody's image. These girls are fuse-wire thin and unbelievably tall. Their legs are like grissini, barely capable of taking the weight of their etiolated bodies. They move in an odd, careful, swaying way that is newborn and unco-ordinated, like creatures who would be happier slithering on their tummies and have just been made to walk upright. Their shoulders look like universal spanners, their chests like xylophones, their tendoned necks sway and jerk their bony heads with ears that look like folded bats' wings. They have glazed, sedated eyes, and the ones who don't seem terrified look to me to be psychotic. Nobody normal could aspire to look this way.

The models teeter and sway down the catwalk, pause momen-tarily and grimace at the giant flashing bug eye. It's impossible to say how many girls are in a collection because so many of them look the same. At the Dolce e Gabbana show I thought there were only eight girls. At the end, about 30 came out and clapped and took a bow. One who is instantly recognisable is Nadja Auermann, a terrifying-looking specimen with hair like the chrome bumper on a Chevy and eyes the colour of mineral water. She's not the sort of person you want to meet in a dark alley. All the models have minders who run them from show to show on the back of scooters. Nadja looks as though she probably has a trainer and travels in a circus cage. The minute the show finishes there's a smattering of applause from the planted claque and we all crowd for the door, ten steps behind Menkes whose bobbing quiff hits the street at a sprint.

This scenario is repeated every half-hour from nine in the morning to eight at night for five days. The models do it over and over again always late, always uncomfortable, shouted at, gay-manhandled, bullied and permanently starving. The top two or three might get a couple of thousand a show, but most of these poor creatures count their earnings in hundreds and a few free shirts. I stumbled out of my first collection feeling as if I'd taken part in something degrading. The closest thing I'd ever seen to this was a pub strip show. This is striptease for fetishists who want sexless girls to put clothes on. By the fourth show I was talking hem lengths and pastel shades with the best of them.

At lunch a shrill posse of London fashion editors are talking with blasé excitement over the mozzarella and rocket: "Oh my God, blusher's back." "And more corsets!" "Is smoking in again?"

215

I ask whether they don't think the models look, well, sort of strange. "Oh, yes, Helena's got so fat. Did you see her tummy!" (Helena Christensen is about 5ft 11in. She's reported to be size 6-ish.) Has the fact that so many of the design houses have been accused of fraud and bribery affected the shows? Six pairs of hard chic eyes stare at me uncomprehending. Am I mad? Versace, Armani and the rest are above the law; the law is for people who shop at Next. They could have accused Messrs Dolce and Gabbana of having dead puppies in their fridges, but they'd still have excellent tailoring and do wonderful things with ostrich feathers.

At night, after the shows, there's dinner, and parties for those who've still got the energy. I went to the bash for 30 years of Italian *Vogue* in an architecturally fascist gallery. It was full of black and white and beige people, silly cocktail frocks worn with gumboots. I doubt if there was a room anywhere in the world that night with more titanically lusted-after people in it. It was so, so utterly sexless. Everyone looked as if, given the choice between a demon lover and the perfect handbag, they'd go for the bag. They were so bored, so miserable, so slidey-eyed and self-conscious. It was as if every invitation had come with an RSVP suicide note. This was one of the top ten industries in the world having a good time, letting its lacquered hair down, and I couldn't fathom why it was all so joyless. Fashion is, after all, great fun; shopping is the second of life's great pleasures. How come, here at the centre of it all, they're bonkers and gloomy? We, you and I, wear clothes as outward and visible signs of our internal desires, aspirations and characters. We bring our lives to our wardrobes, but here on the catwalk and in the Stygian auditoria, the clothes are the people. What's outside is also what's inside.

In the arcade, the small, solemn huddles of old men continue their peregrinations. "So, signor. I hear that blusher is back?" "Si, si, and more corsetry." "More corsetry, you say, good, good."

Hunforgiven

Hunforgiven

Germany, July 1999

Time between leaving Berlin's Tegel airport and mentioning the war: eight minutes, ten at the outside. And it wasn't me, I swear, Iron-Cross my heart with oak-leaf cluster. I'd been told in no uncertain terms: "You're not to mention the war, we know what you're like. The war is *verboten*, out of bounds, off limits, bad form, we've moved on from all that." Well, it wasn't me, it was the taxi driver. "Berlin, in area, is the same size as London," he informed me in that emphatic, punctilious way that Germans have with English, as if there were a euphonium playing in their heads. "When it was laid out at the turn of the century we had the fastest birth rate, but then came the war, and the Nazis and, well . . ." Gong! Sorry, you mentioned the war, no prize, Fritz.

The first thing you notice about Berlin is how few people there are compared with other great capitals. It feels like an overlarge patchwork suit worn by a man who has gone on a crash diet. The people rattle around the streets and there is a 1956 amount of traffic. Actually, that's not the first thing you notice. The first thing is the cranes. Berlin's skyline is a forest of cranes, a navvies' rollercoaster theme park of elegantly circling girders. "What you must remember," the driver says, with added oompah, "is that what you're seeing in Berlin is a moment in a process. We are building the future." Or perhaps just burying the past.

The Mercedes slides round a vast column with a gilt-winged victory on the top. "This used to be outside the Reichstag, but Hitler moved it brick by brick," he adds, with barely disguised admiration. It's the Siegessäule, a monument to wars against Austria, Denmark and France. The gilt and marble Teutonic exclamation that marks the beginning of a united Germany. The Prussian Bismarck, with typical German tact, chose Versailles to announce the formation of his new *Uberstaat*, made up of the diverse and disparate German-speaking principalities, dukedoms and self-governing cities, and collaterally instigating the longest-running, most eternally popular hate affair in Europe. For we all hate the Germans – come on, it's all right, admit it, we're all agreed, we hate them. Of course we don't hate them individually, one at a time they're fine, thoughtful, polite, cultured – above all, cultured. But collectively, in columns, we hate them. "Oh, he's a German," is a dismissive remark that speaks reams in every European language. As political correctness irons out the parenthesis of prejudice, there will always be a special, sour dispensation for Bismarck's baby; hating the Hun is perhaps the only thing that truly emulsifies the rest of us. By any measure you care to choose, the creation of a greater Germany has been the greatest disaster, the cause of more misery than any other political act in our continent's history. In fact, in the whole bloody story Germany has only been a united country without foreign occupation for something like 65 splintered grey years. For all its vaunted economic metal-bashing success as a homogeneous nation, Germany has been an unmitigated, ghastly failure.

At the other end of the martial avenue that boasts the priapic column stands the Brandenburg Gate, Berlin's most famous image, and it's rather a disappointment. Smaller than you imagined, and coarser. It's not the Arc de Triomphe, it's not even Marble Arch. Just the last of many city gates of the old Prussian capital that was always famous for being a rather dull, parochial, unimaginative city except for a brief exotic and vicious loucheness in the 1930s. Beside it stands the phoenix of the new Reichstag, the seat of the Bund and, so the persistent whisperers insist, the hub of a new European superstate-in-waiting.

Norman Foster is having a party to hand over his remarkably beautiful re-creation to the city. It's very impressive, with its glass dome and mirrored funnel for extracting all the hot air of German irregular verbs. It will, Norman tells a soberly nodding audience, run on vegetable oil and has already conserved 95% of its energy year on year. Well, that's what we can do with the olive-oil lake, then. Incongruously, Carol Thatcher is here: "I haven't told Mummy, she'd have a fit, unless I brought some matches." Margaret Thatcher was virtually alone in voicing strident reservations about German reunification. She may have been alone in saying it but, as usual, she wasn't alone in thinking it.

It's now ten years since the Berlin Wall came down, and Germany has been swinging cranes and pouring concrete day and night to build something that works this time. The new Reichstag has preserved some of its old scars: the bullet and shrapnel holes, the graffiti. Germans know they are constantly treading on eggshells, tiptoeing over cemeteries, that they're observed from outside with distrust and concern. They are careful to keep their natural arrogance *sotto voce*. But this obvious gesture of humility turns history into an exhibit, pacifies it into culture, which is a trick I'm to discover the Germans do a lot.

Graffiti is something of a tiresome obsession with young Berliners. The border wall was covered in impasto layers of the most hideous daubs. It elevated the artless into important political statements, and a whole school of wall-defacing artists sprang up. The wall may have gone, but the graffiti of incomprehensible pneumonics lingers. Every perpendicular surface in Berlin is smeared with it. It has none of the wit and panache of New York. German, it need hardly be said, is a written language that uniquely fails to lend itself to the precision of hit-and-run spray painting.

The wall itself has essentially vanished. Literally Jerry-built in the first place, the few remaining slabs are being ironically resprayed with signs asking for them to be left standing as memorials. Symbolic irony is also something I found Germany has a surfeit of, mostly entirely uncomprehended by the natives. The stressed concrete of separation has been chopped up into tiny pieces for sale as souvenirs. You can't see the Berlin Wall any more but you can see any amount of Berlin gravel. Presumably this is done by former East Germans who saw the thing as their last natural resource, to be exploited after they all got made redundant when their factories were bought for a song (probably "Tomorrow Belongs to Me") by West German entrepreneurs to be converted into BMW showrooms and lofts.

So, in ten years what has happened to East Berlin – indeed, what has happened to the former German Democratic Republic (GDR)? The answer is that greater Germany has managed to do to it what it so nearly did to Austria, Czechoslovakia and Poland. It has made it disappear. It's impossible now to tell whether you are in East or West Berlin – even the taxi drivers don't always know. You can't tell by looking at the buildings, because hideous communist architecture looks remarkably like hurriedly built, hideous capitalist architecture, and anyway, it's all being pulled down to make way for hideous and precipitously constructed postmodern unity architecture. Whatever you thought of the old GDR – that it was grey and dingy and fearful and cynically created as Russia's gum shield – it was for all that a real country. There was a national anthem, a flag, a parliament, a civil service, an infrastructure, people got born, married and died in it, but now, just a decade on, it has ceased to be; vanished, without a tear or a discernible whimper, beneath the balletic cranes. Only a handful of tarnished Olympic shotputting medals remain to show that East Germany ever existed at all.

What is being put in its place? Well, nothing. Really, Berlin is as close to an awful lot of *Sturm und Drang* signifying absolutely nothing as you'll wish to find. It's a non-place, it has less atmosphere than Uranus. I thought it a lukewarm Knightsbridge, or a watery Hull, or a black-and-white Torremolinos. Apart from the Reichstag, Berlin is a dumping ground for the back-of-envelope doodles of unemployable architects. It's a city that comes up to you and says: "That's enough about me, what would you like me to be?"

Of all the people of Europe, Berliners look the most like us. And yet I think I have more sympathetically in common with Kalahari Bushmen. It's like *Invasion of the Body Snatchers*. They're good, but there's always some tell-tale sign that they're not quite right. There are the clothes, for a start. The men are into this mix'n'match jacket-and-trousers thing, often wearing two or three parts from different suits. You'll look at some chap and think: "Well, I can understand the whistle, and I could just above live with the tie, but where on earth did the socks and sandals come from?" German men must all go into Burberry and say: "*Ja*, this fits perfectly, I'll take it, two sizes bigger." Couples like his-and-her windcheaters, sunglasses and hats. I saw one pair who had matching Versace ties and headscarves. You've got to be pretty jolly Junkers to do that.

There are other little things which tell you that, although they may look like us, they syncopate to a different beat. They can't walk in crowds, for instance, which is surprising because they're so good at marching. Germans are constantly bumping into each other with barely restrained looks of fury; perhaps they're just habituated to invading other people's personal space. But then again they'll stand for lengthy minutes with a bovine serenity at completely empty crossroads waiting for the little green man to tell them to cross. As it happens, the little green man is the only bit of the former GDR that anyone wants to save. He's a perky little cartoon chap, *Apfelmann* (apple man), who has fallen foul of modernity and EC traffic light directives. Nobody seems to have noticed that, with his jaunty hat, crooked arm and pointy feet, he looks disturbingly like an anthropomorphised swastika. I'd be lying if I said there wasn't a touch of *schadenfreude* in seeing quite how clunky modern Germany really is (*so* German to have invented just the right word for this). The design of everything from lighting to street furniture is abysmally transitory, modern gimmicks that look nerdy and tired the moment they're erected. Form follows whim rather than function. If most of what you know of German quality and polish is lardy-voice car commercials, then the truth of the place comes as a pleasant surprise. It doesn't work very well, the service is as stroppy and sloppy as anything you could expect to find in provincial France, there are fewer mobile telephones, computer terminals and annoyingly integrated banking machines than you might expect from Portsmouth.

There are, however, great dolloped turds of dire public art. Berlin is pocked with meaningful erections that make the cranes and concrete mixers look aesthetic. Apart from the Reichstag, the building that Berlin is proudest of is the new Jewish museum. It's on the cover of guidebooks, on posters and postcards, very futuristic, very liberal, very part-of-the-process. This is the new, caring, cutting-edge Germany, a smart, angular bit of kit, all flat metal and futurist slots and holes. There is one problem, though: call me old-fashioned, but it doesn't really work as a building. You get inside, and you're in a murky labyrinth of dead ends and sloping walkways and spaces that might be rooms, but then again might just be spaces. It comes with the sort of wordy, art-autopsy bollocks that Germans respect with a furrowed awe: "Represents the three journeys of European Jewry, based on the 3,000 angles found in the Star of David." That sort of tosh. And there's another thing: you and I might think this is a fundamental kind of thing. It's quite empty. The perfect emperor's new museum: totally, nakedly bare of exhibits. And a persistent voice whispers in my ear as I get lost: "If this is the Jewish museum, then where, pray, are the Jews?"

Apart from the traffic signals, the only other bit of East Germany you can find without a shovel is in the flea market that at weekends runs up from the Brandenburg Gate. Here you can buy the mistakenly confident tat of the Warsaw Pact, boxes full of thin medals in lieu of freedom. You can purchase an East German border guard's underwear or a fireman's gas mask. You can have as many busts of Lenin and posters of nubile gymnasts as you could shake a Stasi at, but nobody's buying much. It all seems a bit tiredly previous. With capitalism you get fashion, and totalitarian chic came and went. An old woman offers me a chain-link evening purse. "Very good value," she oompahs, "very beautiful." And then as the clincher: "Made entirely from human fillings." You don't say. How riveting. I'll think about it.

Beside the market is the Tiergarten, Berlin's park, the biggest inner-city park in Europe, once a Prussian hunting ground, once turned into matchwood by RAF Bomber Command. Here, strangely, is somewhere with some atmosphere. On a bright May bank holiday it's full of families, cycling in strictly descending order like mobile Russian dolls, and picnicking, elaborate picnics with gas barbecues and trestle-tabled buffets. Dogs and children run after balls around the naked men. Oh, didn't I mention the naked men? It is a truth understood across Europe that, given half a chance, a German will whip off his kit, and here they disport, Teutonically akimbo, blond, paunches and willies lolling as the families grill their symbolic bratwurst. In the middle of Berlin, so unlike our own Hyde Park. Germans have a unique and mystical relationship with trees. If you understand their feeling for forests, I'm not sure that you understand them any better, but you come close to understanding how they understand themselves. The forest is the spiritual, mystical heart of Germany, the engine and the ultimate metaphor of their literature, poetry and music. Nature's cathedral is always young and still timelessly ancient. Constant but regenerating, the great German forest is the cradle of German identity. It has hidden and protected and nurtured them and it goes to their very bloody origins.

In AD9 was the Battle of the Teutoburg Forest. The Roman commander Quinctilius Varus led 25,000 legionaries into the heart of Germany and was slaughtered by Arminius's spearmen, who rushed from their holy groves. Six years later, their skulls nailed to trees, their bones piled in torture pits and on votive altars, the Roman Army was discovered by the appropriately named Roman general Germanicus. It was the greatest tragedy ever to befall the Roman Empire and it sent a shudder of horror and shame across the civilised world that has vibrated in our subconscious for a thousand years. The slaughter in the Teutoburg Forest divided Europe into the warm south, who forever saw forests as dreadful places to be avoided and cleared, homes to dragons and trolls, antitheses of the civilised city, and the north, who understood them to be healing, protecting, mystical, spiritual places. How you feel about a silent birch forest at twilight says more about your blood and kin than your passport. The Germans are children of the woods, people of the dappled half-light, the secret glade, the silence and camouflage.

Driving east through the former GDR, you're flanked for mile after mile by forest, breaking occasionally into flat farm land and squat, ghastly, prefab boxed industrial towns, like goitred fungus clinging to the swathe of wood. The autobahn hisses towards the Czech border and we pass streams of lorries that all seem to be carrying either cement or live pigs. For us, Dresden is one thing, it's the away draw for Coventry. Not a lot of people know that it produced the world's first beer mat, the first toothpaste tube, the first mouthwash (Odol, still available), the world's first coffee filter and has the second largest Dixieland festival. And there's more. It has a cherry stone with more faces carved on it than anyone else has ever bothered to manage. On the Elbe, it is also the capital of Saxony, sometime birthplace of the kings of Poland, the cradle of Lutheranism, and was once called the Protestant Vatican. It has

Europe's finest porcelain collection and an art collection that beggars expectation.

It is also, of course, home to the most successful bombing raid in history. But for us to rather parochially compare Dresden with Coventry and think one-all stretches jingoistic relativism to breaking point. Dresden was one of the finest baroque cities the world has ever seen; Coventry made bicycles. Dresden, like Berlin, is a forest of cranes. They're building a bright, glorious future here too. Only here they're constructing a perfect replica of the 18th century, stone by stone, blasted chard by chard, they're putting Humpty Dumpty back together again and it's impressive in a macabre sort of way. The centre of Dresden is a *Nutcracker* fairy-tale setting but it's surrounded by the most grotesque and personally abusive state-ordained city imaginable – public spaces that make you physically recoil, vast, squalid, careless housing projects, factories that offer nothing but soul-destroying state-school-to-state-pension graft. Old/new Dresden sits incongruously unconcerned in the middle, listening to its fountains splash and its multibelled clocks tintinnabulate politely.

But Dresden isn't a reconstruction. It's no Disneyland, not to the Germans. It's a moment in the process. And it is here that I realised possibly the most profound truth about them: their attitude to culture. Germans are very big on culture, big and smug and arrogant. They have *Kultur* with a capital K. Everything from sausages to Schiller fills the Teutonic heart with pride. They have the most profound writers, romantic poets, incisive philosophers and mobile-Christmas-decoration woodcarvers. And above everything, they have music. No other country in the world can hold a tuning fork to German music. A to Z they only have to get to the Bs and Germany has a globe-trouncing team with Wagner still on the subs' bench. But they see culture as divorced from history, parallel but separate. We, on the other hand, understand our culture as being inextricably entwined with events. Indeed for us, culture and history are almost interchangeable words – not for the Germans, and with good reason.

If you were German would you want to look back at history? For them it's a century and a half of undiluted misery, humiliation and grovelling apology. By keeping the culture separate, immaculate, eternal and timeless, the Germans have a sense of national pride and unifying glory. The skein of their art is far older than their country. Dürer had no concept of a united Germany, but none the less he was utterly German. Dresden isn't a retrospective re-creation, because it exists in a separate continuum from the events that formed it. This is a very bizarre, even psychotic way to get on. It means that you live in one place, but exist in another esoteric, imaginary plane, unshackled by fact or memory. It's like admiring the china, but ignoring what's on your plate. There should be a large metalwork sign erected over the Brandenburg Gate: Amnesia *macht frei*.

In the basement of the grand, reconstructed hotel is a restaurant that features authentic old-time German food. It's a theme restaurant for authentic old-time Germans, where they can eat dumplings and sauerkraut at long trestle tables, there are birch and oak trees nailed to the wall, the waitresses wear bosomy peasant costumes, and a bloke dressed in lederhosen strums a guitar and sings old folk songs. The diners sing along with gusto. This isn't for tourists. If I had to choose the best thing about Germany, it's that there aren't any tourists. These are Germans coming together for some bogus, bucolic heritage, oblivious to how absurdly ridiculous they look or indeed how vile their food and singing is. They also appear oblivious to the fact that on February 13, 1945, Dresden was bombed, causing a firestorm that sucked cyclones of boiling air out of cellars like this – no, this exact cellar – suffocating an entire city. Thirty-five thousand souls vacuumed into the roaring Baroque flames. And these old folk who were children then can sit here scoffing pig and Pilsner and sing hodie-ho songs about the woodcutter's daughter.

To be perfectly honest, three months ago I had no idea that Weimar was a town. I thought it must be a district or piece of paper, the Weimar Republic and all that. But then someone at a London dinner party said, you simply must visit Weimar, it's this year's Prague. So I'm back on the autobahn listening to the appalling German pop stations. For people with such a vaunted musical heritage, they play the very worst British and American 1960s and 70s stuff across the dial. As "Mighty Quinn" comes on for the third time, I push the button; I'd rather listen to the squealing pig trucks. We skirt Leipzig and its chemical factory, which produced the phosgen gas for the Great War and the Zyklon B for the second. "You get the war, we've got the gas." Weimar is this year's European capital of culture and, boy, does it have culture. Goethe ran the theatre, Schiller wrote the plays, Tolstoy made pilgrimages, Kafka fell in love here. Any number of composers beginning with B and Wagner composed here, the Bauhaus was started here, the Liszt is endless. Weimar is Stratford squared and looks like Port Isaac made out of gingerbread. It's everyone's idea of a perfect little German market town. There is a square with a maypole and a stall selling roast sausage. It was flattened by the Americans, of course, but they've cloned it. There's even a hurdy-gurdy man. He grinds out "Colonel Bogey" without irony. I don't think any of the milling culture Krauts know the words.

We sit in a café, drinking hot chocolate with an entire cow of cream on top, looking at the town festival guide and wondering why so many Germans carry walking sticks with those little metal place plaques nailed to them. Do they have Rotterdam, Stalingrad and El Alamein? And then I noticed in very small, bracketed, italic letters the 16th recommended thing to do in Weimar: Buchenwald. The name leaps from the page. I hadn't planned to see a concentration camp but in retrospect it was Wagnerianly inevitable that this is where the story would end. I've never been to a concentration camp before. I'm glad I went. I never want to go again.

Two miles out of town, past the ironic rifle clubhouse, on a ridge up the road of blood built by the inmates, is Buchenwald, or what's left of it. Rightly it was flattened. There are no cranes here resurrecting a moment in a process. Now it's no more than a shadow of bricks and concrete and horror. The main gate and the watchtower still stand with their ironwork inscriptions, "Each to his own". There is a monstrous Russian-inspired memorial. Buchenwald means beech wood, and the forest is still here. When they cleared the land for it, they left one large oak standing inside the barbed wire. The locals called it the Goethe oak, Goethe who wrote *Faust*, a man who sells his soul to the devil. I won't describe the sense of the place, not because there aren't words to describe this monstrosity, but because there have been others better qualified to utter them than me, and to add to them is to detract, to bury the sin again in language. Unbelievable, though, there is a restaurant here, set in the woods, rustic and jolly, with a view and a children's plastic slide. I've always thought that professionally I could eat anything anywhere. But I found my limit. I couldn't eat German food in a concentration camp.

After a couple of hours, we returned to Weimar and any residual sense of cosy marzipan charm had vanished. It is a ghost town, a town of unquiet shades. This railway station was a transit stop to the death camps. This city was the base for the first Nazi regional council in Germany, the delightfully named Junior Crossbow Society grew up to be the Hitler Youth. The *gemütlich* hotel I'm staying in was Hitler's favourite; he even helped design it. And some grey committee in Brussels has thought about all this, considered and decided in their infinite wisdom that this place of genocide should be the European cultural capital. God forgive them.

It's not that Weimar has wholly denied Buchenwald, it has just wrapped it in its ethereal, Teutonic, clean-anything, whiter-than-white culture. There is an exhibition of Hitler's kitsch nudi-art collection, and a crapulous, thick-tongued deconstruction of good and evil as if Buchenwald were an artistic problem, like perspective or metre. It was here that I understood quite why we hate the Germans. It's not "don't mention the war" – the war is understandable, explicable, we've all had a war or two. The war is soldiers reminiscing, and combat comics and Jack Hawkins movies. What we don't mention is the Final Solution, the lengths and the breadths and the depths of German genocide. That's unique. Only they in the history of humanity have built Buchenwald, and others like it. The crime stands beyond credulity or forgiveness. But there is also pity. I pity the Germans. The helpful, smiling young waitress, the children on school outings. They weren't born when Buchenwald gave up its ghosts. Why should they bear the weight and the mark?

"It wasn't us, it was our fathers," is what your fathers said of your grandfathers. Germany is the country that invented the idea of predestination, the Lutheran concept of being born into sin, and it is only in Germany that I've ever really understood what that truly means. What can a good German do now in our bright, shiny, millennial togetherness, our community? What can they do to stop us seeing them as Europe's psychopaths? They can run to the future, stride for new dawns. Never live in the past, barely step into the present. They can run but they can't hide, and we can't stop remembering. There is nothing they can do other than live with the stain and the guilt, because so many millions can't.

Of course in the end it will fade, like all pain, become dull in anecdotage, and the German forest will grow over the Final Solution. We walked in silence through the beech woods. The ruins of the SS falconer's cottage and the commandant's schloss were cluttered with vegetation, looking almost picturesque. The evening sunlight dappled through the leaves, casting shards of light onto the bridle paths. It was the saddest place I've ever been. A breeze sighed through the branches and we came to a glade, a secret place of fir and silver birch. It hid a pit, deep and broad. It isn't empty; only the bodies had been disinterred. Their heavy silence still filled it. The grave's edges were softened by spring wild flowers, the earth's cyclical promise. And because the symbolism of this land is as thick as loam, the blood-and-earth metaphor was inescapable. The coloured blossoms were like the rough, triangular patches sewn on striped uniforms. And the greatest number of them were dandelions, long swathes of yellow heads clinging to the rubble, each individual and wonderful, yet all the same. Here and there, they'd already run to seed, the wind caught at them and the delicate spores danced through the wood like puffs of smoke.

Dripping yarns

Iceland, March 2000

Why in all of God's good earth did anyone ever come here in the first place? And having got here, why didn't they take one look and turn the family-people-carrier longship right round and go back? What threat, lie, bribe or bet could conceivably have induced anyone to look at Iceland and suck their teeth and nod their heads and say: "Yes, I reckon with a bit of hard work and some jolly curtains we could make this place home"?

The first people settled here in the time before Gore-Tex, convection heaters, Velcro or Cup-a-Soup. When Europe's population was that of present-day Barnsley, they could have gone anywhere. They were Vikings, for Christ's sake, nobody was going to argue. "A beach-front property on the Côte d'Azur, Olaf? Help yourself."

Coming here was Jeremy's idea, Chipping Norton's Eric Blood-axle: "Iceland is just [pause, drop voice a gear] the best place in the world." So there's him, me and the Monkey driving across the moon in winter, from Keflivic "We never close" airport to the capital, Reykjavik, where half of Iceland's 250,000 souls live – for want of a better word. I wouldn't normally mention the Monkey. Monkeys are a wearisome fact of working abroad, like lost luggage, inexplicable street signs and public holidays. Monkey is a journal-istic term for a photographer (monkeys climb up things, break stuff and you don't want to sit opposite them at feeding time).

We all arranged to meet at Heathrow at 11.30; the Monkey had been here since 5. That's a bit keen, isn't it? "My wife was flying in from Thailand – I haven't seen her for six months." Ah, how romantic. "We're getting divorced." Right. I just had this feeling that the Monkey was going to be trouble.

Reykjavik clings by the frozen skin of its teeth to a bay of black pumice, a huddled, head-down, white-knuckle town made of corrugated iron painted in pastel ice-cream tones, the steeply pitched roofs hoarding light and warmth, the streets a slick grey slalom. On one side the North Atlantic, the metallic colour of frozen-to-death, smashes and grabs at the impertinence of human habitation with corpse-white fists. On the other side stretches the hinterland, a jaw-dropping, face-slapping, eye-pricking, awesome empty space of mountains, crevasses, glaciers, geysers, vertiginous waterfalls and a garden centre, trying to blow the limpet city off its face. Nobody owns the middle of Iceland: the natives haven't found anything you can usefully do with it. After 1,000 years they are still caught on the beach, huddled behind their derelict whaling stations and cod-drying racks.

The list of what Iceland hasn't got is a saga, and includes trees. In fact, it hasn't got anything that grows except moss, the closest nature has yet come to inventing nylon. It hasn't got neighbours, it sits bleakly isolated in the killer sea, the nearest landfalls are Greenland or Orkney. It hasn't got public transport – don't even think of building a railway. It doesn't have any crime to speak of: anyone who hung around with thoughts of mugging would become a speed bump till late June. Neither does it have signs in shop windows saying: "Lowest-ever prices". Iceland is hysterically, laughably, expensive. A round of drinks for the three of us? No problem, that will be £60 (and I don't drink). And that's not even including nuts for the Monkey.

What Iceland has got are taxes, avalanches of taxes. What it spends them on is something of a mystery. There's no crime, no public transport, no military except a couple of wind-up fishery boats, and the jail is the size of a small post office. Most of it seems to go on clearing snow, which is a bit like paying God Danegeld. A task that makes Sisyphus look like he's got a hobby.

It also has active volcanoes. Oh, there goes Mount Hekla spitting lava over an area the size of the home counties, and spuming a mushroom cloud that should give the Japanese tourist a bad dose of *déjà vu*. Iceland is the youngest place on the globe: it's still cooking, steaming and cracking after its journey from the oven at the centre of the earth. Because it is so new, contrarily it feels profoundly ancient, like being morphed into a natural history museum's dawn-of-time diorama. There is enough raw geothermal power to supply Europe for a very long time and, of course, Iceland has fish – 70% of its income comes from the sea. It's caught by 5% of the population. The other 95% go shopping.

But most of what Iceland's got is bundles of weather. This isn't anything as benignly balmy as a climate: this is weather that is like living with a giant psychopathic bouncer, weather of heroic, mythic proportions. The air around you is a sensate physical presence on a mission. For nine months of the year, outside the clattering window stalks a man-killer that wants your guts for popsicles. Welcome to Iceland, twinned with Valhalla.

Finally, what Iceland has got are the most beautiful women in the world. I'll say that again, just in case you missed it. The most groin-throbbingly, pulse-revvingly beautiful women (drop a gear) in the world. Not just one or two, not a handsome few, not a judicious nubile sprinkling, but flocks, shoals, herds, coveys and prides of the most stunningly direct and confident, perfectly formed women. In answer to the timeless question "How far would a man go for a pretty face?", the answer is, at least in Jeremy's case, Iceland. The ice-blonde, ice-eyed icing on the icing.

First thing, then, is to get kitted up. We need jerseys with more patterns on them than a blind folk musicians' convention, and we need fur. We don't want to just endanger a species, we want to pull evolution's hair out. The great thing about fur in Iceland is that it's not some sort of dainty fashion detail, it's work clothes, it's a practical necessity. The man in the shop says there's a problem with seals: "Just too damn many of them, by the way, please smoke. We can't club them fast enough, do you fancy a sealskin donkey jacket with salmon-skin trim?" Do haddock shit in the fjord? I just want to bring all the rodent-hugging animal rights activists in their nylon windcheaters here, stand them on the tundra, and say: "Look, just before your bodily functions cryogen-icise, tell me, who's the dumb animal now?" So we get big hats, big, big, hats made out of Ivana Trump, and a fox scarf with the head on, and it's time for dinner. At the homely Two Overcoats, whose name is a small Icelandic joke because the overcoat rack takes up most of the room, smoked puffin to start, followed by whale steak *au poivre* – whale is man's meat as meltingly soft as fillet, it has a round, brown flavour with just a touch of iron, where else do they fry Willy? – and Iceland was starting to grow on me.

The clear-eyed relief of so much profligate political incorrectness, and it was still early.

Downtown Reykjavik is a winding shindig of bars and clubs, arranged so that you don't have to go more than a couple of freezing pixie steps between drinks. Every Friday and Saturday, anyone who is solvent and ambient gets out and crawls. Jeremy, with the assurance of a seasoned tracker, leads us to a bar that he knows is so bodaciously stuffed with Scanda-totty we'll need flame-retardant underpants. I have to keep reminding the Monkey to keep his tongue indoors or it'll freeze to his chin. The bar is a wooden barn on three floors, stuffed with 14 Icelandic men in dun-coloured Crimplene parkas, sipping pints of lager and sliding their little piggy, albino-lashed eyes.

It is one of the remarkable features of Iceland that the male and female of the species should be so diametrically different. The men are universally, unremittingly hideous. There is a definite look, a sort of weedy, crumpled, dim Hitler-youth thing with seal-coloured hair that grows in random tussocks and moults in rotation. The answer to this fundamental disparity, I suspect, like so much else, lies in DNA. Iceland has a unique communal gene pool. A thousand years of being Sven No-mates, and regular cataclysmic genetic bottlenecks where the population has been whittled down to a freezing handful, mean that they all share the same genes. Iceland is one glowing advertisement for incest – just as long as you're female, of course. There appear to be no other ill effects. In recognition of this, the Icelanders have very sensibly dispensed with surnames. The phone book is alphabetical by first name and profession; Thor the Fisherman followed by 20 Thor the Shoppers. Your second name is your father's first name with either *son* or *dottir* added. Illegitimacy is therefore never an issue. Well, it is an issue, but not an issue, if you see what I mean. Just as I was considering the complexities of all this, a brace of girls of a perfectly humdrum radiance and suicidally few clothes passed by, trailing a glare of piggy-eyed lust. "What are you doing here?" one said to me. "This is a bar for parents." "No, grandparents," corrected the other. It was recommended by a very sad old man, I replied. "Oh, let us show you all the really happening clubs and bars in Reykjavik. I'm Angeline, by the way, and this is my friend. I'm twenty; she says she is twenty, but she's only nineteen. I won a prize for having the prettiest eyes in school, but I don't think it's very important. My worst feature is my bum, don't you think so? No, feel it. Do you mind if I sit on your knee? I've got a boyfriend, but he doesn't like me having fun. I like having fun. Do you like having fun? I'd love a drink, surprise me. Is this uncomfortable? I'm a gymnast, you know, I can do the splits right here (she could). Do you think I talk too much? Everyone says I talk too much." I turned to Jeremy just in time to hear him say to his nearly-20-year-old: "Right, given that Iceland's not in the EC, does the common agricultural policy, and in particular the fishing policy, have a specific impact on the island's GDP?" I promise I'm not making that up.

What followed is something of a blur, of being led by the hand from bar to bar. A translucent cheek pressed to my cheek, while a stream of prettily lilted inanities poured steadily, unquenchably into my ear. All around, the most beautiful girls and troll-like boys drank and danced and fumbled and snogged in a surging tide of 1970s pop classics, beer and hormones. In one shambling interregnum I do recall Jeremy saying that what he liked best about Iceland, apart from all the other things he liked best, was that he could be completely anonymous. Nobody buttonholed him about gaskets. Then, finding a long, ice-sculpture queue for a club, he marched up to a bouncer and produced his BBC identity card, which says: "I'm that bloke on the satellite telly." He spent the next half-hour surrounded by excited, sweaty Scanda quick-fit fitters arguing about gear ratios.

Reykjavik on the razzle is cool without cynicism. They don't pose or preen, there's a barely restrained sense of enthusiasm and expectation. They go at the drinking and lust in an elegantly unselfconscious manner and there is no Icelandic word for "excuse me". I was particularly impressed by the girl in the gents' loo, who took her turn at the urinal and peed standing up. By 5.30am we'd washed up at the bar of a sardine sauna club, the girls had finally drawn breath, and Jeremy and I were doing what middle-aged men do best and most often, just watching.

The punch that decked the Monkey was a good punch. Not that I'm much of an authority on punching. But it had a meaty, compact ferocity with plenty of Viking shoulder behind it. It caught the Monkey right in the kisser. He came up spitting a satisfying amount of blood, doing that "Hold me back, hold me back, I'll kill him" routine. Jeremy and I caught each other's eye and in a flash of deep male recognition knew what had to be done. We were three travellers alone, joined by a professional bond, but also by a deeper, playground-learnt camaraderie – all for one and one for all. Without a word, for none was needed, we made our move. As the barman wrenched him to the door by his neck, we turned our backs and pretended we didn't know him. "His flash didn't work, for all practical purposes he's pointless." "Absolutely, no reason for all of us to get the bum's rush." "None at all, what are you having?"

Outside, in the coldest, bleakest hour before dawn, the glittering icy streets shoaled with avid Icelanders giving each other saliva transfusions, twining eelishly in doorways, blowing like whales in gutters and just having lost the battle to remain bipedal on the French-polished pavement, lying on their backs waving at the brooding bungalow sky, like stranded crabs. Marvellous.

Next morning, the Monkey stumbled into breakfast with a scab that satisfyingly resembled a nasty dose of herpes, and a look of abject misery. Before you say anything, I've got your box, Jeremy's got your camera. He slumped with relief. "And the bag?" What bag? "The bag with all the lenses and film." Oh, good grief.

Reykjavik is this year's European city of culture. It's taking the honour with a remarkable humility. In fact, it is so humble about it that it hasn't even put up a sign. Iceland's one great gift to the world is the 10th-century sagas, a collection of prose, myth-history and legend that includes the origin of Wagner's Ring Cycle and the discovery of America (another reason Jeremy likes Icelandics is because, having caught America, they threw it back). The sagas are utterly compelling and violently beautiful; they make *Beowulf* read like the diary of a gay hairdresser. Reading them here, with the ravens raggedly soaring overhead, makes them seem spookily like plausible current events.

Icelanders are very cultured people. They stay in school until they are 20, mainly because it's too cold to go into the playground. They are phenomenally well read. They travel widely and dress fashionably. Per head they spend more in London than any other nationality. But Reykjavik isn't an ostentatiously aesthetic place. True, there is a natural history museum that reputedly has a stuffed great auk that was the most expensive piece of taxidermy ever.

But there is only one absolute must-see. The penis museum, appropriately secreted up a back passage. What's extraordinary is not so much the penises – though you do see that nature is as inventive as a Swiss Army knife when it comes to the nozzle of reproduction. What is extraordinary is that someone (a man) woke up and said: "Eureka! I know to what great end I shall devote my life. It'll be the great end. I'll collect a penis from every species of animal in Iceland." There are no animals in Iceland. It's a very small collection, with the exception of the sperm whale. Which isn't. There is an affidavit signed by a farmer promising his own pocket gristle to complete the set. "Why wait?" said Jeremy. "We could just leave them the Monkey."

After taking the Monkey to buy a new flash and film at gratuitously Icelandic prices, we walked down Reykjavik's Bond Street, which is pretty indistinguishable from our Bond Street. Jeremy pointed to a café. "The last time I was here I interviewed Miss World, who was Miss Iceland, in there. Let's go and have a cup of steaming euphoric recall." And at that very moment, with a synchronicity that would make you puff out your cheeks in disbelief if this were fiction, a voice called, "Jeremy," and there she was, Miss World, like some fabulous heroine from a sword, sex and sorcery saga, with a brace of handmaidens who even by local standards were dropdead poleaxing. "Come and have coffee. I know, why don't we all have dinner and then go out clubbing with all the current Miss Iceland contestants that we just happen to be judging?" All of them? Another 24 dazzling blondes. I was planning on having an early night and arranging my woolly collection by zigzag. Another icy blonde? I don't know that I could. I'm right up to here with gorgeous, blue-eyed Valkyrie. You only get invitations like that once in a lifetime. No, you only get invitations like that in 10th-century sagas.

But before clubbing with goddesses, there was Jeremy's fun to get out of the way. He was ever so overexcited. "I can't wait, I can't wait. I can't wait to see you do it." Driving a snowmobile is stupid.

Driving a snowmobile in convoy in a blizzard is deeply stupid and frightening. I now know that oblivion is a real place, and I have been there. If you want to know what it's like to turn your face into a Christmas decoration, then hop aboard. But frankly, growing icicles off my eyebrows and out of my nose is not a party trick I wish to repeat. Then Jeremy and I fell down the Jules Verne memorial crevasse and only his vast beer gut prevented us from plummeting to the centre of the earth. Oh, and the Monkey hit a rock and landed on his new flash gun, which broke. That was funny, that made us laugh – a lot.

I got my own back by feeding Jeremy shark, not just any old shark, but shark that had been buried for a year. Nowhere else in the world has anyone else thought of burying a shark for a year and then putting it in their mouths. It looks innocuous enough, like yellow blocks of caramel, and it tastes like nothing else in the solar system. No, it tastes like one other thing. Sharks have cartilage skeletons, not bone, and as it rots, cartilage gives off ammonia – a lot of ammonia. After a year this tastes precisely like urine, ferocious, vicious, diseased urine. You know the burning sensation of an Extra Strong Mint or Victory V? Well, imagine that, but with the flavour of a Turkish long-drop lav – in August. Oh, his face was a picture. Or it would have been if the Monkey hadn't been pointing the other way.

Oddly, the place Iceland remind me of most is Cuba. Another no-mates, quarantine island where they gyre and gambol long and hard and in public. Where the sense of isolation has bred a sort of self-sufficient, self-generating, cool confidence. As the rest of us in mainstream Europe become more harmonised, precious, pasteurised, sani-wrapped and timid, a one-size-Fritz-all culture, Iceland shows that you don't have to be in it to have a life. Today more than ever, this last frontier seems spectacularly attractive and remarkably enviable. It's the end-of-term dance at the end of the world.

By the way, apropos the evening out with the putative Miss Iceland Dottirs, I don't like to boast or anything, and I'd never divulge an indiscreet confidence, but they did all get together and ask if I could possibly be a judge. What a country – become a legend in a weekend. Sadly, Jeremy will be filming in Birmingham.

The coolest beauty contest in the world

Judging Miss Iceland, October 2000

So there's me and Miss World and the candlelight. It's the end of dinner, that soft post-prandial moment when conversation gets mellow and the hands start searching for something else to do. The current world champion is Miss India and she is everything you could wish for in a first-class stewardess. It would have to be first class because she's a bit broad in the beam. Don't get me wrong, you wouldn't throw her out of a sleeping bag for taking up too much room.

When I say there's me and Miss India, there are a few others here in the private dining room of the Rex Bar, Reykjavik's only Conran-designed restaurant, but they're mere shadows with the sound turned down. Mademoiselle Le Monde and me only have eyes for each other. I feel as if I'm falling into two mysterious, velvety, deep brown pools full – as they used to say on the telly – of eastern promise.

"Well, what would you do?" Miss India enquires, slightly more sharply than my mood requires. "What would you do if you were Miss World?"

And because my mind is already playing pass the parcel with her sari, I don't really think before opening my mouth and have that all too common experience of hearing a voice that sounds remarkably like mine say, "Me? If I was Miss World, well, goddam, I'd go to bed for a year and play with my tits." Hee haw.

It wasn't the right answer. It wasn't even the wrong answer. It was so utterly beyond any sort of answer that fell within Planet Reasonable that Miss India's face closed up with a clang, like off-licences on a Sunday afternoon used to. She in turn searched for the appropriate final riposte.

"You are," she said from the bottom of her soul, "a very stupid man."

It was, I must say, a fair comment. I was a very, very stupid man.

How often does one get to chat up Miss World? Well, exactly – and I had to go and make with the smart-ass remark. It was my first day on the job, the dream job, and I'd fucked up. Stupid, stupid boy.

Ever since we were about 15 we have had this collective fantasy about the job. We had the interview with the careers bastard and enthusiastically said we'd like to cash in our GCSE metalwork for a job as Ferrari's design consultant and part-time bikini-line waxer in the *Playboy* Mansion and he said, "Ha ha. Be realistic. What about the cardboard box factory? There are a lot of openings in cardboard boxes." I don't think anyone's ever actually quantified the furious spur to achievement the careers bastard has been to generations of boys. I've never met anyone who was told, "Son, you can do something exciting and fun and innovative that'll make you respected and rich." It was always the cardboard factory box or something. And, from that moment on, we started to have hot fantasies about the job. The perfect job. The ideal, I-don't-believe-it, pinch-me-I'm-dreaming job, and when we landed it we'd go back and find that careers bastard in his hideous suburban semi and we'd grab him by his spindly neck and tap his head on his Georgian-style doorjamb and say, "I", thump, "got", thump, "the job", thump, "cretin".

When they say that men think about sex every 20 seconds they're wrong. What we're thinking of is the job that has endless, crude, pneumatic sex as a perk. Well – and let this be a beacon to those of you who think the offer will never come – I landed it for three days. I had that job and it came out of the blue. I didn't even have to apply for it.

I was sitting in a café in downtown Reykjavik – actually there is only downtown Reykjavik – and a woman I had just met gave me an odd look and said hesitantly, "You wouldn't like to be a judge for Miss Iceland, would you, by any chance?" Of all the questions since the question mark was invented where the answer "No" is not even a conceivable option, that's right up there with "Would you like to minutely examine Christy Turlington for imperfections?" and "Would you like to run over Carol Vorderman in a steamroller?" I knew that this was one of life's exclamation marks. That the glittering lottery finger from CV heaven was hovering just over my head. This woman called Linda, who by chance was arranging the Miss Iceland finals and by further chance had herself once been Miss World and was another woman I'd happily examine for imperfections, made me a job offer I couldn't refuse.

So two weeks later I was back on the afternoon flight to Reykjavik airport, having torn up the diary. I was supposed to be in Hollywood reporting on the Oscars. Forget it – a lot of neurotic, self-obsessed plastic diva-dolls wearing designer net curtains and talking about egg-white enemas. Forget it. Stuff the money, stuff the sun, stuff table-hopping at Spago. I'm going to the frozen north to a city that looks like a tin model of Dundee, where the ground bubbles, a tree is a landmark and everything smells of rotten egg. I'm off to the northern-most capital in the world where they have man-killer winds and they grow the finest women in the universe.

That's the thing, you see. Being asked to judge Miss Switzerland or Miss Israel or Miss Wales wouldn't be worth bothering directory enquiries for the number of your careers bastard, but Miss Iceland is something else. Icelandic women are the benchmark against whom all others are found wanting. It's all a matter of taste, I hear you say. Well, up to a point. You may personally yearn for the fiery dark-eyed voluptuousness and thong-fraying buttocks of Copacabanas; you may grow purple-tipped thinking of the elegant, swaying, cone-breasted princess from the appropriately named Horn of Africa; or, indeed, there may be a few who lust after nothing but the softly fawn-eyed, caramel-tummied, blossom-bedecked teenagers of the South Seas. But the point of Icelandic girls is that it's not just skin-deep. We're not talking some two-dimensional centrefold fantasy.

In Iceland, what's under the bonnet is quite as erotically high-octane as the bodywork. While other nations may boast women of a sublime pulchritudinocity, convention and caprice, custom and culture mean that the eye writes cheques the body is never going to cash. But not in Iceland. I have never been to a place where predatory sex is such an equal-opportunities employer. The girls have a directness that borders on rudery. There is a vaunting national self-confidence that almost amounts to Posturepedic arrogance.

That's not, I hasten to add, to say that the place is one long, easy lay – an 18–30 Nordic shagathon that's just gagging for charabanc-thank-you-mam sexual tourists. Quite the opposite. Icelandic girls tend to cut the crap. They're nobody's fools or floozies. They're not just anybody's, but they do think that anybody could be theirs and that's what makes them so attractive. Sexuality, sexiness and nubility are all things that come from the inside and with Icelandic girls it shows on the outside.

How they got to be like this and so unlike the lasses down your local is a mystery. It also turned out to be a bit of a blow for the Miss Iceland competition. You see, a blind man with a sense of smell could pick the contestants for Miss Iceland and come up with a good selection. My initial reaction to seeing the contestants was, "Well, yes, this is a fabulous collection of very pretty, self-assured girls but why isn't the waitress one of them? Or that girl I just passed in the street?"

Beauty pageants are, as we all know, faintly ridiculous, reducing sexuality and attraction to the dimmest lowest common denominator but, even given this premise, choosing Miss Iceland is still invidious. It's like choosing the prettiest apple in an orchard or perhaps the tastiest without being able to take a nibble. Oh, what the hell – I should complain.

My fellow judges were Claudia Schiffer and, unfortunately, Tim Jefferies plus the ex-Miss World (1988), Linda Petursdottir, and a couple of Icelandic gents, one of whom was called Thor. But despite all the excitement and rioting beauty, I became obsessed with Miss India. It's a sad truth that I always want to impress the one person in any room whom I know despises me. I couldn't take my eyes off her. I'm ashamed to say I came close to stalking her. Apart from her obvious and sickly addictive antipathy to me, she was just so odd. The window into the life of a reigning Miss World was fascinating. She spends a year as a sort of glittering refugee – being shoved from one airport to the next, picked up in taxis, taken to dinners, photographed and shoved off again.

Miss India travels with a chaperone – a plain, middle-aged lady with all the gimlet-eyed thin-lipped malevolence of her calling. A woman who knew, on her charge's behalf, how to say "No" in 37 languages, she'd been chaperoning Miss Worlds for most of her career. "I love every minute of it," she lied. Imagine that as a job – caught forever carrying the tickets through someone else's glory years. Changing the hotel rooms, explaining that she won't eat pork and won't be photographed in the swimming pool with the Minister of the Interior's son. The world rolled past her: Miss Turks and Caicos; Miss Fiji; Miss South Africa; Miss Lost Life.

The two of them together were a sad couple. I spied them going back to the hotel after a gala banquet with speeches. Miss India doesn't stay late; she doesn't nightclub or dance; she needs her beauty sleep. Miss India towered over her minder. Neither spoke, having obviously run out of conversation a dozen airports ago, having never become friends, joined by this ridiculous title and its absurd ambassadorial role of bringing love and peace from no one who matters to people who aren't listening.

The phoney, semi-diplomatic role of Miss World is highlighted by the fact that the chaperone at all times carries a plastic bag that contains a special box. In it is the crown and sash of office, like those of the presidents of Russia and America. It is always there in the background – the peace and love version of the nuclear button. Miss World the special envoy from Planet Smile, here to spread the word on behalf of hugely tall, pneumatic girls with hard-hat hair and 1976 make-up.

Miss India herself is a perfect example of the catwalk diplomatic corps. She is utterly, utterly humourless. I'm not just saying that because she didn't laugh at my jokes. For her, humour is plainly a gigantic human failing and an expression of an absence of gravitas. She has dozens of degrees in things as disparate and appealing as accountancy and zoology. She also plays the classical sitar, but what makes Miss India particularly suited to her role of ambassador is her attitude to sex. She's against it. Not in principle, but as recreation. She thinks most men are silly. Their attitude to her huge, bouncy-castle body and sphinx-like face is demeaning and pathetic. It is obvious that the men she meets on her travels are only after one thing – well, maybe four or five things, but all in the same general ballpark. Sex belongs in marriage and marriage, contrarily, is best brokered without thoughts of sex. In this she ideally evokes the Miss World ethos, which is sexless sex.

You don't have to be Desmond Morris to understand that lining up a lot of girls and picking the most beautiful is all about humping, but Miss Worlds are supposed to be sexless. They aren't just virgins for a year, they have to be Barbie virgins. Even to imagine they might own organs of fun is a heresy. Girls have been stripped of the chaperone's sash and crown for having children, an irrefutable sign that sex of some sort must have taken place on or near them. Boyfriends or husbands are not only discouraged but are also a heresy.

This was Miss India's first visit to Iceland. It was her first sight of snow, something she approached with the insouciance of a Persian cat being shown a hot bath. I tried to imagine Iceland as seen through her eyes. This cold white land of hot blonde women was the antithesis of everything she believed about intergender bodily contact and attraction. All us judges were taken for a morning's snowmobiling. It's funny and fast and silly. Snow makes you silly. We threw snowballs, fell over, laughed, pushed each other and generally behaved like children. That's the point of snow. Miss India sat in a hut and watched through the window. The heavy weight of her responsibility as ambassador of poise forbade her from joining in.

"I expect you've eaten all our lunch," I said in a jolly, joshing manner, in an attempt to build bridges. She just rolled those huge eyes at the ceiling and whispered, "Stupid, stupid man." Done it again.

The pageant itself was remarkably good fun. Dinner in a revolving restaurant that made everyone else feel queasy, and then, before the televised catwalk bit, we judges were left backstage to do the all-important questioning of the contestants. This is very nerve-racking, for us not them. It's difficult not to appear as a sleazy slave dealer looking over the merchandise. The girls were wearing sheets while they had their hair and make-up done. Some of them were wearing more sheet than others. Tim's big question was, "Could you change the wheel on a Land Cruiser?" This being Iceland, the girls laughed at him pitifully. Of course they could change the wheel on a Land Cruiser. Could he? Er, no he couldn't. "Never mind, just stay with your vehicle," they shouted. "One of us will be along shortly."

Claudia asked if any of them wanted to be models. Very few of them did. They wanted to travel, to have fun, to get on with their studies. Not one said she wanted to work with children or for world peace. None of them said their turn-ons were kindness, sunsets and baby animals; or their turn-offs bad breath, argumentative people, pollution and intolerance. They thought Miss World was a bit of fun. None of them took it seriously. Neither did their friends. They didn't much mind who won except that the travel scholarship would be useful. There certainly, definitely, wouldn't be any tears.

Miss India looked on with blank horror. What, I asked wittily, was their favoured form of contraception? I might as well have asked what their favourite fabric softener was. You have sex; you take precautions. Who's so weird as to have a favourite bit of rubber or gel or chemical? Quite right – it was a dumb question.

One girl flirted outrageously, standing very close, giving it lots of eyes and teeth and lots of touching. Now I have no illusions about my irresistibility – well, of course I probably have tons of illusions, but not when it comes to 46-year-old men in suits interviewing 19-year-old girls in sheets. She did it just to see if she could, just as a bit of amusement.

The parade was a weirdly Nordic affair. A mix of in-your-face leering and a social workers' convention. In between the parading girls there was a speech by a Down's syndrome girl. Anywhere else this would have seemed like screamingly bad taste. Here it was a natural setting of priorities. Some things are just more important than others.

The final decision was quite quick. We weren't going to argue the toss and, actually, watching Miss India in her supermarket monarch crown and end-of-the-pier sash, I suddenly thought, "I don't want to inflict the possibility of a sterile year in VIP lounges with a chaperone on any Icelandic girl. Perhaps if you've come from the middle classes of Bombay and the corset of steely etiquette and polished smiles chimes with your own culture, then being Miss World mightn't be an unreasonable way to spend a year. It might even be a title she could wear with modest pride in the years to come. But for an Icelandic girl, for whom everything it represents cuts against the sophisticated and deeply liberal modernity, I can't think of anything worse. To inflict that diplomatic sexless baggage on one of these young women would be simply cruel, although I insisted my flirt came third. I thought it would amuse her.

The winner was a very photogenic girl who did want to be a model. She already had an agent. Claudia said her face was "very now". She could be a great success. The title might help. There was a problem though. As Claudia had to announce the winner, she wrote down the name.

"How do you spell that? D . . . o . . . g. She's called Miss Dog?"

At the party in the disco afterwards the girls got faceless, danced until their clothes fell off and snogged lucky boys. There were no tears. Miss India went home to bed. I caught sight of her the next day in the airport, trailing her nanny and the bag off to God knows where in the waiting Mercedes. I shouted, "Don't do anything I wouldn't do." She flashed a big smile, and didn't mean a single tooth of it. What a woman. I've never met anyone who was so suited to being Miss World.

Scumball rally

Monaco, October 2001

Odd stuff, money. It doesn't always do what you think it will do. It's like water. Not just as it slips through your fingers but as it finds the path of least resistance. And it's not always pretty. Or clear. Or cool.

Monte Carlo is a money puddle. A cash delta. It is as if all the wealth from the rich northern European pasture has run down the Continent and found its way here, to form a sort of mangrove swamp of avarice before running into the Mediterranean. Maybe swamp is the wrong term. Maybe some of you like swamps. Perhaps sewage outlet would be a better description.

There are two sorts of slum. There are slums that grow out of too little, and slums that grow out of too much. Monte Carlo is the sort of slum that rich people build when they lack for nothing except taste and a sense of the collective good. The one thing a poor slum has over a rich one is dignity. What Monte Carlo has instead of dignity is CCTV cameras and policemen. It's been said that Monte Carlo is the biggest trailer park in the world. An itinerant collection of wasters, drifters and self-delusionists. It's also an example to the rest of us of what money actually does buy you. And the truth of the rubric is that any place that has the appellation "tax haven" will be a waiting room for purgatory.

It wasn't always that way. Monte Carlo managed to remain an independent principality caught between Italy and France because neither of its neighbours ever wanted to take it on. It simply wasn't worth the effort. After a thousand years of not being anywhere or doing anything much, the wheel of fate spun the ball of chance into Monte Carlo's lucky slot. It got a casino. The south of France became fashionable and invented a new tribe of people who called themselves the Jet Set.

And finally, in a coupling that would have pleased a medieval court, Prince Rainier pulled Grace Kelly. As far as Hollywood was concerned he might well have been short, ugly and boring, but short, ugly and boring was how powerful men were in Hollywood, too. And he was a real prince (who cared if it was only of some Old World Las Vegas?). They agreed he could have Grace mainly because everyone from the Mexican border to Big Sur had already had her.

The new rhinestone royalty produced a family that befitted Monaco. A trailer-trash aristocracy. A princeling who was so characterless he'd get off in a police line-up of one. Princess Caroline, the beautiful public school girl touched with laughable tragedy who ended up marrying a German with more GBH accusations than quarterings on his coat of arms, and the only prince since the Black Death to be accused of pissing in public (he's suing).

And then, of course, there's Stephanie. Where do you start? She's just the Queen of Kitsch, the mother superior of lowbrow, a pin-up princess of pristine trashiness. A real, live, walking, talking, humping and sulking country and western lyric. The Grimaldis – bless every one of them – have gone from being highnesses to lownesses. They just are Les Dukes du Hazzard.

After money, Monte is famous for two things. The Monte Carlo Rally and the Monaco Grand Prix. Now, you might justifiably think this shows a distinct frugality of imagination. Well, it's no accident. If you have loads of cash but are technically bankrupt in the taste account, then motorcars come as close to culture as you are likely to get. It's so much easier to boast about a million-pound Bugatti than a Branscusi. "Oh yeah, the Modigliani. I had one once. Marvellous acceleration, lousy road holding." Cars become the imitation of civilisation in a land where no one does anything, or knows anything. The brief history of the motorcar is the High Renaissance Monte Carlo never had. The fact that Princess Grace died in a car crash is symptomatic. It's the equivalent in the rest of Europe of having a Titian fall on your head.

Once a year, Monte Carlo plays it down for the Grand Prix. It is, uniquely, a road race. And where every other European city is desperately trying to get rid of motorcars, Monaco lies on its back in the street like a trucker's prostitute braced for a petrolheads' gang-bang. The truth is, there's nothing better to do and even if it knew how, it couldn't do anything else, anyway.

Naturally, we arrive by helicopter. The drive from Nice airport along the pretty, barren corniche is tortuous. A refugee column of rich folk and folk who want to stare at rich folk.

From the little heliport, we're whisked round the harbour to our boat. Now, a boat in Monte Carlo sounds glamorous. One of those phrases you throw into the conversation like Ferrari keys: "Oh, we are just popping down to the bateau in Monte." Actually, in truth, the harbour is an aquatic favela. A hugger-mugger horizontal tenement of ugly, awkward, moulded plastic bathroom fittings bobbing in cess. Both ex and the other sort.

The boats are built as Portakabins for cocaine, metered sex and competitive lying. They grab the harbour wall with desperate, straining gangplanks. You see, the thing about these waterborne shag pads is that none of them can swim. You know that if they were to be unkindly set adrift, they'd bob and wave until they drowned. The boats in Monte Carlo aren't going anywhere. Which is a good thing because the people on them don't want to go anywhere. Just being here means they've arrived.

Inside, they are designed with all the elegance and savoir-faire of a Swiss proctologist's waiting room. Perhaps someone can explain to me why boats inevitably have pictures of other boats on their walls? It's like being at home on land and decorating your living room with the framed photographs out of estate agent's windows. Anyway, never mind, we are here and we are pleased to be here. And forget the satellite stuff. The most important bit of equipment, the fridge, is working overtime. There's a prostate, emetic dribble of constant champagne.

Boats force intimacy. Whatever you are doing, you are never further than six inches from your neighbour. The next floater's chemical bog is only two sheets of marine plastic from your pillow.

From the sun deck, roof deck thing we can look out over the marina at everyone else looking at us. And everyone else is here. Why motor racing should attract so many people is one of the stupidest mysteries of modern life. Millions and millions of Euro gawpers arrive to be shuffling pedestrian extras and background atmosphere. They shamble along the lines of moored Port-a-loos whose backs are opened up like dolls' houses so that we can be seen. Every ship a little tableaux more Dantesque, a glimpse into a *faux*-glamorous life. Champagne bucket on table, couple of girls in halter-neck bikinis, steward with botulism on a tray, big bowl of maternity flowers and three or four blokes getting beered up in their devil-may-care shorts and T-shirts, advertising other no-brain holidays that stretch over their fat, hairy, pink bellies which have held more than their fair share of the good things in life.

These boats are living billboards for envy – part matey Budweiser ad, part lap-dancing poster, and a good part recruitment flyer for the Workers Revolutionary Party. Frankly, honestly, hand on heart, we look ridiculous. Not just posy and prattish, not just loud and cheap, but flatulently venal. Repellent. Mostly because we are a big lie. We don't live here. We don't live like this. We're ligging. Or renting. Or being bought and used. It's all a lie.

Monaco isn't a grand place. It isn't a racing track. And none of it is remotely smart and sophisticated. The whole port has a sense of being a *Monty Python* epic recreation of a medieval pilgrimage or crusade. There are flags and banners bearing heraldic symbols, *hoi polloi* sport the livery of their favourite mechanical knights. And it smells like the middle ages of softly decomposing canapés; baking pizzas; ocean-going whores; tan cream; smeary lipstick; baby oil; slippery condoms; clammy G-strings; wrinkled, sodden nylon armpits; frying oil reheated to the consistency of acrid sump sludge. And over it all, the abiding nasal ebb and flow of hot sewage.

Monaco is the lid to its own cavernous, bubbling, torpid septic tank. It's the stink of consumption and corruption. The sun bakes us into a mellifluous bouillabaisse of stewed fat, flesh, gristle and Nike trainers.

I expect you want to know about the birds. Well, there are a lot of them. Ugly, unshaggable ones mostly, holding their German boyfriends' Ferrari flags, lumpy bumbags bobbing on lumpy bums.

There are slightly prettier ones. Akimbo le bateau: the famed boat girls. Boat, by the way, is an acronym – Bordering On A Tart. The boat girls have two looks. Unavailable and bored. They look unavailable to strangers and bored to people they've been introduced to, and whose names they don't remember.

They lie on the plastic like anorexic shaved seals and like racing cars they have been chosen for their aerodynamic bodywork. These aren't family saloons or loved, polished classics. They are not reliable or economic, and you wouldn't take one home to meet the family. All they do is go. They are goers. Except, like racing cars, mostly they don't go. They promise to go but they break down. You push their starters and nothing happens.

And then there are the blokes. Photocopier salesmen to a man. Drunk, pee-stained, clingingly insecure, baritone, loud and hideous. Even if they aren't actually photocopier salesmen they have the sounds of photocopier salesmen. And if they are not actually hideous, then they're larging it with the lads – kit wraps them in hideousness. The lads make up the majority of this sweaty, champagne-breathing rookery.

And even though the place semaphores sex, reeks of sex, yammers, dribbles and bays for sex, you just know there's very little, actual one-to-one, face-to-face, perky, genital, real-time sex going down. And if it does, it's because there was no way of avoiding it. And, PS: it was very, very unsatisfying.

So, we're all here for the weekend, sniffing out a bit of slippery and an icebox full of San Miguel. What do we actually do?

Well, not much. In fact, very little. We talk about doing tons. Most of it involving getting out of Monaco. We could go to St Paul de Vence and find a restaurant out in the hills. We could visit the Matisse chapel. Go shopping. Do Jacques Cousteau impressions in the Aquarium. But the truth is, doing anything is a Technicolor nightmare. The only people who can get around Monaco with ease are the racing drivers, and they can't get out to do anything either. The town is a labyrinth of crowd control barriers, manned by the sort of policemen that very rich people like. That is, furious head waiters with guns.

If you do decide to make a break for it, the best way is by tender or water taxi. But they can only take you to another bit of shore that you can't move on. Or another boat that's very like the one you're on. So why bother?

The one thing we have to do is go to the Grand Prix Ball, which is touted as being one of the premier social events of the sophisticated Euro season. It's black tie, which on land is a bore but on a boat is ocean-going torture. We all get into the tender in sequins and penguin suits, and are stared at by the surreyed ranks of photocopier salesmen and Finnish petrolheads. I have never been so aware of what it might have felt like to be Captain Bligh, set adrift from the *Bounty*.

The dinner is like every other large corporate bash. Brain-numbing, slow, uncomfortable and organised like a learning difficulties junior school's nativity play, made that soupçon worse because it's supposed to be fun. How is it that, with all this money and experience, you can throw a party that not a single human being can enjoy? That sort of negative enthusiasm takes some doing, as would Caprice on video. She introduces the good cause that has invariably been stapled on to this gala event (which tells you something about the quality of the glittering guests). You've reached some sort of barrel bottom when you clap to a virtual Caprice. A photocopier salesman wins a Harley-Davidson. The Harley contemplates phoning the Samaritans. It's time to go. It was time to go before I got here.

Next door, Monte's premier nightclub has a scrum of furious don't-you-know-who-I-ams and their scrotum-withering rented totty. And there are a lot of young men arguing with moonlighting waiter policemen with wires in their ears trying to park mummy's Porsche.

We take the tender out to see to a party on a boat, which turns out to be not one boat, but two huge ferries stuck back-to-back like vast, mating sea dogs. At a long trestle table, 100 Germans sit and eat Thai-ish school food; our host turns out to be a 40-stone gay Kraut in bespoke cream shorts and jacket with a baseball cap. It's worth the trip just to see him; in this city of utter hideousness he gets the golden apple.

This party is to promote the dotcom business he sunk a Third World debt into. We arrive just ahead of a load of pole dancers who pretend to be lesbians around the pool. The Germans chew

Asian cud and stare. On the dance floor, three sorry hookers simulate sex. It would only take Vincent Price striding out of the dry ice to make this a scene from the Hammer horror movie they didn't dare show.

It's so deeply depressing, so comprehensively devoid of any amusement, expectation or glamour, so utterly tacky, witless, empty and sad that I can't even stand back, wrapped in the pashmina of my hack's cynicism, and laugh at it. Getting off this boat takes on paramount shove-the-women-off-the-life-raft importance. I couldn't want to leave more if it hit an iceberg (and I couldn't wish for an iceberg more). This party is social Ebola. The blonde wants to try another one on another boat. I can't face it. Not even for the lives of my children.

We return to our floating bidet and Jamie Blandford just happens to be passing. By comparison to the rest of the evening, it's like a visitation from Aristotle.

Monte Carlo is an attack on the senses, the most violent of which is the noise. Our gangplank is ten feet from the racetrack, which sounds great when you say it, but sounds as if your brains are squirting out of your ears like toothpaste when you live it. We spend all day with yellow plastic McNuggets in our ears, every so often raising an eyebrow or shrugging a shoulder by way of conversation.

It's a hurricane of sound. If the racing cars aren't practising then there's something called Formula Three, or go-karts, or racing Porsches. And when they are all done, the local mummy's boys get into their Ferraris and zoom and pretend. It's as pathetic as taking your own football to a Cup Final. And if it's not them, it's the synchronised knockabout street sweepers.

The aptly named pits are a self-contained city of Portakabin cafés and motor homes. They perambulate around the world as the modern equivalent of the circus. Today, naughty boys and girls from nice suburban families run away to join Formula One. The money that it must take to make these little plastic cars go round and round is staggering. Embarrassing. And I'm not someone who naturally spies conspicuous consumption and then thinks of starving black babies or Third World disease. But motor racing is bulimic consumption on a psychotic level. I look over the side of the jetty and lo, there is what pays for most of it. Millions and millions of fag butts. The bay is one huge ashtray. The confetti of a great cancerous wedding.

Waiting for the race to begin, we are entertained by the Swiss Red Arrows. I know that sounds like a joke. Little crimson turboprop trainers buzz and dive-bomb Monte Carlo and on every sun deck every photocopier salesman shouts, "Tora! Tora! Tora!" high-fives his mates and collapses into self-congratulatory giggles. Switzerland Blitzkrieg-ing Monaco is funny. One fat tax avoider declaring war on another, dropping anti-personnel inter- est rates. But Switzerland and Monaco are never going to fight a war. You've got to care about something to be prepared to die for it.

As a human being there are many, many things you can feel ashamed of. Things that leave a metallic taste in the mouth, make you promise to do better. Try harder. Reorganise your priorities. And physically or symbolically, every single one of them is here for one weekend a year.

Monte Carlo is a gaudy parable. A speechless Sermon on the Mount. But no one's listening. And they couldn't hear even if they were. The noise has reached concrete-splitting levels. It's the roar of selfishness, greed, vanity, avarice, addiction, lust and pointless stupidity. On the giant screen above the slurping ashtray, shimmering in the petrol haze, the start lights are flashing. Red, amber, green. And they're off.

Return of the native

Scotland, May 1999

"There's an end to an auld sang," remarked the Earl of Seafield, Scotland's Lord Chancellor, as the Scottish parliament voted itself out of existence in 1707, thereby writing himself into the quotation books and out of history.

The amount of money England had to spend in bribes for this decision was derisory. The provost of Wigton pocketed £100; Lord Banff sold his country for the princely sum of £11 2s. Perhaps even more shaming was the fact that so many members didn't even bother to turn up and vote at all. However you look at it, Scotland's last parliament was dissolved and the nation given away loch, stock and herring barrel without a shot being fired.

Most independence movements are made cohesive by a common people drawn together by ancestry, a shared language, a religion and a defined land. Scotland has none of these. The first problem of where Scotland actually is has bothered everyone since the Romans, who built two walls because they got the first one wrong – the Hadrian and the Antonine (after which, incidentally, I'm named). Most of the north of England as far south as Yorkshire has been disputed Scots territory, the Isle of Man was Scots, but parts of Galloway were English and the northwest and the isles, Viking. The western isles and part of the mainland were Irish.

Nobody knows what the original people of Scotland were – cold is probably the best informed guess, and wet. They were, in the comforting phrase of anthropologists, absorbed by the Picts – a Celtic people who probably made their way from Spain, though nobody could possibly fathom why. We know little more about them, not even what they called themselves. Pictae was Tacitus's name for them: painted people. Whether this meant tattooed or looking like Quentin Crisp, again nobody knows. (If you're looking for an archeological subject to study, the Picts are a good bet;

anyone with a beard and a purple windcheater can be an expert.) They lived somewhere called Alba.

The Scots were northern Irish and had a country on the west coast called Dalriada. They absorbed the Picts and were eventually sent back to Ireland by Cromwell where they became foreigners and British. In between times, there had been various migrations of Norsemen and Anglo-Normans (Normans, of course, were originally Norsemen) with various degrees of violence and absorption. Robert the Bruce was more Norman than he was Scots, and William Wallace's surname means that he was Welsh (who in turn claim to be the original English). So I hope that's all clear.

The Scots Nats rather sidestep the question of who is and isn't a Scot by saying anyone who lives in Scotland can be. Unless one lives in an awful lot of it, that is, as people with estates are to be deemed absentee foreigners. People with Scots antecedents are more difficult. There are 90 million of them worldwide. There are more Macdonalds in the New World than there are people in Scotland. (Trevor McDonald and Naomi Campbell, though, are not thought to be applying for citizenship.)

Scotland started as a place of superstitious animists and pantheists, much as it is today. But the Irish brought Columba, who converted the Picts to Celtic Catholicism prior to absorption. This was in turn absorbed by Roman Catholicism. Then half the country signed the covenant and became Protestant Presbyterian.

As for language, the hideously bereft Gaelic, with a vocabulary that makes the *Sun* sound verbose, never was Scotland's national language; it was spoken by the Irish. The closest thing to a national tongue is the pidgin Lallans, or Lowland Scots, which is what Burns wrote his poetry in and is the most pyrotechnically expressive, lively, intuitive and humorous language in the world.

Accent is what most immediately identifies a Scot but it's more of a class distinction. Upper-class Scots tend to sound English, and Aberdonians don't sound like anything human at all.

Perhaps Scots are best defined by what they're not. They're not English. The country has for most of its alleged existence been held together by competing and contradictory rifts and violent hatreds – not just the Highland–Lowland or interclan rivalry of romance but deep divisions between east and west, Catholic and

Protestant, Viking liberals (only in Scotland is this not a contradiction) and central belt communists. One need hardly mention Rangers and Celtic.

Scots haven't even been united under a king. Barely one died in his bed before the Act of Union. They have two flags – the lion rampant and the saltire – but no national anthem.

What all Scots have in common is history, or rather a hotly argued current mythology. For a small country of 5 million people at the far end of a European cul-de-sac, Scotland has been plagued and adorned by more events than is polite, almost all of them fabricated in the 19th century. Tartan was invented by two snobbish Poles, the Sobriski-Stewarts. The noble Highlands and its castles were invented by the German Prince Albert. The clans and Highland dress were cobbled together by Sir Walter Scott for another German, King George. Whisky is made in sherry barrels and is Irish and never was Scotland's national drink; that was brandy.

Scotland's martial glory was invented by the English after they thrashed us for the umpteenth time to get the Scots to fight their colonial wars. Ossian, Scotland's Homer, is a fake. Scots meanness was actually invented by a Scot, the comedian Harry Lauder; before him, Highland hospitality was a universally used phrase meaning generosity. Bagpipes come from Asia, and haggis from sheep.

But for all that, there is incontrovertibly a place called Scotland and a people who think they are Scots. Perhaps the fact that none of it is real and is based for the most part on fantasy shouldn't matter. Perhaps, in a very modern way, Scotland is the first virtual country, a collective chat room where you can exchange lies, wistful thinking and boast.

The harsh and simple answer to why Scotland voted to be absorbed in 1707 is because it was bankrupt, stony broke. The one constant in Scots history is lack of funds. England had cash and trade but precious little glamour or imagination. Scotland had myths and legends and painted people; in exchange for money it gave the Sassenachs romance. And who can say that wasn't a fair swap?

The site allocated for the new Scottish parliament looks like a bomb has hit it, which, all things considered at the moment, is rather appropriate. Until it is finished in 2002, the born-again parliamentarians will have to sit in the Assembly Hall of the Church of Scotland up on the Mound with a coldly disapproving John Knox looking on. Because of him, the new parliament will be dry, not even a dram to welcome it in: "Hea's tea us, wha's like us? Damn few seem to care . . ."

I've come to Edinburgh to report on a capital eager to get to grips with its new democratic responsibilities. I expect to find a politically savvy, educated city, animatedly debating devolution on street corners and in bars. I've come to observe a populace itching to get off its knees and shake a constitutional leg after so long with its hand out.

Some hope. There's nothing. Auld Reekie can't even summon up the energy to be apathetic about this election. There are no posters, no billboards, no vans with loudspeakers. I've seen church council elections that have elicited more enthusiasm. The sense of being fundamentally, deeply underwhelmed is, even by Edinburgh's purse-sphinctered standards, almost spooky.

In the south Edinburgh headquarters of the Scottish National party, Margo MacDonald is sitting under the treaty of Arbroath, giving a press briefing to 300 hacks. She's trying to engender some heat over private funding for the Royal Infirmary by rubbing two disenchanted members of Unison together. This is not a vote-winning issue, and we all know it. Where is the *Braveheart* stuff that's going to send the proud people to the ballot box shouting "Albanaich! Freedom!"?

MacDonald herself is inspiring, a sort of Caledonian Mo Mowlam – the type of woman who has been all that's stood between the Celts and maudlin communal suicide. Isn't she depressed that this campaign has got off to such a slow start? Where's the broad rhetoric, the grand sweep of history, the heathery horizons? For 50 years the SNP has been blowing relentless romantic pibrochs into the electorate's ear. But now, when nationhood is merely an election and a referendum away, it's gone coy and parochial about small change and hip operations.

"No, no. It's quite the reverse," she says. The dull campaign shows that this is a serious, grown-up election about real issues – and the infirmary is important. (Oh, I know. I was born there.)

"We've got to stop thinking like a big country and start thinking like a small one," she adds emphatically. A barber shop quartet of party workers echo that thought. "Aye, 10 million legs good, 100 million legs bad!" Then she spoils it by adding: "The real issue in this election is going to be the war."

The war? "Aye." Well, I'm sorry, but if you get out of the Union and out of Nato then who's going to give a hoot what Scotland thinks about Kosovo or anything else? How big's the Scottish air force gonna be?

"We've got to be more like Denmark, or Sweden, or Finland. Finland's done really well. Or Ireland. Look at Ireland." And that's supposed to be a winning alternative, is it? Finland, a nation of drunk Captain Birds Eyes – or Ireland, the *Big Issue* seller of Europe with added clapped-out rock-star tax avoiders. Why does Scotland have to take a leaf out of Drogheda's or Tuupovarra's book? Why can't Scotland be, well, like Scotland?

Fed up, I go off in search of a kilt. I always like to have a kilt around the house. I never wear them, of course, but – like a fire extinguisher and a cross-head screwdriver – I feel better knowing I've got one.

Buying a kilt is hysterically good fun. Nobody would ever ask you what your family's name was or where you came from if you wanted to buy a Guernsey fisherman's sweater or if you really throw a lasso before selling you a pair of cowboy boots.

The lady at Kinloch Anderson tells me there's a kilt war going on. Despite the disdain for tartan shown by the SNP, Scots are buying kilts by – well, by the yard. Caledonian pride is stepping out without knickers.

A young designer from a kilt shop on the Royal Mile is making modern kilts for the club-going generation (not that Edinburgh has any clubs worth mentioning). You could, if the mood took you, sport a plastic see-through one, which would stop all those questions about what you wear underneath. Or you could try a camouflaged one, or something denim.

Looking both ways, he produces from a locked storeroom the most incendiarily offensive garment ever made. I can hardly believe my eyes. Oh, the horror: a kilt made entirely out of Union Jacks. If this doesn't sting Edinburgh into a home rule frenzy then nothing will.

I put the ghastly thing on and stand underneath the castle on the Esplanade. After the third American wifey has asked to have her photograph taken with me, I'm on the edge of losing my nerve completely. Then a numpty, walkie-talkie jobsworth in a parka sidles up and tells me to shove off.

"It's not me, you understand, sir; they're watching you." He nods ominously towards the granite crenellations. "You'll have to go."

It seems that there are some things that even here, at the heart of the city of reason, protected by a castle, are simply too dangerous – that overrule freedom of expression, freedom of the press and even freedom of tourism – and a Union Jack kilt is one of them.

So back to the election trail with Dr Ian McKee, the hopeful SNP candidate for Edinburgh Central, a nice, well-meaning general practitioner and a political virgin on his first election campaign. You can tell he's a beginner because he canvasses council flats from the bottom up. Old hands know to take the lift to the top and walk down. But there's something else odd about him. I can't place his accent. Then it drops. He sounds just like me! He's that rarest of mythological beasts, an English Scots Nat.

We traipse up the council flats behind the hole in the ground that would be a parliament, retrieving the leaflets left by the Scottish Socialist party from letter boxes. ("Decriminalise cannabis now" – a pipe dream, pal.) I point out kindly that this is quite possibly illegal. He grins. It's obviously the most radical political act of his decent life.

These blocks are the oldest municipal housing in Edinburgh and, although they are stark, staring hideous, they're also neat and clean and the lift smells of lift. Even though Edinburgh has done its damnedest to become a truly cool, contemporary, Channel 4 city, its Midlothian heart is not in it. It can't work up an indecent head of urban decay. It may have turned Leith into Godalming-on-the-Water, and the city fathers may have dotted the place with the most horrendously brutal civic architecture this side of the

Warsaw Pact; but this only highlights the stunning beauty of the place.

True, getting *Trainspotting* as a tourist brochure was a stroke of luck. The Japanese tours can go on Irvine Welsh heritage walks and watch the junkies queue up for their traditional Highland methadone at the quaint chemist on the Royal Mile – which is positioned, like a symbolic postscript, opposite the Museum of Childhood. Yet Edinburgh is still the most perfect city in Europe. Bracketed by braid hills and the Salisbury crags, the waters of Leith and the great volcanic fist of the castle rock, it looks like nothing so much as a city designed by enlightened angels. Naturally, and by tradition, this means it's always been loathed and despised by the rest of Scotland.

Edinburgh is the least Scots place. That Morningside accent sounds like a Swede trying to talk Surrey. The vestigial snobbery and probity of Edinburgh have always made it look enviously south rather than patriotically north. With its Hanoverian street names and its lawyers, judges and civil servants it is also the least likely place in which to find hot nationalism.

That was always Glasgow's department, with its antediluvian unionism, its poly-Trot lecturers and its internecine tribalism. But a friend in Glasgow says they're even less interested in the elections there. "Oh we're forty miles away; it's Edinburgh's thing. All your smiley, interlocking circles of power where they manicure their nails on each other's backs."

Indeed, Edinburgh is a small incestuous town, where everyone who matters swings together like the pleats of a kilt, presenting a uniform pattern. If you're stitched into the warp and the weft you can see this as an efficient network of reasonable folk who get things done. If you're out of it, you probably think it's a self-perpetuating oligarchy of self-righteous social climbers.

Try as I might to be even-handed about Edinburgh, I can't. My commitment to this place doesn't stop with a bawling entrance at the Royal Infirmary. This is where I come from. This place is home, if anywhere is, and I love it with a deep passion. If, against all the best advice, this country and this city do take the high road to independence, then I'll be first in the queue for my passport, because, right or wrong, this is who I am. I'll never be anything else.

But I'm also a defensive Scot in the sense of being an expat. I walk around like a tourist, aware that there are only a handful of Edinburgh numbers in my phone book. I'm neither the warp nor the weft. It may be home, but like the 90 million Scots of the diaspora, to me home is somewhere you leave.

Looking at a supplement on Great Scots, which this newspaper recently produced for its Scottish readers, it was sobering to count quite how many of them took the one-way ticket to greatness – people who defined themselves not principally as Scottish but by their talents as engineers, poets, soldiers and artists. The list is impressive, perhaps unmatchable. But the fact that it needed to be made at all is indicative of the schizophrenia that blights Scotland: the sense that we think we're superior but feel inferior. It's no coincidence that Jekyll and Hyde was from Edinburgh.

I remember a man from my childhood who, if you mentioned anything, would suck his teeth and say: "Aye, we invented that. Rubber tyres? Television? Modern economics? The rifle? Aye, we invented that. Dental floss, daytime television, pop tarts, coloured tile grout, puking – aye, we invented that . . ." The whole world owed a debt not just to Scotland but to him personally, and he was waiting in his lambswool tartan slippers (aye, we invented those) for it to start paying up. Even at an innocently young age, I recognised that he was very, very Scots.

At the front parlour end of the Royal Mile – the other end from the hole that would be parliament – is the new Museum of Scotland. The blood runs cold at the very mention of a new museum in Scotland. Museums are Scotland's cancer; Edinburgh has terminal museum-tumours. There are museums for absolutely everything – whisky, tartan, sharp metal things, ghosts, the police, weaving, murder. There are probably museums devoted to spitting, facial hair, cobblestones, belly-button fluff and giving directions in a very slow voice. Scotland doesn't have a history; it has tea towels.

But the Museum of Scotland is something of a revelation. For a start, the building is the first thing erected in this city since the war that can hold its pediment up next to its classical surroundings. Inside is even more of a revelation. I know what a Scots museum looks like. It's a lot of rickety mannequins with dusty plaids and stick-on red hair looking like they're facing terminal constipation. A tinny tape of Bill Paterson usually intones "but then something far worse happened . . ." The new Museum of Scotland is not a Scots museum. True, the bloody treaty of Arbroath is graffitied on the wall as part of the fallout from *Braveheart*. This treaty, with its passing mention of freedom, has become Scotland's mission statement. But I don't see a single kilt and there are no quaichs down the ages. It's a very un-Scottish view of Scottish history.

The exhibition starts at the beginning, right at the very beginning with the oldest thing in the world: a 3-million-year-old rock. It's Scots. (Ancient geology is rather the coming thing; beside the absent parliament there is a very transient Blairish dome tent-thing that's going to be a museum of geology. The poster outside strangely fails to mention the treaty of Arbroath. But it does, with vaunting hubris, claim Scotland is the father of geology. Rocks? Aye, we invented them – and gravel and wee stains and dirt.)

Back in the Museum of Scotland, the top floor is given over to an exhibition of things that people have donated to represent the future. Alex Salmond, with the innate cunning and subtlety that makes you want to entrust your future to him, has given a picture of Mel Gibson. Tony Blair has donated his electric guitar – at least, while it's in a glass case, he can't play it – and Sean Connery, this year's prince over the water, offers a milk bottle to remind us of his humble origins. Within it is a message. Of course, it's the treaty of Arbroath. There's also a smart-looking restaurant where the warp and weft of Edinburgh's pleats hang together in the evening. It has a great illuminated view of the castle. But they switch this off at 12. "You'll have had your view then, sir."

A lot of the city is romantically lit at night, but the one building that conspicuously doesn't glow with civic pride is the Greyfriars church, where a far more important document than the complaint of Arbroath was signed. It was here that Montrose and Argyll signed the covenant, which did more to Scotland than any other piece of paper. But Hollywood hasn't made a film of that yet. The museum's press officer tells me that a lot of people consider this place to be far more important and symbolic building for Scotland than the parliament, and he's probably right. Given the choice, Scots wants to know where they've come from rather than where they're going. Why, I ask, is everyone so uninterested in the election? "Oh well, they want a parliament, they just don't terribly care who's in it."

Jamie Byng, the young, enviably talented and well-connected boss of Canongate Publishers, tells me: "We wanted the parliament because we didn't want to be taken for granted. But the politics of devolution are very introverted, inward-looking. This is a city that has international connections and expectations; it's looking out to the rest of the world."

Perhaps there's a truth there. For all the Scots Nats' touchy-feely expressions of good neighbourliness with England as equal but separate bestest mates, they make independence sound like Richard Briers and Felicity Kendal opting out for the knit-your-own *Good Life*. However you spin it, devolution and possibly independence is cutting yourself off, not joining in.

With her exclamatory trip round the world's bonsai countries, perhaps Margo MacDonald is right that the grubby little Balkan war is going to be the decisive issue in this election, but not in the way she means. It's an example of what unchecked small-time introverted nationalism leads to; and the image of the Scots as Serbs in skirts is just too plausible to be funny.

What you vote for in elections is not more freedom and more democracy but more politicians. It's Scotland's politicians that have sold the Scots short, sold them cheap and sold them out. It's the politicians who led the nation agin the world in romantic lost causes. Aye, we invented them, too.

The Wilmslow boys

The Wilmslow boys

Cheshire, October 1999

Welcome to Cheshire. More precisely, that golden triangle of Cheshire that stretches between Prestbury, Alderley Edge and Wilmslow, the suburban trim'n'tanned aspirational nirvana that is the Virginia Water of the north. We must assume a dozen weddings over a weekend in Cheshire. Weddings are a bit of a local obsession. While national marriage figures drop, in Cheshire weddings are booming; you can almost hail an antique white Roller with ribbons in the street. A wedding costs a great deal of money, so that's a good thing, and your neighbours and friends can see every penny of it spent. Weddings are uncomplicated, romance with sex and drink, and there are photographers. Where would Cheshire be without photographers to prove that it really existed, and mantel shelves and occasional tables that bear testament to what a good time your life is?

But more than all that, weddings are symbolic of new beginnings and a bright future. They are hope over history. And if Cheshire believes in anything apart from discount cards, it believes in hope for the future. Everyone is here through choice because they've broken away from history, escaped class predestination, proved the headmaster's assessment wrong, got on and got out. Cheshire is the arranged marriage of cash and cachet. A true love match.

It's easy to mock Cheshire, but then that's hardly a reason not to. Cheshire is mock everything: mock gentility, mock Tudor Georgian, mock family, mock style, mock casual and mock happiness. Cheshire thumbs its nose job at mockery. More Ferraris call this twisty lane, 30mph place home than anywhere else in Britain. There's more champagne sprayed over Alderley Edge than anywhere else in Britain. There are more millionaires to the square mile here than anywhere else in Britain. And every garden gnome, carriage lamp and novelty door chime here has been earned, if not entirely paid for. This is *Hello!* country, Posh-and-Becksville, Cheshire twinned with *Dynasty*, a *faux* Florida with rain.

Earlier this year the curate of St Bartholomew's Church in Wilmslow got himself transubstantiated into the national news with a shot to his congregation in the parish magazine. They were, he said, a godless, pagan lot, more interested in money and snobbery and motors than saving their souls. Admittedly, saving isn't a particularly notable habit. If you could save a soul with a 10% cash deposit or put it on the credit card, then they'd all be on the waiting list for a pair. One for running about in, the other for showing off with a personalised number plate.

Bearing the curate's reprimand in mind, I didn't come to Cheshire empty-handed. I brought it a present, something it needed. I brought it Jeremy Clarkson. For a place where the showroom is a cathedral of pilgrimage and the double garage a family chapel, Clarkson is the Second Coming. People don't mob him so much as genuflect to him, and they speak with awe and in tongues: "Five valves, ABS, GTi with spoilers, eh, eh?" "Mazda, Toyota, Vauxhall, Honda, Lada, amen." They sway after him in ecstatic Hare Krishna lines, chanting: "Jezza, Jezza, Jezza, Jezza, Clarkson, Clarkson, Jezza, Jezza." Here the car is an outward and visible sign of an inward and invisible insecurity, a yearning of the soul. It fills the garage of spiritual emptiness. When you've got the back-pocket folding, when you've made it out of the smoke, how do you let people know? You buy a car that is three times your bank manager's annual wage.

Cheshire is surprised and not a little hurt by the ridicule it attracts from us in the media. What have they done to deserve the sneers, I'm asked defensively by the Stuart Hall (that's his title up here: *the* Stuart Hall). They're not bad people. All they've done is follow the instructions on the box and in the glossy magazines. Got on and consumed, cut their lawns, learnt to ski. If Clarkson is God up here, then Hall is Elijah, Cheshire's longest-serving celebrity, a man whose best friends' party list is the Cheshire phone book.

We are sitting on a blustery patio with a pair of men whose nicknames end with O. It might be Chico and Harpo. They've been playing doubles with Jeremy. Actually they've spent an hour calling each other poufs and double-faulting. In the middle distance, cows set their noses to the north and watch the battleship-grey clouds roll in. This part of the country gets more rain than anywhere else in Britain. It trundles in from the Atlantic, remorselessly pissing on Cheshire's fireworks.

Cheshire is an unremarkable county. Set on the Welsh Marches beneath Lancashire, its name comes from the Latin for Place of the Legions. After the Romans left, it reluctantly became part of the Saxon kingdom of Mercia, then foolishly resisted the Normans. There is a myth that King Harold survived Hastings to live as a hermit in Chester. The county was made palatinate under the Earl of Chester, a title that now belongs to the Prince of Wales. During the civil war, Cheshire was so equally divided between royalists and parliamentarians that they tried to declare a draw, but in the end the King got Chester and Cromwell got Nantwich. The industrial revolution that transformed the northwest largely bypassed Cheshire. Though bisected by canals and railways, it remained a lump of clay-clagged farmland. It produced the meat and milk for its industrial neighbours. If you wanted a county to represent the serviceable weft and web of our island story, you couldn't do better than Cheshire. Its two staples were cheese and salt: hard cheese and the salt of the earth.

In *arriviste* Cheshire terms, Prestbury is salt in a silver cruet. It's old money. It probably means you've got Paul Simon on the Range Rover CD instead of the Corrs. Prestbury is a pretty enough village, with cobbles and half-timbers and an impressive Norman church, but that's just a front. Actually, it is the seething pit of hell. If hell is other people, then the other people's hell is Prestbury people. I've always known that the devil's most preciously loved vice would be smugness, and Prestbury is smug central. It wrote the book of smug revelations and you can buy it in the church. Called simply *Prestbury: A Little Piece of Olde England Still Survives*, it goes: "So Prestbury retains something that is really England. It is quiet even when the day-trippers are here and there seem to be more visitors than ever wandering the village main street gazing in the olde chocolate box windows. And some always say they wish they could live here. It's something to do with the village friendly feeling. That's why Prestbury folk are not too proud to pick up sweet papers or beer cans. A sort of home pride."

Home pride, pass the Uzi. You get the drift. The barely unspoken "You filthy oiks with your sweet papers and beer cans. You can press your crusty noses up against our fake bottle-glass windows, but join us and live here? In your dreams." This is a place where the council won't put up street lights because they're common, and won't allow an Indian or Chinese restaurant because they lower the tone. More specifically, un-white people hanging around the place being industrious would be a style solecism wrecking the mellow colour scheme. Brown people are immigrants. Immigrants live in poor areas. Prestbury is not a poor area. *Ipso facto*, it can't have brown people or street lights. The presence of an Indian restaurant would qualify the prestige of their his-and-hers BMWs and, you know, not one person in this self-satisfied corner of olde England would see that as racist. They'd point out that they don't allow McDonald's here either, or young offenders' hostels or naked morris dancing.

There is a pub that used to be named the Saracen's Head but has a sign calling itself the Black Boy. This is the place where, on election night, according to the local grave-digger (a man who is sadly under-utilised), the friendly folk huddled so terrified you would have thought the Sandinistas were massing in the hills. No group in England is as appalled by the threat of hands-on socialism. Most of them have never experienced it as grown-ups. As it turns out, they needn't have worried.

I sat on a bench in this little bit of olde Newe England devoutly wishing I was an artillery spotter, and considered what a vile, deluded mockery Prestbury is. A dormitory fantasy of a place, constructed out of holiday Aga and blow-job novels and bucolic daytime soap operas, a childish Edwardian Shangri-La with a greengrocer that only sells flowers, and no peasants or dung. A furtive local sidled up to me holding a pad and a ballpoint. "You're with Jeremy Clarkson, aren't you? We heard he was here. I just wondered if he'd . . . you know, for the wife." Sure, he's just hanging out in the long grass round the back of the graveyard. He's a predatory homosexual, you know.

On to Alderley Edge. In the minute pecking order of Cheshire, if

Prestbury is old money, blazers and tweeds, caps and huskies, then Alderley Edge is new money and more money. It's Dolce e Gabbana sandals, Prada rucksacks and suede-peaked baseball caps. Alderley Edge is where Manchester footballers bring their tin-opener-voiced, pony-mad, disco-found brides to set up home. It's where loveable, long-serving characters from *Coronation Street* settle. The real Rovers Return is a Mexican cappuccino bar. This is the funky, sociable, envious home to fast-food millionaires, mobile-phone chain-store owners, carpet layers who won a corporation contract, brickies who got smart and got into plant hire, out-of-town do-it-yourself merchants, and above all the franchise – that little fallout of corporate success that is a licence to print money. They franchise anything from crispy chicken dipping sauce to Punjabi terracotta tiles, to plastic bolt-on things, to sports cars. Alderley Edge is the place for the middleman's cut, for geezers who saw a gap and went for it, made a space, used their heads. It is an ugly place. It has a railway station that's two sizes too big, an inheritance from the last century, when Manchester's cloth merchants and mill owners moved out here and built the chalets and laurelled mansions that are now the most sought-after properties. The low-slung High Street is a collection of car show-rooms, estate agents and newsagents sandwiched by cafés that have franchised the names of more exotic locations: Cuba and Capri, Sorrento and St Tropez, all selling the same Bedfordshire battery bird in a bap.

On the street, furious women in sunglasses slam the doors of all-terrain runarounds and march into little boutiques that sell what used to be called "notions": comedy alarm clocks, executive desk ornaments and pot-pourri. The first thing you notice about people here is their colour, a hue unknown anywhere else in the world. The colour of fired-earth kitchen tiles, applied with all the care of a French polish. Everything else about them is gleaming white, snowy jeans and T-shirts a size too small. And off-white hair cut either as variations on *Charlie's Angels* or *Ally McBeal* that make their owners continually nod and toss like a mare bothered by flies. White and orange are the county colours, representing biological cleanliness and healthy vitamin C.

In a newsagent we buy a copy of *Cheshire Life*, a glossy magazine that yearns for a question mark after the title. It's thick with ads for cars, bridal photographers, fitted kitchens and private schools, and looks like a spoof of a 1980s *Tatler*. Hundreds of social pages with passport photos of identical radioactively glowing women in white hair worn as a loose chignon for the evenings, holding flutes of champagne, their grinning husbands in designer dinner jackets with that dash of stand-out-from-the-crowd personality that only a brocade waistcoat and Day-Glo bow tie give you. My favourite article was on Dee Cattom, a sad but cosmetically smiling lady who says, "I'm 45 going on 25," in the mistaken belief that it's clever and amusing. Dee was, as she readily admits, so desperate to join Cheshire society ("beautiful county, beautiful people") that she had herself built in Cheshire's image. "I've had a brow lift, nose job, tummy tuck, jaw re-set and gone from 32AA to 34DD." She's also been fitted with a yellow Lotus Elise number plate, S111 EXY, which at £27,000 cost only the skin off her nose more than the plastic surgery. "I don't regret one minute under the surgeon's knife. Now I really feel as if I belong here in Cheshire." There's really no answer to that.

Attracted by some boggling particulars in an estate agent's window, we go in. "Oh, would you mind?" says a girl with a mansard bra extension and no room for development, holding paper and pen. "It's for my brother. He's mad about *Top Gear*." As Jeremy scrawls, I whisper: "He's gay." We spend a good hour in the shop. If you're thinking of buying property in Alderley Edge, I do recommend you consider an estate agent: there's hours of hysterical fun to be had. We began by trying not to be London style snobs, to keep our metropolitan insouciance zipped, but the sheer volume, the boundless gaudy vulgarity of it, overwhelms you, and you just have to howl with derision. Here is a short compendium of things you need to have to get on in Cheshire:

A bar. It can be of the traditional Dean Martin sort with maroon buttoned leatherette, matching stools and illuminated shelves. Or it could be the rustic halved barrels with horse brasses, pumps and a stuffed fish. Or, discreetly, a globe that lights up and doubles as a cocktail cabinet. You must have a music system prominently displayed, with speakers like dwarfs' coffins, and you must have curtains made out of Liberace's knickers, incorporating enough two-tone dressing-gown cord to fly a kite. You have to have a freestanding kitchen island, terracotta tiles and lynched utensils hanging at concussion height, a his-and-hers bathroom vanity unit with infinitely reflecting mirrors. You'll need an inglenook display space for porcelain dolls, and a Wimpole Street occasional table of magazines. Ceilings are low and everything that could be described as a feature must be exposed (that goes for your wife too). What you won't need, and I never saw one, is a bookcase, but you will need somewhere for your video collection. Stylistically, feel free – in fact, indulge yourself. Old El Paso is a popular theme at the moment, as is your chintz Mrs Tiggywinkle look. As for pictures, use them sparingly. But do mix traditional prints of horses, churches, etc, with modern stuff bought in the open air when drunk on holiday. Of course, you can never have enough wedding photographs.

The one style that is never going to catch on in Cheshire is minimalism. It may be the fashion at the moment and Cheshire may well watch fashion like a Northumbrian monk watches for Vikings, but minimalism just doesn't compute. The idea that less is more only applies to skirt lengths. No, up here your home is an Egyptian mausoleum of all the kit you need for the afterlife.

Alderley Edge *is* the afterlife: life after Lancashire. House prices are fantastically high for the northwest. I asked the estate agent what most people were looking for. "Oh, somewhere to prominently display a skip. It's vital that you can be seen throwing away the virtually new Smallbone fitted kitchen while putting in the new Smallbone fitted kitchen."

Driving up millionaires' row, with its Edwardian Lutyens knock-offs and its 1970s haciendas and a you-can't-go-wrong Jacobean, you can see that no opportunity to shout, "Oi, Mr and Mrs Lucky Bastard have arrived" is overlooked. Gardens are pub-bright with lots of geraniums and red-hot pokers and little spiky palm trees. The cars never see the inside of a garage, because you wouldn't notice them there and because the garage is full of archaic games and pinball machines. There are nonchalantly dropped mountain bikes, swimming pool gazebos, arc lights for tennis courts and the *de rigueur* electric gates, as if no burglar would have the nous to push his way through six inches of privet. Attached to every single home is a conservatory – there must be a couple of dozen conservatory millionaires up here. Ornate ironwork and glass lean-tos are mandatory, and you can see why: you can see through. They are the perfect Alderley Edge room for people who want to live in glass houses and throw parties.

Jeremy turns the Cadillac out of town and we drive in silence. "You know," he says after a while, "it's worrying. Some of that stuff looked a bit like the stuff I've got at home – only a bit, mind." Yes, that is worrying.

In the grey, sodden country that surrounds Prestbury and Alderley Edge, crossed with motorways, intersections and roundabouts with bright geraniums and spiky stunted palms, along with the essentials of out-of-town shopping centres, automatic-louvred security blind warehouses and more car showrooms with grubby flags, we come across gated private estates like Dark Age forts in a dangerous land. They have classy feudal names like conference centres. These arching culs-de-sac are an idea imported from America, but here in Cheshire who do they think they're trying to keep out? The fences and barriers, speed bumps and empty watchmen's huts are the trappings of wealth, the buffers of avarice. What they're actually keeping out is the gnawing doubt that all the things you've dreamt of don't really amount to very much. Hideous little family homes with gratuitous Victorian and Georgian detailing, all hung about with baskets of geraniums and carriage lamps. Outside the gates, landfill landscaping sports first-growth scrub and weedy saplings. "Cover for child molesters and peeping toms," notes Jeremy. If Prestbury is olde hell, then these drizzle-washed private internment camps are a sort of new purgatory, and proof of the old warning that you should be careful what you pray for – you might get it.

Now the big one: Wilmslow. I had trouble getting Jeremy into Wilmslow after dark. "I don't want to go," he whined. You've got to, it's important. "You go – they'll only point at me and tell me about their Porsches and repeat what I said about their Cherokees." And they did. Drunkenly they queued up to talk torque. Girls asked him to autograph their thighs in mascara: "Can you put, 'To a 911 driver with love'?"

Most country towns the size of Wilmslow are no-go areas after sunset. Their pedestrian precincts and American-style bars are given over to gangs of vomitously aggressive youths and shrieking Greek choruses of underage girls, and prowling police cars, but not Wilmslow. This is the centre of Cheshire nightlife and it attracts partying folk from as far as Blackpool. It rather resembles Miami Beach as imagined by Catherine Cookson. We'd been told of a couple of bars to try. "That's great for the naughty forties and randy birds," said a squeaky-voiced bellhop. "Anyone can pull there."

Well, Jeremy could. Jeremy pulled like Geoff Capes, like the old man of the sea. The bars were packed with people ranging from 16 to 60, all of them 25. And the first thing I noticed was how thin everyone was, how toned and worked out, the women all expensively dressed in Prada and Voyage, last season's Dolce e Gabbana and Ghost. Not Kookaï versions, the real thing. And they all had white hair. It wouldn't do to get fat and greasy in Wilmslow: you'd be letting your car down. The men were gelled dark yobs on best behaviour, leery geezers uniformly dressed in untucked Gap casual, the tasteful style choice for blokes who don't know the first thing about anything. And they all looked beautiful. I don't think I've been in a room in this country with more active pheromones.

A pretty girl with hair you could have eaten your dinner off spoke to me while she waited in line for Jeremy. "It's my birthday today, I'm having a bit of a party. I got given this." She flashed a vast ring. Oh, lovely, it's very, em, discreet. She beamed. "Do you really think so?" Discreet is the most difficult look to manage in Cheshire. "What's he like?" she asked, nodding at Mr 0–60. "Gay, I'm afraid." Altogether the fashion was very Harvey-Nicks-last-week, but the music and the atmosphere were 15 years old, completely 1980s, Radio 2 favourites blasting away. The feeling in the bars was of splashing out, going for it, live today, live better tomorrow. The 1980s was Wilmslow's spiritual decade, and you might think that this was the last stronghold of über-Toryism, Thatcher's children hold out as the Saxons did against the Blairish Normans. And though I'm sure they'd all vote Tory to a man if they voted at all, would hang and flog everything that broke the laws of property, actually this place and these people are the legacy of, and indeed the great success story of, socialism.

It was the Labour movement, the unions, the co-operative societies who crusaded to educate and empower and, most importantly, motivate the labouring classes that made Cheshire possible. Cheshire is what happens if you let people get on. From the outside it may look like a risible chimpanzees' tea party aping Notting Hill or Godalming or Los Angeles, but it's more than that. It's the very end of the industrial revolution. This rocking bar in tasteless, crass Wilmslow is the graduation party of the old working class. Their children won't be seen dead here, this is just a pit stop. Their kids with their private educations, their flattened accents, their university places and their gap-year travels will move on, calm down, button up, buy a Honda and become invisible among the rest of us in the shifting middle classes.

It had to be done. "It's got to be done," said Jeremy. I suppose so, but have you ever done it before? "No." No, neither have I. Do you think it will be embarrassing? "Undoubtedly."

Golf. We want to play golf. We sauntered – no, more sidled – into the club shop, and said we wanted the kit. Head to foot, the full Monty, as gaudy as you can make it. We want to be Men in Pringle. By the time we got into the buggy with our bags strapped to the back and our two-tone shoes going tippety tappety, we were hysterical. Dangerous, life-threatening laughter. Jeremy was laughing because we were funny. I was laughing because we were funny, and because when he'd gone to the changing room the man behind the till said: "I hear he's gay."

Golf is just as stupid as it looks, but harder. We got lapped three times on the first lawn. We swung our bats in the prescribed manner, but frankly it would have been quicker if we'd kicked the bloody thing. So we retired to the driving range and spent a frustrating hour ploughing. We eventually got the hang of it and went back to play a couple of flags at a tenner each. When you get into the swing, golf's more like housework than a game. You're forever brushing and smoothing and putting things back. It's a lot like Hoovering, and like all housework it's never, ever, finished.

The clouds parted and the late-night sun washed everything, making the countryside if not actually breathtaking, then a bit panting. "So what do you think?" asked Jeremy, after a hole where we were only nine above par and I'd hit a very sweet fifth drive. You mean the golf? "Yes, what do you think about the golf?" The golf – well, it's rather embarrassing. But you know, I quite like it. There's a sense of achievement, like dusting the dado rail. "You know, I rather like it as well. I could take this up, but then I'd have to pretend to the wife that I had a mistress to get away at the weekend, and hide my kit in a friend's house."

This is it, then. This is Cheshire's revenge. We've caught a dose of golf. "You're not going to write that we enjoyed it, are you?" Jeremy grabbed my pully. Oh, I think I've got to. "Christ, that's torn it. That's the end. I'd rather be thought a pouf than a golfer." Ah, Jeremy, I've been meaning to talk to you about that.

Look who's stalking

Look who's stalking

The British Army's sniping course, Wales, January 2000

You have no idea how difficult it is to give the army a gun. The guard at the gates of Derring Lines, the headquarters of the infantry school in Wales, approaches my car gingerly, armed with a cocked bathroom mirror on a stick. "Open the bonnet and boot please, sir." "There's a gun in the boot," I tell him helpfully. The reality of actually finding something in a visiting boot seems to confuse him. "You'd better take that to the guardroom, then." The gun comes as an unwelcome novelty in the guardroom too. "A gun, eh, what are we going to do with that?" I swallow the desire to reply: "You're the army: if you don't know, then the independent nation state's in deep trouble." Nobody wants my gun. Finally they say I can put it in the armoury, where my poor 12-bore gets a terrible dose of barrel envy. Stacked in decks in racks are hundreds of rifles and machine guns. I hand over a bag of cartridges. The storeman recoils in horror, as if I were offering a regiment's worth of CND badges. "No, no, this is an armoury. You never keep ammunition with guns, didn't you know that?" I feel even more of a pillock than I did just standing here in plus fours and woolly socks.

Decimating waves of partridge is as close as I've come to military life and, as I think with most men, there is a grain of regret that I never followed the flag – only a grain, mind – which is easily assuaged by a blokeish fascination with killer kit and war films, but which draws the line at collecting hat badges or commando daggers. I have a nerdy love of military history, and I've never been able to walk past a window of toy soldiers without a second look, without indeed squinting Gulliverishly and wondering if I'd ever have fitted into the thin red line, behind the mealie-meal palisade at Rourke's Drift, waiting for the whistle on the firing step at Ypres, crouched in the bows of the wallowing landing craft, bucking the surf for Juno Beach. I'll never know. Like most British men, I am the first adult male in my family for 100 years never to have worn uniform.

I go off in search of the officers' mess. Captain Rupert Steptoe, the adjutant, is there to meet me, a man who is the blissful evocation of his name – soldiers generically call all officers Rupert. He's floppy-fringed, blond and pinkly handsome with slightly buck teeth; even in civvies you'd pick him out as an army officer at 500 yards in the rush hour.

His regiment is the Devon and Dorset, which sounds not so much a fighting force as a flower show. An army report once marked him as tall, blond and affable, a distinction that would be attractive in any civilian capacity, but in this camouflaged other world is deeply risible. He's nervous of journalists: "What I really hate is the way you go on about the ridiculous, old-fashioned stereotypes. It's not like that any more." He introduces me to Capt Rob Connolly of the King's Own Scottish Borderers, another movie-stock type, 6ft 6in in his gartered socks, a straight-backed, red-haired, steady-the-ranks paragon.

I am here to observe the army's sniping course, and Rupert and Rob are here to answer my questions. Between them they compete for the world-title affability contest. The army has only recently decided to reinstate snipers and now runs this course twice a year for 19 hand-picked mature NCOs (noncommissioned officers) who, in turn, will go back to their companies and pass on the skill. It also takes a number of foreign students for cash. At the moment they're training an Italian Navy Seal who takes a lot of reverse-gears stick, a Dutchman whose liberal government takes a dim view of sniping, two Singapore policemen and a Gibraltarian who has already flunked out because he's homesick (though how anyone could be homesick for Gibraltar is beyond me).

There is something very un-British about sniping. Lurking in bushes taking pot shots is what They do to Us; we stand in lines volley-firing to the sound of brass bands, then go in with a bayonet. Since the cold war, the ethos of modern, rich, industrial bullying has been technological – get the computer and laser to do the dirty work, fire and forget. Soldiers are seated middle managers in headphones. The Americans have reached the point where they can't afford to risk a single life or piece of kit – apart from anything else, it all costs so much. Money is the grunts' best body armour.

But it's a truism that generals invariably re-fight the last war, and the assumption that the next one would be a Dolby Imax version of the second big one – that we would tip up in Belgium again and have a mega November 5 – has been proved unlikely over the past 20 years. They still talk about theatres and battlefields as if there's a United Nations consensus. But the paradigm has been made redundant by the Gulf, the Falklands, Somalia, Bosnia, Kosovo, East Timor and Sierra Leone. They proved that the high-tech, big-bucks battle is a tank in a china shop. The stream of Serb military vehicles that left Kosovo proved just how ineffective our technology is, and Sarajevo showed how devastating the amateur sniper could be. Wars have been dragged back from the computer screen into the modern rubble.

Before Rob marches me up the hill to see them, I have to play a courtesy call on the CO, a man who manages the seemingly impossible feat of being both loquacious and taciturn, simultaneously producing gusts of incomprehensible chaff. He's not alone in this. I barely understand an entire sentence anyone in authority says. Military language is cancerous with TLAs: three-letter abbreviations, like PUP for pick-up point, DOP for drop-off point.

They say this makes orders clear and concise; on paper they're an ugly Morse code that would make Wilfred Owen sound like the ingredients of field rations – and of course, out loud, DOP has the same number of syllables as drop-off-point. What it really is is an exclusive gang slang, invented 3,000 years ago when the first Israeli Army said shibboleth to differentiate them from the Philistines (David with his slingshot was the first recorded sniper). The CO (commanding officer), who, by the way, is not the same as the OC (officer commanding), tells me there's a sergeant in the Irish Army on the course, and he manages to drop one phrase that resonates: snipers are force multipliers. "He told you about the Irishman?" says Rob. "I didn't think you were meant to know that."

Rob and I hop into a Land Rover and head for the hills. Unfortunately for military panache, owing to defence cuts, all the army's butch kit is driven by Welsh civilian taxi drivers, so the effect of leaping into a revving combat vehicle and shouting "Go, go, go!" is rather spoilt when a retired long-distance lorry driver from Aberystwyth replies: "Where to, chief?"

Few places on earth can have been more roundly and heartfeltly cursed than the Beacons of Brecon. This is unquestionably the most loathed spot in Britain. To the civilian eye they may have a rugged beauty, high moorland creased with burns, and soggy like a massive organic sponge. The lung-exploding hills rumple into the distance; it's as close as the Welsh get to wilderness, and that's close enough. But to the military perception the Beacons are a monotone vision of hell. While the boys with big-barrelled toys bang on about Salisbury Plain, the infantry slog over Brecon and hate it with terse tommy's loathing. As Rob sweetly puts it, "Because we can't re-create the real fear and danger of a battle, we push them with cold, wet exhaustion and pain as far as they can go, and then a bit, so they can see what they're made of, see whose head drops. It's not about making them fail, it's about making them exceed."

Across the moor, fierce, drenching squalls and low-level Hawk trainers chase napkin-size patches of sunlight. Brecon has its very own military microclimate, as depressing as a February eisteddfod. "There they are." Rob points to a stand of regulation Forestry Commission pine trees. There's nothing to see, no sign of life. Inside the dark, pillared wood, precious little light seeps, there's only the noise of the wood and the crunch of pine needles underfoot.

Then in the gloaming I can just make out a series of variegated camouflage sheets, the size of lonely single beds, strung between the trunks about 2ft off the ground. It could be a Turner Prize installation. Underneath each, in shallow scrapes, lies a sleeping sniper. They've been here for a week. Beside each *faux* grave is a bergen, a rucksack the size of a chest of drawers; in it is a soldier's life, an entire outdoor activity caravan on your back, a knee-buckling, spine-crushing dead weight; in war as in civilian life, the ergonomics of miniaturisation and technology have actually increased the amount of stuff. Soldiers used to have knapsacks; now they have Imelda Marcos's winter wardrobe.

A sentry, rifle held low, slowly and silently pads guard. Rob tugs at the nearest bergen. "This is what they wear." He pulls out a

damp ghillie suit, the camouflage all snipers tailor-make for themselves. It's a waistcoat garlanded with strips of hessian that have
been frayed, daubed with paint and Greek restaurant nylon
foliage. There's a hat that might belong to an aggressive morris
dancer. I put them on over my fatigues; Rob hands me a compact
with three shades of earthy face paint: "It's cream, not make-up."
Sweetie, it's make-up.

Being able to shoot straight is only part of what makes a sniper.
He must be able to deconstruct a map and reconstruct it on a
horizon, and read a landscape the way that you and I see a face,
and then he must be able to become part of that landscape, not a
figure moving over it but a wraith moving through it, never being
skylined, seeing cover the way that we see pedestrian crossings,
noting dead ground and lines of fire enfilade and defilade; and he
must look for other men like him stalking the earth – half the
training here is in hunting enemy snipers. Set a poacher to catch a
poacher. The ghillie suit breaks up a silhouette, the recognisable
configuration of line that is how we recognise a fellow human.
We're expert at picking each other out in confusing terrain over
great distances, it's important to us, we're sociable creatures.
Unless we're snipers. Recognition gets a sniper killed. Anyone can
curl up and cover themselves in leaves and hide, but a sniper must
see without being seen, he must constantly watch and be just as
constantly aware of his relationship to every tussock, branch and
gully. He must revert 10,000 years and think like a lone predator,
become pre-civilised in the service of civilisation.

And then there's judging distance. Rob pulls at another bag that
will be attached to the sniper by a long lanyard, the L96, soon to
be replaced by the L115, the sniper's rifle which fires a small-bore,
full-metal-jacket, high-velocity round-head shot at 600, 700, 800
yards. It wasn't what I was expecting.

Childishly, I wished for something sleek and menacing, something matt and high-tech. This is a disappointment, clunky and
heavy with a bolt action, a thick stock and cut-out pistol grip,
daubed in paint, like an amateur dramatic prop. I lie in the grass
and peer through the sights and suddenly everything looks quite
different. The delightfully named Schmitt and Bender sight simply
insists you see things quite differently. The cross hairs impose a sly

menace on the land, the small dots of calibration turn a life into an algebra problem; at 100 yards a 6ft man takes up two dots, adjust accordingly. Placed in a new theatre, a sniper begins by measuring things; the average door frame, 7ft in the UK; a brick, 4in; the width of a road, 9ft; a hedge, 4½ft, so he can judge distance. A 5% error is x feet at 200 yards. The scope has a huge 50% peripheral vision and starts at three magnifications; turn the bezel and it goes up to 11 magnifications. A button on the side clicks millimetre correction to the fall of shot. Allowing for wind and light, you shoot differently in full light from in shadow.

The sniper must consider all this in instant calculus. In the far distance, along the humping road, an army truck crawls up the horizon towards us. A terse order: "Take out the driver." The scope slides over the windscreen, the wipers are on. How far? 400, 350? The cross hairs skitter through the cab, searching. And there he is: a man in a cap, worn jauntily on the back of his head, late 50s, could be a grandfather, he hasn't shaved. He turns, sharing some joke with the man next to him, he laughs, he's missing a tooth, 300, hold a breath. The thread of life and death, vertical and horizontal, meet on his creased eye, hold a breath, squeeze . . . click. I stand up, skyline myself. The truck growls on. Without the telescope's frame, it's oddly loud and solid and prosaic. The driver doesn't look round as he passes. In the back is a group of Welsh fusiliers, and here's me, a ragged scarecrow creature from the swamp, an image from a schlock nightmare. They stare without interest or surprise.

Rob takes me to the nerve centre of sniper school. The concrete hut in a dip in the hills is like a cattle byre. Inside are half a dozen camp beds strewn with sleeping bags, around the walls jerry cans and heaps of kit. The windows are holes in the wall hung with sacking, there's nothing as nancy as glass in them. The door is a slightly lower window; at one end there's a tent like a proscenium stage, the set for *Journey's End*, perhaps. It glows with a warm light, a generator hums. There's a bank of radios, a heater, a gas ring bubbles happily.

Inside, arranged hugger-mugger on a selection of chairs and boxes, are the NCO instructors. This, then, is infantry *Top Gun*. The best of the best. Hard, hard men, eagle-eyed, stag-footed, stallion-muscled, Jack Russell-haired. The *crème de la crème* who rose to the top of the paras, the marines, the highland brigade and the SAS to come here and pass on spartan skill; these are the gods of war. Their motto isn't some fancy Latin or Norman French *bon mot* about steadfastness and glory – it's plain, single-syllable English: "One shot, one kill."

"The trick is getting a proper amalgamation out of the garlic and ginger," says a marine, using a plastic mug and a stick as a mortar and pestle. "Have you deseeded the chillies?" A fearsome highlander slices a chicken as easy as jerry neck. They're making a man-sized Thai curry with steamed rice. Nobody gets up as the officer enters, there's no saluting here: in the field a salute can send an officer to an early body bag. They don't even call him "sir", just "boss", and there's an easy, knockabout camaraderie.

Snipers are different. The normal rules don't apply. Their uniforms are a motley collection of personal taste, they're like the privileged prefects at the top of school, but, as Rob says, everybody knows where the line is and they don't step over it. And neither do I.

Officers are the snipers' target of choice, so nobody wears overt marks of rank. Can you tell who's an officer, I ask. "Oh, aye," says the chicken dicer, Staff Sergeant Marr of the Small Arms School Corps. Can you always tell his rank? "Aye, pretty much by his age." Could you tell an officer from, say, a Welsh or Scottish regiment? "Of course, they'd both speak with English accents." Marr is as instantly winning as a shampooed, playful Angus bull. He, along with another instructor, has just come second in the international sniping contest in Austria, beaten by one shot and twin German territorial policemen who nerdishly made their own ammunition. "They were more marksmen than snipers," he says, by way of explanation. "We missed an egg at 300 yards."

Staff Sgt Marr is the ultimate emergency exit; he's the man who'd get you out. He's also the best advertisement for never joining the army. "What I like is to make them really suffer. I love it when they cry for their mothers." As if this freezing bunker on this godforsaken heath, the 18-hour days, the crawling about in the mud and route marches weren't bad enough, he's brought his own weights with him. They lie about like the *Flying Scotsman*'s bogeys. I very badly want to be Staff Sgt Marr's friend; the alter-native is too horrid to contemplate.

If officers pass down their own arid three-letter language, then the non-commissioned ranks pass up the trench slang. Theirs is gutful, livid and visceral, almost Shakespearian. A sleeping bag is a maggot, sleeping is gonking, smelling is mingeing, food is scoff, cake and arse is a mess, a cock-up; sentry duty is a stag, shimfing is moaning – there's a lot of shimfing. To show faith is to be there, a young recruit is a crow, and only the marines yomp, the infantry tabs (technical advance to battle). If you're asked how you want your brew, you say nato – that's standard issue: milk, two sugars. My favourite is gucci as an adjective, as in they're gucci boots, or he's got a really gucci knife. Gucci is good kit, and kit is an obsession. The men are perfunctorily complimentary about army issue but then buy their own boots, sleeping bags, down waist-coats, Gore-Tex socks and cookers. When you're out there in the wet and cold, a scintilla of extra comfort is a prize beyond medals. A radio operator from the Green Jackets says he reckons he's spent over £2,000 on extra stuff, his own money, just to look after you.

As a civilian it's impossible to be among these men without add-ing your own patina of envious Boy's Own romance, without seeing them as latter-day Pistols, Bardolphs and Poins, without imagining these earthbound, bantering tough men waiting round camp fires at Agincourt or Plassey, on the Heights of Abraham, at Ladysmith or Nijmegen, spelling out the dusty battle-honour names that exist not in topography or time but high up in church naves. It's impossible not to see marble memorials and bronze statues or hear snippets of Rattigan dialogue and catch the shadow of varnished imperial canvases and grainy film. But the soldiers reject any fantasising of their jobs; however I try to wheedle them into con-sidering bravery or fear, heritage, pride, morality or doubt, so they just as remorselessly avoid it, replying only in the most under-stated terms about their vocation. And this makes them more heroic. They've pared their lives down to a thin obstacle course of problem-solution-action, problem-solution-action. In the small, professional peacetime army, training in courses like this is endless – they apply, they endure, they pass and move on.

A single failure can finish a career. The NCOs will go to extreme lengths to attain the boy-scout sharpshooter badge that proclaims the elite snipers. They struggle on with weeping sores, raw blisters, temperatures and twisted ankles. Lying in the earth out there is a paratrooper whose wife is about to undergo surgery for cancer. He's been offered honourable compassionate leave, but he's here, he'll swallow the personal anguish and finish the course. All failure, however undeserved, however excused or dogged by ill fortune, is treated the same. It's not business, it's personal. You break a leg, it's because you weren't walking properly. This may seem cruel, but I suspect that these soldiers can only face death or crippling because they see it not as random luck or fate, but as a lack of concentration or skill. These blokes are part of the best-trained army there has ever been and they don't take their eyes off the job for a second. By and large they've sloughed off civilian friends, and wives and girlfriends must know they come second to the three-letter abbreviation, come childbirth or cancer. Marriages are often casualties, and contrarily they do think that's bad luck.

It's late afternoon and the light is already packing up to go somewhere more appreciative. Tonight there is an exercise. The snipers will collect in teams of five – two guns, two spotters and a co-ordinating commander. Three teams will crawl and wriggle and slither to stalk and triangulate on a small guarded bridge. All night they'll watch and at first light they'll shoot every damn man within sight. That's the plan. Rob Connolly goes off to brief the designated commanders, who include the two Singapore police-men. Their grasp of English would just about get them a job in a Soho dim-sum restaurant.

Rob starts with that calm, reined-in eagerness that is such a feature of war movies. The TLAs flow thick and fast; the Singapor-eans hunch over their notepads. It's all very tense and exciting. The atmosphere's building nicely, then he falters. "Tonight's code name will be, will be," the military mind reaches out into enemy territory, the land of imagination, "green haddock." Green had-dock? There's a shifting in the ranks. "Glin Radrrock?" repeats an Asian copper, "whossit mean?" Unforgivably I lose it and chortle at the back of the class. It's contagious. The room is a shoulder-heaving, cheek-biting act of superhuman restraint. Rob rescues what's left of the aura by synchronising watches. The men go back to the darkness and we wait. Where did you get green haddock from? "You're not to write that, it has nothing to do with sniping." Of course.

A few hours later we go into the dark wearing night-vision glasses. It's a clear, star-filled place of deep, colliding shadows. Through these goggles the Beacons glow green and the air seems filled with fairy fireflies. This monotone world is another country, a dangerous place where you feel alone and exposed. The rational certainties of an adult sophisticated life are wafted away on the keening wind, and I become a wide-eyed child in a bedtime horror story.

I understand in my bones why snipers are force multipliers. It's the fear. Out there, where every shadow, every stand of trees, every curl of the land could hide the cross hairs of extinction, your skin crawls. A pair of well-trained sniper teams can hold up a platoon, a regiment, a brigade, send men scrabbling face down in the earth, huddling for cover, mewling and sobbing. The panic makes them useless liabilities. You take out the officer, they're blind; the radio operator, they're deaf; the driver, they're crippled. All snipers carry not only the L96 but also a 5.56mm regulation rifle. Rob says it's for emergencies if they're in a close spot. That's half the truth. It's also so they can ditch the sniper kit and return to being just PBI: poor bloody infantry. Snipers don't get taken prisoner. They're so hated and feared that they're inevitably killed or worse out of hand. The terror cuts both ways.

On the bridge the enemy are slapping their shoulders and stamping their feet. Welsh fusiliers wearing motley uniforms and Rambo headscarves, clutching decommissioned Kalashnikovs, a multi-purpose Arab/East European/Balkan enemy. It's 2am. Back in the bunker, I crawl into my arctic maggot, wearing four layers of everything, and gonk out for a couple of hours. It's 2° below with a biting wind. What it must be like up there on the hill, cold, wet, exhausted and watching, is beyond comprehension.

I go to make a brew. The room's quiet, only the hiss and click of the radio, and I'm startled to see a man standing behind me, one of the instructors who has kept to the shadows. He looks like an eagle that has been turned into a man by a trainee wizard. He has piercing, unblinking blue eyes and he knows all about me; the shotgun, the car I'm driving, he's very spooky. We discuss deer-stalking in the Highlands and the kit, he doesn't like the infantry's new rifle, he loves the Heckler and Koch. He's wearing square-toed ski boots, breaking them in for Norway. What are you doing there? "Can't tell." Look, I venture, I too know who you are, the reference to Hereford was a bit of a clue. An SAS sergeant whose father and grandfather were snipers before him, I've heard about him. He bet Rob a bottle of port (nice officer-teasing touch) that he could hit a man-sized target from a standing shot at 1,000 yards, close on a mile, and he did it. That's mythic shooting. Then he did it again. What do you think about training foreign soldiers? And the Irishman? "I don't like it. It's just money, isn't it? Oh, I'm sure he's fine but I don't know who his friends are. Who he'll pass the training on to. I've lost friends in the border country. They're not snipers now, they're just amateurs with a good rifle, but it would make a difference if they were." He takes his cup and goes back to the shadows. A man on a mission that exists only in his own head. A quietly, softly terrifying killer.

Before dawn we jump into the Land Rover. The taxi driver goes up to the bridge head, where the enemy are smoking and chatting disconsolately. Rob checks with the snipers on the radio, the landscape is shrouded in early morning mist, the hills emerge like someone twitching consecutive net curtains. "Teams, have you got a primary and secondary target?" Yes, yes, yes, stop – no. One of the enemy has chosen this moment to take a dump behind a bush, and it has added a precious two minutes to his life. Finally, inevitably, yes, yes, yes. The radio crackles. "Fire at will." The enemy tumble over histrionically, one starts running up the road. Bang. The photographer is so excited by the sight of bodies, he leaps out of the truck. The radio squawks: "There's a man in black on the bridge, a man in black." Bang. It's a moment any journalist would savour.

The longest night is all but over. In the distance, ragged groups of men emerge from the earth like the undead, walking scarecrows. They could be medieval or figures from *The Seventh Seal*. Hot breakfast. A nice surprise, brought up from camp, eggs, bacon, beans, fried bread, tea poured from a jerry can. The snipers gather outside a deserted farm. They don't look so bad. Stripping off the wet gear to put on damp gear, checking their guns and feet. It's the end of a long week and they've made it, just the debriefing and the ritual bollocking, then a bed, a real bed, with a warm girlfriend and beer.

"Right," bellows Staff Sgt Marr, "get your kit on, we're tabbing over that hill, the far one, then live firing. You've got forty minutes to get there." Another surprise, not so nice. Let's see whose head goes down. They trot off with that short, bent-kneed sherpa's gait. A man falls over in a chest-high river, his bergen holds him under; another man goes back to pull him out. They tab on, gasping and sodden. The Italian nearly severs his trigger finger. Rob picks up his rifle and examines the breach. "Look at that: rust. That would be a court-martial offence in our army." Staff Sgt Marr jogs past like a happy spaniel. "I love it, love it," he says. "Suffer, you bastards." I know what it is about these men that makes them so enviable: it's their confidence, a confidence we never have in the world, where we can choose our own clothes. Far from being unreconstructed testosterone-junkie cavemen, they're amazingly well balanced; they cook and sew, wipe surfaces, take out the rubbish, and kill. They're aggressive, but not violent. There's none of that half-cocked, late-night thuggishness about these soldiers. Their aggression is focused and appropriate. They prove themselves as professionals every day, they don't need to do it as amateurs, and they have an utter belief in their own ability to complete what they start.

They've arrived here not just by single-minded diligence and grit, but by discarding everything that might be confusing or contradictory. They have no life outside their service, and they look inward to each other, to the banter and shimfing and the gucci-kit chat, to be a constant reassurance that their discipline is right. The civilian world is a place of uncertainty and shifting focus, where their skills count for little; only the officers peek over the barricade towards banking or land management.

Seeing them through civilian sights you judge the distance and realise that for a generation that has never served, this small-knit band of men are further from us than ever before. It's easy and convenient to patronise them, but we should never forget that the force these men multiply is actually us.

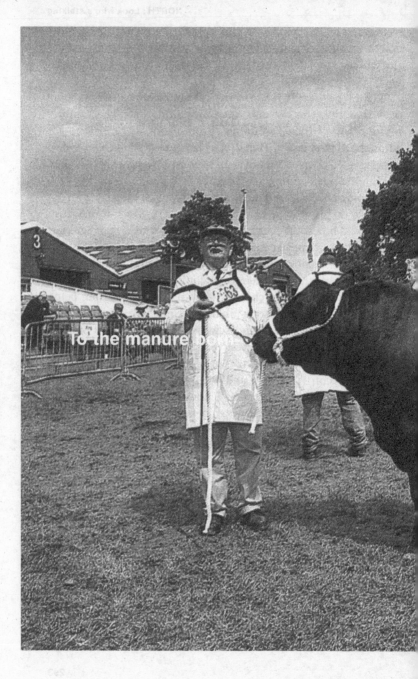

To the manure born—

To the manure born

The Royal Agricultural Show, September 2000

Once upon a time, I flew through the night in a helicopter from the Lancashire coast to London. It was a full moon. A thousand feet below stretched England, its cities, towns and villages neatly delineated by house and street lights. Bradford, Huddersfield, Sheffield, Worksop, Nottingham, Kettering and Milton Keynes glittered like distant constellations, threaded together by the meteors and shooting stars of motorways.

Mercifully shorn of their grim, grey, close-up civic ghastliness, they looked pristine and enchanting. The country, crumpled and folded, patched and darned with centuries of use, resting from its labours, lay snug, invisible. The jigsaw fairy lights appeared ephemeral; the dark, immemorial and timeless. Over it all, spinning flakes of snow fell to glaze every field and hedge, copse, covert, root and branch. It all looked so heart-stoppingly, pitifully fragile.

We live, you and I, in a communally agreed white lie. We believe this is a rural country, a "country" country. Of course, empirically we understand that England is one of the world's most densely populated nations, more hugger-mugger than India or China or Switzerland; we know that, having put industry into revolution years before anyone else, there hasn't been a soul who could honestly answer to the name of peasant for 200 years.

We know that the nation's wealth is all made indoors, that power has passed from the Whigs of the land to the Tories and socialists of the smoke-filled room. We hardly need reminding that the country is peristaltic with cars, screaming with claustrophobia. All this we know and yet . . . and yet we also know that, if we had a mind to, we could all stand shoulder to shoulder on the Isle of Wight and see in the distance an empty, green and pleasant land. When we close our eyes and think of England, we see country lanes and thatched cottages, a patchwork of fields, the organised randomness of a Georgian park.

Even though the chances are that you're reading this in a place where your neighbour is just the other side of a wall, and your horizons are never further than 15ft, and where if you saw a sheep you'd call the police, you still persist in thinking we live in a country with dotted urban set-aside, rather than a rolling, sprawling suburb with occasional fields. It's there, just up the road, out of sight. This real England, your unreal home, turns us all into maundering John of Gaunts, sighing over sceptred isles, demi-paradises, other Edens. So how come the country is in such a parlous state, crippled and bankrupt, depressed to the point of eating the shotgun?

If we love it so, if it's the cradle of our identity, why are we complacently rubbernecking as it's turned into our own home-made Kosovo? The litany of sorrows that afflicts the country is wearyingly familiar. Debt, poverty, exhaustion, burglary, vandalism, vigilantism, migration, depression, poisoned land, poisoned food, organic loonies, no transport, closed post offices, closed shops and wandering bands of offensively dressed ramblers.

Some of these also afflict towns and cities, but somehow they seem worse in the delicate green bits. Even songbirds are leaving. Ruralists are mad, mad with despair, call-the-Samaritans mad, with the righteous fury of victims made second-class refugees in their own back yards by weekend-dream property prices and rock-bottom farming. They are surrounded by an ignorant urbanity that on one hand ignores them, and on the other tells them how to keep sheep and grow onions.

I set off into the mud and the blood to uncover the strategies the heart and soul of Olde England, with its back to the dry-stone wall, is planning for its survival. The Royal Agricultural Show at Stoneleigh seemed the place to find out – a great beer-tent-and-bacon-butty get-together of the clans of round-vowelled, clotted-faced ruralists.

It starts badly. You have to go to Coventry. Through the train window the Midlands drifts away into the sodden mist. To a city boy it looks as it always has. The bucolic war of attrition and scorched earth of the past 20 years they keep telling us about have had little visible effect: this is still the landscape of my childhood. Those hundreds, or thousands, or hundreds of thousands of miles of hedge that have been grubbed up every week since the war, well, I'm damned if I can see where they went. Olde England must have been a sunless maze that stretched from Penzance to Carlisle. I think they're lying. Lying, or selective embellishment, is one of the things I associate with rural folk, that and sex without foreplay.

Disappointingly, Stoneleigh isn't actually in the country, it's one of those golf-club and ornamental-willow, Jag-and-water-feature suburbs. The first thing you see is that all the humans have huge hands, and everything else has huge testicles. Perhaps that's no coincidence. Huge, smugly thuggish bulls are led by the noses by equally smugly vicious lads with shaven heads and shit-kicking boots. Having a Hereford on a rope beats a rottweiler any day. The black Angus bulls have such short legs that their gonad clearance is less than a Lamborghini's. Bit-swinging bovines are paraded in the ring in a simulacrum of a Mr Universe competition; absurd judges in bowler hats and mothy suits dribble over muscle and leather like old queens in a biker bar. Each yob has a long stick with a hook on the end, with which they gently and rhythmically rub the bull's pizzles. Now, I'm sorry, but slowly cluster-frotting a rib roast comes right at the end of truly weird things to do. Sheep have their tails lifted, pigs scamper and swerve like fly halves, chased by ready-rubbed, shag-breathed men waving trays advertising banks. Why pigs will be impressed by low-interest flexible mortgage TV dinners is beyond me, but then what do I know?

The sheer ingenuity and variety of breeds are a wonder. Could you tell your Beltex from your Berrichon du Cher, or Black Welsh Mountain, Bleu du Maine, Clun Forest, Hampshire Down, North Country Cheviot, Southdown, Romney, Wensleydale, Exmoor Horn, Herdwick, Lleyn, Oxford Down, Vendéen, Bluefaced Leicester, Devon Closewool, Dorset Down, Texel, Rouge de l'Ouest, Swaledale, or the fabled, mysterious Lonk?

I thought not. But there are men who can and do, and they feel unloved, harassed and marginalised as they tenderly wander their hands up and down shaved inner thighs. Those are just sheep. Cows come in an equally wondrous diversity, from the psychopathic midget dexter to the bovinely provocative Belgian Blue with its double-muscled buttocks. It all makes you wonder what God could have done if he hadn't rushed the job in a week.

Each breed was carefully forged from forced copulations over hundreds of generations. In these rings it is possible to see the countryside as one vast Nazi brothel, producing specialist *über*-races. Take Yorkshire's large white pig, bred with long legs, york-ham legs smoked over the sawdust and chips from the oak beams that for a century were used to make York Minster. Crossed with the Landrace, it was taught Italian and sent to live in the damp northern Po valley, where it became the parma-ham pig. Its long legs were bred so that it could be driven to market across remote Yorkshire dales (pigs aren't naturally great walkers). Every breed of beast has a similar story, a quaint specialisation that is mutely told in muscle and hide, in hoof and horn. For 3,000 years they have been our help meats. They've been led to slaughter, through feast and famine, feeding an urban progress that would make their uniqueness obsolete.

It's the heavy horses that reveal just how *de trop* they all are. Great dumb things, Shires and Percherons, Clydesdales and cobs, with moon-boot feet and brains the size of walnuts. Nobody can pretend that these equine oiks are anything more than garden furniture, but they do pretend, they put them in front of carts and drays and make believe that the world is still cobbled.

An utter belief in the goodness of horses is one of the totemic truths that separate town from country. In the town, nobody in their right mind would put a 14-year-old girl on a motor scooter with the engine of a Magimix, but in the country every pre-teen is encouraged to sit on top of half a tonne of frothing, glossy, bonkers imbecility which can go at 40mph across six lanes of traffic through a barbed wire fence, roll over and pogo and then kick a Range Rover into its constituent parts. There are said to be more horses in Britain now than there were before the invention of the internal combustion engine. That they serve no useful purpose other than to give work to strapping girls with pitchforks, and to act as a catalyst for rural adultery, is something you couldn't conceivably question at Stoneleigh. Heritage trumps utility, or even common sense, every time. It's no accident that the issue ruralists have chosen to dig in their heels about is horses. Of all the fields they could have made a stand in, fox-hunting is the least fortuitous: an expensive, faintly absurd recreation. But it is a clear demarcation between them and us. Hunting is clearly, unequivocally rural. In the ring, no equinity is left unworshipped: hitching, harnessing, plaiting, braiding, kiddies on leader reins, contests by age, height, breed and sex; they skitter past for three days, like Genghis Khan's Girl Guides. My favourite, far and away the most camply ridiculous, is a woman whose nag syncopates to light opera as she tells her life story over the Tannoy, rider and mount erotically heavy-breathing as one.

Extraordinary, weirdly beautiful though the animals are, they're no more than nostalgic pets, couture catwalk creatures, amazing but impractical and expensive, and you won't see them in the shops next season. The bulls with their mighty meat-and-two-veg have been cuckolded by the rubber gloves and turkey basters of the artificial inseminators, mild-mannered little men who have achieved macho nirvana. A schooner of bovine DNA is the price of Sunday lunch at a Harvester.

Insemination stalls dot the ground, their walls boasting large, glossy photographs of provocative heifers, posed to display their mighty, round, pink udders. They're just page-three lovelies with obscenely eager teats. A brochure for a bull called Figaro ("who ranks with Jed, Jogger and Jolt" – even the names seem like a tacky porn movie) has a cover like a Beatrix Potter *Penthouse*, a huge, globular cleavage with two erect nipples and a headline that shouts: "Udders that are a joy to milk at 5am!" A pinstripe salesman in a company tie with matching grin comes over: "Have you been seen to?" This is not a good opening gambit if you're selling artificial insemination, but then that's the other thing about the country: they don't get their own innate, rude, mechanical, comic irony. They think a sticker saying, "Young farmers do it twice a day with manure," is funny. They don't see anything risible in handing out posters of gargantuan ruminant knockers for your bedroom wall.

There are tents selling the potless countryside things they didn't know they needed: nonslip cattle flooring, portable milk pasteurisers; banks and Shylock companies that will kindly squeeze a few extra drops of interest out of the mortgage; a coffee tent run by fundamentalist Christians, estuary-vowelled Elmer Gantrys. Along with the Nescafé, they are offering, if not divine hope, at least an

Old Testament explanation of the evil and wickedness that got farmers into this mire.

I picked up a useful pamphlet, *Where Did Cain Get His Wife?*, by the wonderfully named Ken Ham. If Ken has found out, the young farmers would love to know – they are desperate. No, they're really desperate. In the door of the young farmers' tent stands a jolly, rotund chap. "Sign our petition, sir." He rattles a tin. For a couple of coins I get a bit of knotted rope with a pin. It's the young farmers' *Blue Peter* version of an Aids ribbon. It looks like a noose. Is this to remind us that you're all hanging yourselves? "No," he says, with a mildly shocked incomprehension. "It's to show your support for young farmers. Would you like to look at our home-made puppet competition inside?" Do you know, I don't think I could bear it. There's only so much pathos a man can handle in a lifetime. "Are you a young farmer?" I ask. Not exactly, he lives in Guildford, but he'd like to be.

Well away from the four-legs-good paddock is the four-wheels-better prairie. A great herd of no less glossy and pampered machinery, whose heritage is as noble – from the first bone ploughs, through Jethro Tull's seed drill and the Georgian fascination for technological farming. Primary-coloured kindergarten kit the size of Bovis starter homes, costing about as much. Behemoths with retractable arms and articulated grabbers, shovers, cutters, wrappers, stereophonic sound and air-con. There's stuff that you couldn't even guess the use of. Sort of Jules Verne meets *Wacky Races*. It all looks so 1980s, a bosky equivalent of the red braces and conspicuous-consumption Porsches and Ferraris.

This is loadsa-agrimoney kit from when EEC grants and set-aside subsidies flowed like milk quotas, but nobody's buying now. Salesmen stand in bored stupefaction, as the sign-on-the-dotted-line champagne goes flat. Only a few small boys play in the cabs. Both the machines and ring animals are generally ignored. Just a smattering of grooms and judges and the salmon-hatted wives of supermarket sponsors waiting to hand out rosettes watch with a wake-like reverence.

There are crowds, not huge enough to make the place look more than half full, but crammed into temporary arcades of shops. They consume with a duty-free fervour. Shopping is, after all, the great pan-rural and urban pastime. No longer do the grey legions of workers spend their precious leisure time walking the chalky downs, or being Mr Polly and bicycling the byways for refreshing half-pints of scrumpy. We are not a nation of shopkeepers but a nation of shop grazers, and this, it turns out, is the real point of a rural fair. Confronted with the catastrophic decline in traditional farming, the best advice Mr Blair and the serried ranks of civil servants from the Ministry of Agriculture could come up with, was that bumpkins should think about starting cottage Macjobs (that's Macdonald as in had-a-farm, not turned-the-surplus-cattle-into-burgers). They've gone at it with alacrity, turning medieval copses into paintball playgrounds or corporate bonding camps. Barns are agri-dating agencies, internet picnic-hamper purveyors. Milking parlours are aromatherapy yoga temples, weekend B&Bs, golden-years knocking shops.

There's this Stoneleigh peripatetic refugee camp of craftiness, where Pacamaced trippers can ruminate on blind-man's-bluff knitwear, rainwear, leisurewear, comfeewear, tacked out in one-size-fits-all nylon and polyester. An Oxfam of elastic-waistbanded nastiness, slobby suburban weekend clothes masquerading as hunting, shooting and riding gear. There are the jolly good ideas born out of late-night-by-the-Aga desperation. Sticks that are plastic shopping-bag holders, wooden fruit, small smiley reptiles, all-in-one twin-footed fake-fur slippers, comic dog-lead hooks, plastic bag storers, unpatented original coaster holders, crumpet cosies, draught excluders, boot removers, drawer liners, scented knicker bags, scented knickers, shoe dryers and cat sensory deprivation boxes. There are department-store tents of amateur watercolourists, amateur kiddie crocheters, flower dryers, mud turners, cancerous candle makers, rag-doll knotters and metal benders. And sad, defunct craft proselytisers: coracle makers, three-legged-stool bodgers, fletchers and a dozen men doing a dozen pointless things with birch twigs. All these finger-and-thumb people eke out a living going from game fair to stately-home vintage-car rally, flogging this remnant-and-rag rubbish, that brightly screaming kitsch. A polite underclass of hatchback and picnic-table tinkers.

There's the bottom-line thing about the country. It has no taste whatsoever. The closest country folk ever get to aesthetics is whimsy. They have the artistic sensibility of a sugared-up class of seven-year-olds. You can never have too many patterns, too much chintz or frills or clutter. They knick-knack the world in an eye-grating nausea.

The real pollution of the countryside is, unfortunately, country people. Culture is unequivocally urban, the very word "civilisa-tion" comes from the same root as "civic". This island's 3,000-year pilgrimage of progress has been a one-way street towards the city. City ideas, city sensibilities, aesthetics and sophistication, thank God. In the middle of Stoneleigh's vital, vivid vileness I found a thing (it could only be described as a thing) so perfectly, stun-ningly horrible, it encapsulated the yawning gap between us and them. A jolly husband and wife spend a post-retirement gypsy life selling home-made calico cats doused in lavender oil. They are not just hideous Victorian cabbage-patch cats: they have a unique use. They are vacuum-cleaner covers. Nothing in the country is too mundane to avoid a posy cloche. "Oh yes, they're very popular," the vibrant lady tells me. "We're very up to date. We do one specially for the Dyson. They're particularly popular. Dysons are so ugly, aren't they? Mine's yellow, grey and purple, much nicer under a cat." There you have it. In the city, Dyson is a byword for design excellence. A thing of contemporary beauty, almost an icon of metropolitan chic and the way we live now. The synthesis of form and function. In the country they dress it up with an anthropomorphic bedtime dolly, turning Cool Britannia into an Edwardian whatnot.

I once read that in a battle the most dangerous thing you could do was run away. It's primeval. A fight-and-flight deal. You stop being the enemy and become prey; stabbing you in the back gets that much easier. The country is running away. It whinges and begs as it retreats, and we, from the fastness of our concrete-and-steel high-rise castles, despise it. Rural folk no longer earn our respect as the ruddy yeomen of England, the sinew of the nation. John Bull is now John the Semen Inseminator. The countryside doesn't have an identifiable cohesion or identity. They dress like us, but cheaper. They want the same things, but tackier. The country is a kitsch, twinky suburb populated by humourless nostalgia junkies, who demand money not with menaces but mutters. If they put up a fight, parked their vast Tonka tanks on our lawns, burnt wicker men in town centres, turned some of their sulphurous weedkiller into bombs, we'd fear them, and fear is the father of respect. Instead we pity them, and they fly off the handle one at a time, spraying pig shit over holiday homes, waving sticks at ramblers and shooting a dog.

Their conservative, long-suffering stoicism, wilful ignorance, a masochistic, cloud-watching pessimism, and an almost psychedelic pleasure in being able to say, "I told you so," are utterly out of kilter with the modern world. The urban consensus is, well, just let them sink in their own slurry. We all have to live by market forces, let rural folk feel the sharp edge of international commerce and thatched-property inflation. They're never going to put the clock back to 1910. They're never going to be anything more than a profitless, subsidised, medieval craft collective. Why don't we just put them out of their misery, dump the whole lot in a bumper edition of *Country Life*, and flog it to people who can privately underwrite the losses in exchange for the use of the vista – fizzy-brained pop stars, mobile-phone millionaires and time-share antique dealers? They'll replant the hedges and grow insanely expensive vegetables for fun. They'll keep a few rare breeds to beef up the view from the dining room. Country folk can seep into the job market, become housekeepers, gardeners and minicab drivers.

Yet something stops us throwing them to the wolves. (As if farmers didn't have enough to worry about, some Islington loony is trying to reintroduce wolves.) That something is diversity. Cities breed uniformity. Propinquity means sameness, we all wear black, we all own a Dyson. It's the country that grows variation in language, in behaviour, in outlook and mood. The centuries that gave us a plethora of variegated sheep, cows and chickens were symbiotic in turn and forced an eclectic and vigorous difference in people. We would be poorer without that. The country is the urban imagination's raw material, a place of inspiration, albeit better in the mind's eye than stuck on the sole of your shoe. The eliding rural sameness germinates; the frantic city consumes. The country is home to that peculiarly English natural resource, eccentricity. In the city, an eccentric wields a double-decker shopping trolley and shouts at traffic; in the country, he probably shuffles in odd socks to a shed and slowly, organically, invents something. Mostly, it's a stick for carrying shopping bags, or a better mug tree, but occasionally it's a sextant, a Davy lamp, or a jet engine. Or perhaps just some piece of minutely correlated onanism that has a rare and useless fascination. The bottom line? The country's greatest invention is the city. Only through the tireless, plodding seasons have we been able to devise a society where not everyone has to till and reap. Some of us, then most of us, could leave the harvest home, go off and be investment managers, lap dancers, television presenters and poets, secure in the knowledge that others would mind the farm. We owe the country. In the end, wouldn't we all like to finish up in some dappled country churchyard, finally at one with the land? Though personally I devoutly hope I'm dead first.

I don't want to be a Northumbrian dry-stone wall layer. I don't want my children to lay dry-stone walls. I don't even want a dry-stone wall. But I'm quite pleased that someone out there in the darkness is still doing it. For such a small place, this island has maintained a bewildering number of locally specialised human adaptations, and we would be worse off without them.

Oh, but wouldn't it be so much easier to fight for the country's corner if they weren't all so dreadfully, embarrassingly, uniquely, personally unprepossessing?

Last exit to Whipsnade

The M1, February 2001

Haven't you always wondered about the brown signs on motorways, wondered and been a little curious? They plague me, fill the small, sleepless hours with visions, they niggle. What are they? Who decided on them? What lies beyond them?

The green, blue and white signs are all written with a direct, Anglo-emphatic common sense. Travellers' health warnings and timely topographic explanations. But the brown signs are oblique, runic, frankly weird. What, for instance, is Owl and Otter World? Or the American Adventure, in Derbyshire, or Butterfly World, or the mysterious Billings Aquadrome? They're like the goblins' and sprites' incantations in fairy stories, tempting you to turn from the familiar mortal straight lanes into some windy, wooded enchantment. They seem totally at odds with the know-it-all instructions of the modern matt, black-and-white tarmac world, like the guesses and rumours on medieval maps that explain the gaps: "Here be dragons", "a land of blue men with two heads", "monsters and giants", "fountains of eternal youth". They flash past as we humdrum up the road to some pedestrian destination, and we think: "Better not, not this time."

Other men dream of expansive adventures, or traversing deserts on mopeds, circumnavigating in balloons shaped like beer cans, punting up the Orinoco or just walking to some pole. But me, I've always yearned to visit every brown sign on the M1. One day I'd do it, and then one day I did.

In search of the brown signs of Middle England, I needed a car fit for an adventure. Just standing still, the AC Cobra fair takes your breath away. It's every boy's image of the perfect sports car. If you're in the market for an expensive strap-on penis – and these days, who isn't? – then this is the jobbie that summer's gala balls were made for. And if in those dreams your genitals could talk, this is the noise they'd made – a leering, Cro-Magnon glottal guffaw.

But it has one glaring design fault, one terrible oversight, or rather way too much oversight: there's no roof. Not even anywhere to put a roof. Having got the car, I needed a driver, and the promise of being able to belt on the Cobra brought Jeremy Clarkson panting. He wants to go at 100-and-frozen-to-death up the motorway, push the envelope, re-create the good bit from *Back to the Future*, and I should say right here: "Don't try this at home." One, it's illegal, and two, it's unlikely that your hall is long enough to get into second gear.

The M1 ought to start with a triumphal arch. In practice, it sort of sidles out of Brent Cross shopping centre. I've always considered that its real beginning is the Scratchwood service station, now Blairishly renamed London Gateway. It's here that you feel you're leaving behind the safety of the city, all that is comforting, familiar and, well, just civilised. Ahead of you stretches Oop North in progressive shades of ee-by-gum intensity. We ate a last breakfast here and a brace of pastel-shingled, randomly cackling old ladies came up to me saying, "Can we touch you," then, by way of explanation: "We're going to the Isle of Wight." It seemed a suitably surreal omen for the journey.

Jeremy took off with a squeal and a great roar of exhaust. Then we got into the car, which, being red with two white stripes, in a fit of Arthur Ransome whimsy I'd named the Rasher. Sedately we made for our first brown sign like Gawain and his squire on a quest, or perhaps more like Don Quixote and Sancho Panza. Under a blissfully sunny sky, with the wind playing croquet with our sinuses, we motored up the lads' lane of the M1.

The first brown sign wasn't far off: Whipsnade. Not much of a surprise there. I suppose I must have been to Whipsnade before during some desperate half-term, but I have no memory of the place. It returned with the torpor of amnesiac familiarity. Whipsnade was the first of the "I can't believe it isn't a zoo" zoos. It's meant to be a new habitat, somewhere between the interesting high security of a real zoo and the tagged freedom of the Serengeti. A sort of open prison for ungulates. And, like some *trompe l'oeil* painting of a Tuscan landscape on a suburban dining-room wall, it isn't fooling anyone, least of all the inmates, who seem to have been chosen to colour co-ordinate in shades of grey and taupe. The great endangered stand in miserable huddles in the middle of off-season rugby pitches. Rarity is not necessarily concomitantly interesting. Przewalski's horse, the oldest and rarest of horses, looks to anyone who isn't an expert, or another Przewalski's horse, like a herd of skinhead donkeys. Relieved of the need to avoid predators, little bands of animals have not another single thing in their heads, and stand imbecilely chewing gum, staring at postponed extinction. A drab gene museum, their only purpose and excitement is the annual 30-second legover. Sancho Clarkson is as bored as a desert oryx. Even my enthusiastic explanation of the interesting fact that white or black in relation to rhinos doesn't refer to colour (they're both grey, of course) but lip shape, surprisingly, didn't fire his imagination and he headed for the one spot of colour, the souvenir hut – which turned out to be everything a zoo should be, stuffed with bright, animated, pettable nylon nature. I bought a cow with Velcro arms for the car and he got a baseball cap shaped like a zebra head. It was very Clarkson.

Back into the Rasher. Woburn Safari Park and Abbey was the next brown stop, just around the corner. The park too has non-indigenous animals in fields, which, without too much arm-twisting, I agreed to give a miss, only pausing to mention that there must be more rhinos in the home counties than there are in Kenya. The best that can be said for the abbey is that it's big. But then so is the Barbican. Bigness is all it's got going for it. There's a big drive through a big deer park and a big sign at the start like a cricket scoreboard informing how many big deer have been killed on the road this year. Which goes to confirm the suspicion that the aristocracy is two quarterings short of an escutcheon. Any ten-year-old could have told them deer can't read.

The house is a dusty auction waiting to happen, no less endangered than Przewalski's donkeys. Georgian knick-knackery, crippled furniture and the dust of decrepitude wait behind red ropes for the inevitable tumbril. Someone, presumably a wandering marchioness, has added homely touches like embarrassing family photos and the odd jokey soft toy, which only counterpoint the uninhabitable pointlessness of the place. The Russell family have evidently spent a couple of dozen generations rapaciously buying pictures by the yard. They have yet to snag a good one. Sancho's favourite object was a stuffed canary. Now, how bored do you have to be to consider getting the canary stuffed?

The Rasher sped on. Gulliver's Land was the next sign. Ah, but which land? Would it be a land of civilised horses and violent yahoos? No, that's Gloucestershire. Would it be lots of brilliant scientists living with their heads in the clouds? Hardly, for this is Milton Keynes. We almost didn't find out. I asked the lady in the kiosk for two adult tickets and she said: "Where are your children?" Choosing to believe this was Midlands warmth rather than insufferable nosiness, I told her: "In the south of France, actually." "Don't you have children with you?" "No, do I need some?" "Everyone else does." "Well, can I rent any?" "You want to come in without a child?" Preferably, yes, I've already got him. Her eyes wandered over to Jeremy, then to her lap, where I expect there was a cut-out-and-keep *News of the World* I-spy monsters page. "I expect it's okay, but there's nothing in there for you."

And there wasn't. Gulliver's Land is the sort of place I'd imagined disappeared with teddy boys and the Pathé News. The sort of can't-complain, jolly decrepit Portakabin and cardboard funfair with rides that anywhere else in the post-moonwalk world would have been mechanised. But here the customers provide the power. Let me tell you, pedalling up a scenic switchback isn't something to be undertaken without a fit seven-year-old. There was a misshapen sculpture in the middle of the kingdom just before you got to the MDF fantasy castle. I think it was meant to be Gulliver. Michelangelo's *David* it wasn't.

Back on the road, Jeremy put his foot down. One of the nice things about an open-top sports car is that you can really enjoy the view. It's a Cinemascope experience with Dolby static. You simply can't talk. In space and in a Cobra nobody can hear you scream, so best of all I didn't have to listen to the running if-this-car-were-a-Belgian-prostitute commentary.

Billings Aquadrome. I had no idea places like this existed. Actually there can't be another place like this, a trailer park set around some flooded gravel pits. There are pubs, shops, roads, a couple of funfairs. It's a holiday park perched on the edge of the motorway. Traffic hisses just the other side of the trees. But here in the meadows is a perfect working-class getaway. I don't mean that snidely. But Billings is, unselfconsciously, tabloid fun. Aesthetically nude. Unencumbered by improving good taste or Tate Modernish, Domish sensibilities. It's a little spot of England where Channel 4, the *Guardian*, Alessi orange squeezers, ciabatta and the Booker short list don't exist. Its denizens, who have paid up to £20,000 for a hut, are all from the north. This is as far south as most of them want to get. This is salty Lancashire's Mediterranean, and earthy Yorkshire's West Indies. The culs-de-sac of mobile homes (not caravans, these stand on sleepers and have picket fences, satellite dishes and decks) make up a small back-to-back nostalgic fantasy of what working-class life should have been if the industrial revolution and the welfare state and trickle-down economics had panned out. It's Catherine Cookson without the cobbles and smoke and abortions. Here all doors are open and it's safe for the kiddies. Men stand and chat on the communal lawns, handing out beer cans, watching their crop-haired sons juggle footballs. Men and boys are dressed identically in bright polyester football shirts and tracksuit bottoms. The only things that distinguish the generations are the beer guts and tattoos of the mature adult.

If watching the laddie endlessly dribble palls, there's all that jet-skiing on the lake, or monkey bikes and go-karts, or more football on the TV. And there's a big tent with a koi carp show. Koi carp are distressingly large palomino goldfish. There are dozens of blue paddling pools full of the nightmarish things for sale for thousands of pounds. Big, bouncerish men with scarred, annotated knuckles struggle to hold squirming plastic bags. Koi are unlikely working-class pets. They don't bite burglars. You can't take them to the pub. They won't watch *EastEnders* with you and you can't eat them. But there you go. Those who only know the English working classes as awayday thugs know only the half of it. There is also a deep, sentimental streak that idolises childhood, loves noisy motors that travel in pointless circles and worships fish.

It was with great reluctance that I left Billings. I was truly envious of this comfy, ugly Elysian field. As we scraped over the kiddie-friendly traffic humps, past the pedalo swans, it struck me in a sadly typically smart-arsed, brittley intellectual, cosmopolitan way that this was far more like one of Swift's kingdoms than anything I'd seen. And I would dearly love to be unshackled from my bookish heritage and have the culture, freedom and the nerve to join in.

Continuing north to the American Adventure, another tacky, low-rent theme park that exploits every cowboy film cliché from American adobe burger bars to Monument Valley-style Geronimo heads. Well, what do you do with reclaimed pits and slag heaps? You turn them into a Saturday afternoon B-movie set and truly bury the memory of industry, like putting a supermarket over a war grave all built with Tory guilt money. It's half-full of teenagers; they're here for one thing only, a particularly unpleasant ride. Without the Skycoaster, the American Adventure would be another cowboy cliché, the ghost town. But adolescence will travel great distances and stand in depression-style queues to either get its ears broken or its sphincter loosened. This does both. I watched the youngsters being terrified out of their skulls, emitting jaw-dislocating screams, and thought: "Thank God that's not me." But then one of the many, many disadvantages of travelling with Sancho Clarkson is that the sort of men who manage fairgrounds adore him and want to do things for him. An eager chap in a thin tie with a walkie-talkie came over all wall-to-wall smiles and asked if he'd like a go: "Seeing as it's you, we can jump the queue." Jeremy and I caught and hugged each other's eyes. In unison they silently yelled: "Noooooooo!" But his mouth said: "Thanks." And we were taken to be strapped together in an all-in-one straitjacket. "Who wants the toggle?" said the manager. We tossed a coin. I got the toggle.

Then we were led past jeering youths and clipped to a wire. The other end of the wire was tied round the little finger of God's right hand. Swaying ignominiously face down, we were winched up and up until on my left I could just make out Copenhagen and on my right Seville. The view below was what you're used to seeing from business class. A faint voice shouted: "One, two, three, fly." Knowing that the only way down was down, I pulled the toggle and we fell. We fell for about a lunar month, and I was paralysed by one hysterical thought: "Please, please, dear Jesus, I don't want to die strapped to Jeremy Clarkson in a big green nappy." It wasn't a nappy when we started, but it was by the time we reached maximum velocity. And just as the concrete puckered up we were swinging out faster than a bird, faster than a plane, faster than vomit.

"Ohhhhhh *mach one*," yelled a hysterical Clarkson to an imaginary camera. This was the most distressingly unpleasant and humiliating experience of my life that didn't involve medical staff. Sancho said he wanted to do it again.

The driving changes as you go north. Outside Leicester everyone careens with a fatalistic mania, playing dodgem karma. Suddenly there was a series of rapid explosions, a drive-by shooting from a white stretch limo. But it turned out to be an exotic wedding procession. Onward and northward. Sherwood Forest. I don't know why there's a brown sign for Sherwood Forest on the M1, it's only just this side of Brussels. They were holding a Robin Hood festival. Well, I suppose they're unlikely to hold a William Tell one. It consisted of a lot of rugger buggers in vaguely old-English Xena the Warrior Princess motley whacking each other with broomsticks while over a crackling PA the hospital-radio DJ kept up a jolly commentary: "and Guy of Gisborne takes Alan-a-Dale from behind, a typically dirty Norman trick. Boooo. Come on, everyone, boooo." There's a medieval market where post-Black Death villains practise medieval crafts: groat forgery and gnome decoration. It's pretty depressing.

The smell of the merry band of burghers filled the air. I began to realise that, oddly, the entire holiday throng of several thousand were speaking Italian. Don't ask me why Sherwood Forest and chaps with jesters' hats and penny whistles should be big with the Eyeties. Perhaps it's light relief after the high renaissance, or maybe with his gang of merry men (and Maid Marion), his godfatherly protection of peasants and tax avoidance in very tight trousers, Robin Hood is more Naples than Nottingham.

The Heights of Abraham – how did they get from Quebec to Derbyshire? After a long, windy drive they turned out to be a cable car in Matlock Bath. After the American Adventure I wasn't doing anything that involved vertical wire. But Matlock was another revelation, a pretty Victorian spa town on a tumbling river. And it was stuffed, choked and cluttered with motorcyclists in all their peroxide balding, heavy-metal bondage, romper-suited wonder. In the immortal words of Jacques Cousteau, "Ooo knows where zey come from, ooo knows where zey go to?" There were thousands and thousands of them. Swinging their gaudy helmets, they looked like a gay hanging-basket convention, and they hated Jeremy. They hated him a lot as the proselytiser of four wheels good, two wheels bad. He was Torquemada, and in the Rasher there was no place to hide his big, familiar coconut head. We drove slowly through town to a cacophony of loathing and derision from hordes of Meat Loaf impressionists.

The Yorkshire Sculpture Park. I've always wanted to visit this place. A rolling landscape where Henry Moore's monumental organic statues are exhibited among the sheep that so captivated him. No other modern sculptor has such a symbiotic connection with the landscape. I was halfway through this sentence when Sancho was transfigured into Harry Enfield's Kevin. "Oh, I don't want to walk. I don't do walking. Oh, this is shit. They're all shit. Look at that piece of sheep shit. It's the same as that lump of bronze, isn't it? Explain to me why that isn't a big lump of sheep shit."

I could see this argument stretching wearily ahead like a Philistines' traffic jam with added aesthetic rage, and decided that sometimes silence is the better part of culture. On the way out we passed a particularly fine minotaur on a plinth. "Oh, look, a man with a cow's head," jeered Sancho. "It's Michael Ayrton," I told him. "How do you know, how do you know that?" he huffed, as if recognising sculpture was a potentially evil form of train-spotting. "How do you know what the bloke with the horns is called?" Just drive, Sancho.

Clarkson likes being in Yorkshire. God's own county. Clarkson's own county. The county where Clarkson and God are peers. Still smarting from the sculpture park, he said: "Over there, Sir Walter Raleigh wrote *Ivanhoe*." No he didn't. "Yes he bloody well did. Don't tell me he didn't, because I know. This is where I come from, clever dick. He did." Have it your way, Jeremy Paxman.

The National Coal Mining Museum near Wakefield is a truly

poignant place. Set over a dead pit, kept open for the inquisitive like Lenin's tomb, it's more a battlefield than a museum. The exhibits have the fevered, *Blue Peter* look of a sixth-form project. Bits of chunky, gap-toothed machinery sit and rust. You can go down to the useless hard, black face, but it's sunny up here and the Grimethorpe Colliery Band are playing beautifully. Alfresco brass-band music was ever the most evocative propaganda of the industrial north. Their audience is half a dozen stallholders selling cheap tat to nobody. The remnants of the industry that didn't just make this part of Britain, but forged the lives of a quarter of the world's population, are desperately meagre. Yellowing cuttings, some worn-out clogs and baskets. What's remarkable about the precipitant full stop of the mines is how little is left behind them. After barely a decade there are more Celtic and Roman remains in this country than mining ones. All the workers in the museum are ex-miners. They skitter about in electric buggies emptying the bins, dressed in helmets with lamps and kneepads.

It's ignominious. As the band played "Wouldn't It Be Loverly?", I talked to a gentle, softly spoken miner about the strike, the police and the scabs. He was like a man scratching an itch on the stump of a phantom limb. Behind us a trickle of football-shirted, tracksuited men brought in their sons to show them what their grandads did and what they were missing. But there's precious little sense of what mining meant or was. It was a culture of doing and being, not of artefacts. The resonance is all in memory, and that's fading like firedamp. I bought a small, rude carving of a miner done in coal. Later, I gave it to my seven-year-old son. He took it without interest. "It's made of coal," I told him. "Oh," he said. "Do you know what coal is?" He shook his head.

The miner told me in passing that all the mines linked up underground, and that if you had a mind to, you could have traversed the north of England underground. The image is chilling. A troglodyte echo of the bright roads on the surface, thousands of mole miles of Bible-black empty motorways, streets, lanes and culs-de-sac, gaseous and watery, and in them the ghosts and bones of hacking, hard, inch-by-inch lives. It was difficult to leave this place with the remembrance and the power of its deep ley lines. Finally I asked the miner whether he preferred digging coal or working in the museum. He smiled: "That's the question, in't it?" He stared out at the rolling countryside, remembering 2ft horizons. "This is better," he said quietly.

The M1 stops at Leeds, or rather it used to stop at Leeds. Now it has a tacked-on addendum that joins it to its older competitor, the A1. Why it went to Leeds in the first place is a mystery. What London had to say to Leeds or Leeds to London that couldn't wait was never explained. But the point of roads is journeys, and the point of the journey is the going, not the arriving.

Back in London I was surprised at how moved I had been by this journey. What started out as a jaunt became a sort of pilgrimage. The weekend turned out to have the dreamish narrative of an ancient saga, an episodic archeology through the strata of England from loony heraldic beasts and decrepit stately homes to the industrial set-aside of funfairs. An organic mulch of our culture, the kitsch and oddness, the order and obsession. It had an un-intentional coherence, a plot, a road ran through it. A tale that was more than the sum of its parts. A series of blurred snapshots, of an England I thought I knew and therefore hadn't bothered to examine. And I discovered in passing that I'm far fonder of it all than I imagined. The M1 is one of the world's great journeys and it doesn't go where you think, it goes home. You should set out – just follow the signs.

Roller derby

Owning a Rolls-Royce, October 2001

There are days when you wake up, and you know. Before you draw back the unbleached calico curtain, before your feet touch the kosher forest-hardwood floorboards, before you step into the pulsing, intimately pummelling power shower, you know. You just know that something has changed. That out there in the chaos theory of socio-economic consumption, in the clamorous diorama of culture, the multi-screen iconography, the babble of semiotics, the gaudy gala of fashion and style, a butterfly's wing has beaten, a domino has fallen, a lost piece of sky has been found down the back of civilisation's sofa, and the big picture has changed. A chain reaction of choices has begun.

Thus it was that one morning in the beginning of the year I knew that the bingo balls of the zeitgeist had called the number of a new truth. The Rolls-Royce had come in from the cold. Owning a Roller had become the smart thing to do. In short, a Roller was an object of desire, and I desired one. I desired one fervently, imperatively. The mantra of modern culture I hold closest to my wallet is: "O Lord, grant me instant gratification." The only problem with that is, it's not fast enough.

Everything you choose to own, wear or associate yourself with says something about you. One of the defining characteristics of being human seems to be the ability to read symbols and metaphors. Every generation invents its own, and up until that moment a Rolls had represented all the wrong things. All my life, Rolls-Royces have been symbols of what I'm not, of what my family, my friends, my tribe wasn't. A Rolls was emphatically what we didn't want. If you took everything we thought, believed, worked at and aspired to, it would have been the antithesis of Rollerdom. Rolls-Royces memorialised a risible self-satisfaction. A repugnant image of plutocratic vanity wrapped up in a boorish reactionary nationalism. Gents'-club eulogies about British engineering and standards and roast beef with trimmings and my-lords-ladies-and-gentlemen deference and call-me-old-fashioned values. But mostly they were simply a couple of tons of inequality, where at a sedate 30mph all you could hear was the clock holding back time. A Rolls was the overt secret handshake of us, as distinct from them, and I'd always counted myself among the "them".

So what happened? What changed? As far as I can tell, two things. Rolls-Royces are now cheap. Not just cheaper but really, really cheap. A Rolls doesn't wear out; a ridiculous percentage of all the Rollers ever made are still running. It's owners who wear out, succumb to furry tubes or dangerous sexual practices or the Inland Revenue. So longevity combined with dodgy association and bad karma have released them from the bondage of riches and avarice. Having a Roller no longer means you've made a packet or inherited a stately wad. It could just as well mean you can't afford a four-door Ford.

Now they're free to represent other things. That morning, a Roller had an ironic, iconic wit. It wasn't a Blairish, inclusive, going-my-way people carrier. It's not an airbagged, bull-barred, disco-breaking piece of Kraut hospital engineering that assumes the driver is a haemophiliac dummy with a smaller IQ than his motor. It's not a sad symbol of testicular performance. It doesn't go from 0 to 60 in Rolex seconds. It goes from here to there with good grace. Here's the real reason why Rolls-Royces are suddenly a good thing: shorn of their cash snobbery, you can see a quieter, more sympathetic truth. They're not aspirational, they're not about going places. They were always about arriving. A Roller's natural home is not the gravel of the double drive; it's the cobbles outside the back-to-back. It's what every boy with nothing but pluck dreams of going back in, back to his roots, back to his mates, back to the secondary mod where the teacher said he'd never amount to anything. For me, a dyslexic boy who was told by the careers master to seriously consider hairdressing, it's two heavy-metal fingers. My Rolls was bought with words. It's my story. I wrote it. But I'm getting ahead of the plot. How to find a Rolls-Royce? Where do you start? Well, happily, that very evening the spirit of ecstasy, which, by the way, has the added little irony of becoming a druggable, clubbable pun, took me to dinner with Jeremy Clarkson and Damon Hill. Between them, if they couldn't find a Roller, then Rollers didn't exist. I told them about my pre-cappuccino revelation. They laughed the way Higgins and Colonel Pickering laughed at Eliza. And then they took a beat and said: "By God, I think he's got it." The next day, Damon called to say that he knew a bloke who might just have what I was looking for. So I met Steve. Steve isn't called Steve. I've called him Steve because, despite everything, I still have a sneaking fondness for him. He produced a turd-brown, early-70s Silver Shadow with a vinyl roof. "And I'd better warn you," he said, "a gold lady, it's . . . How shall I put this?"

"An Essex bookie's car?" I offered, helpfully.

"Yeah, that would be the technical term."

Perfect. It was a smidge under £10,000. I wrote a cheque on the spot, still on the phone. The next day, Steve showed me round, his white shell suit rustling conspiratorially, his mullet massaging his neck. He let me into some arcane secrets of Rollerdom. Did I know, for instance, that the driver's seat was fixed? They bespoke-fitted them to the owner. (Not, I learnt later, strictly the truth. It was just broken.) Did I want to look under the bonnet? What do you think? I didn't want to kick the wheels, either.

That night I went to bed knowing that outside was a Rolls-Royce and it was mine. I let the moonlight zeitgeist lap me to sleep, and the next day I sat in my Rolls and marvelled. I sat in it and marvelled because it wouldn't start.

Steve came up from Surrey with a mechanic. He looked through the driver's window and started to laugh. Speechless, he urged the mechanic to take a gander, and he laughed too. Together they laughed and laughed like cockney extras from *Mary Poppins*. There was much side-holding and thigh-slapping. What Steve hadn't told me – and why should he? – was that the thing only starts if the steering-wheel wand is pointing to park. I'd left it pointing to drive. I intoned imbecilic apologies like a mad rabbi. "No, no, don't," gasped Steve. "It was worth it. Really. Oh my, that's a classic."

The next day, it started and it went – but only in a straight line. The power steering had bled to death. This time I called the AA, and a very nice man came and told me the power steering had bled to death, and let me in on some more Roller arcania. Like: did I know that no force on earth can tow one, they have to be winched aboard a tank transporter, of which there are only five in the northern hemisphere? Two days later, I turned it on, and it didn't do anything at all – it was a dead Roller. A deceased Royce. It was no more. Its un-mortal coil had been shuffled off. And someone had tried to jemmy the spirit of E out of her socket.

So I did what all writers *in extremis* do. I called my agent. Ed has Bentleys. (My advice to all aspiring writers: always get an agent with a really extravagant motor and an unfeasibly pretty wife. They only get 10%. Think what you can do with the other 90.)

Ed introduced me to Alan Ledington of Balmoral UK. Alan had three things going for him, which was three things more than I had going for me. He came from the Midlands, and the Midlands still elicits a sense of mechanical probity. He had the sort of moustache that is the stalactite of a Midlands accent. Most importantly, he didn't make fun of me, suck his teeth or roll his eyes. He just took the Rolls away and sent me back an e-mail of things that were wrong with it. After the third page, I stopped reading. Apparently, only the front end of my Rolls-Royce was a Rolls-Royce. The back end belonged to something quite else. Possibly a Bulgarian Zil. The engine was a remand home for tumble-dryer parts, and at speed the vinyl roof acted as an airbag for suicidal sparrows. The good news was that he could let me have a better one for just a little more. Again I wrote the cheque there and then.

He even transferred the gold lady. And so it was that, after a couple of non-starts, I got my blood-clot-coloured Rolls-Royce with nicotine upholstery, Tania Bryer woodwork and whitewall tyres. Only four or five previous owners, the last of whom was a provincial solicitor. I imagined him, pinstriped, in the driver's seat, pink-fingering the volume on *The Black Dyke Brass Band Goes Pop*, patting the Bakelite steering wheel and saying: "Where there's conveyancing there's a conveyance."

I could say that getting it is the best thing I've ever done in my life, but that would be open to justifiable criticism. I also have two children. And any number of ex-wives, whom I love. But I've never owned a piece of kit that has given me so much profound pleasure.

Since the birth of the mechanical age more than two centuries ago, millions of things have been conceived, manufactured and used. Millions and millions of gadgets, great and small. Our lives are awash with the efforts of ingenuity and physics. But how many of these things have ever made that leap from utility to culture? Things may be beautiful, may have an ergonomic aesthetic, but they remain thingy. Very few get to be awarded a metaphorical soul for being more than simply the sum of their parts. A Rolls-Royce is one of the few. If you see a car crash, your immediate reaction is: "Oh, poor passengers." If one of the cars is a Rolls, you think: "Oh, poor car." The Rolls has two spirits: one on the bonnet and an invisible one under it. I could now go on and tell you about the mastery of the Silver Shadow. Its Shire-horse beauty, the Chubb-like weight of its doors, its sarcophagal boot, its touches and flourishes. The kindly vanity: *en suite* cigarette lighters, the shag pile that implores shagging. The ability to park, with one nonchalant hand, in spaces that are 2ft too small because it simply pushes other rude mechanicals out of the way. But let's take that as read.

Let's agree it doesn't so much drive as proceed, that to be a passenger is to view the world from a panoramic first-class lounge. Let's just assume that a Rolls-Royce behaves like a Rolls-Royce, and instead, let me draw your attention to two facets the moustachioed Midlands men don't tell you about: first, its smell. The scent of leather with a hint of woody veneer and warm, oily metal. An indefinable smell of confidence and experience. The other thing is that it makes all my music sound better. Not the speakers or the amplifiers or any of that nerdy wired stuff. It's that we share the same tastes.

In car years, we're contemporaries. This Rolls was born on the forecourt of the winter of discontent. Just as its petroholic engine sidled up to its first leaded nipple pump, oil prices doubled. Ayatollah Khomeini took over Iran, Idi Amin was deposed in Uganda, Zimbabwe was born, Ronald Reagan was declared as a presidential candidate, and Roy Jenkins proposed the SDP. The US surgeon general confirmed that cigarettes directly caused cancer. The first spreadsheet program was invented for personal computers. *Mad Max*, *Life of Brian* and *Alien* was what it saw at the cinema. On TV it was *Life on Earth* and *Tinker, Tailor, Soldier, Spy*. John Wayne bought the farm; Lord Mountbatten blew up at sea; and at 92, the inventor of the bouncing bomb, Barnes Wallace, hit the pillow for the last time. And out of the flat steppe of gloomy shires a new force appeared, sweeping all before it: Margaret Thatcher became prime minister.

For 1979 was year zero of the grab-it-and-run, blink-and-you're-a-loser modern age. My Rolls grew up as Margaret's child. It was her derided and loathed tumbrel. It rolled through the Falklands, the poll-tax riots and the miners' strike. It kept on rolling, past robo-nanny. The iron car outlived the Iron Lady and now it can just be itself. Few mechanical things, outside museums, exist long enough to acquire a story, a history. Regrets? It's had a few, but then again too few to mention.

You know, the pheromones of style are funny things. Now everyone loves the Roller; now people call me to ask if mine is true or merely a legend. Friends ask me to pick them up for dinner and say they've been considering one for ages. This car has become a bandwagon. An old chemist in a white coat came out of his shop and stared. "Wonderful," he said. "Mine's a slightly earlier model." Joan Collins curled her feet up on the front seat and purred. Jools Holland, a man I once stood behind in a taxi queue, sent me an old enamel owners' club badge for my owners' club badge bar, and recommended weekend memorabilia boot sales.

In the end, all cars are only the sum of their journeys. A car that isn't going places is an expensive rabbit hutch. My Roller needed a journey, a lap of honour, a pilgrimage. But where to? Allegorically, symbolically, there was only one place. It had to go to the dogs. Walthamstow dog track is surely the spiritual nirvana of all Rollers.

First I had to fill it with acolytes. People who said as much about the Roller as it had been saying about people like them for a generation. Tim Jefferies, the home counties Lothario, Don Giovanni as composed by Mantovani. He brought a Venezuelan model with the eyes of an alpaca, a body designed by Nintendo and the sexual vibration of a freelance queen bee. On his other arm was a girl of such pristine, radiant beauty that it was safest to look at her as she saw herself, as a reflection. She spoke little but said plenty. There was my Blonde, and the groin-throb actor Tom Hollander, and Sir Michael Gambon. Michael is the thespian version of a Rolls: big, stately, solid, confident and, under the immaculate coachwork, properly common.

No matter where you start, Walthamstow is a million miles away. The Rolls followed the spirit of E north, hunkering down on its soft suspension, certain of the way, sure-footed on the blind canyons and one-way precipices of Camden, Highbury and Hoxton. The old warhorse sensed the chipped concrete and flood-lights of home, it whinnied as it went, there was a flash of the old gadabout, a squirt of adrenaline. We caught it too, by osmosis: the essence of going to the dogs in a Roller.

I don't know if you've ever been greyhound-racing: I never had. If it hadn't been for the motor, I never would. It's a ridiculously unexpected heaven. Gambling is the only grade-A vice I've never been able to get my synapses around. But six dogs with brains the size of walnuts, looking as if they were bred in a wind tunnel, and a tart's nylon pyjama case on rails picked that last lock, and I flung notes at a bookie's runner called Mick with a butch abandon.

We sat in a very modern, commodious restaurant set out like the dress circle of an Imax cinema. We ate prawn cocktails and plaice and chips and cheesecake and drank champagne and watched the hare coursers do their business. And we changed. We changed into people who said "monkey" and "pony" and "carpet", who called "Leave it out!" and "Come again!" and "Your bleeding mother was a mongrel who did it with corgis!" And we punched shoulders and massaged necks, patted thighs and shook hands that had more rings than knuckles. And we laughed a lot, but laughter, serious, crowing laughter that looks very much like anger. And we made a bit of folding, got a drink out of it. I don't know how much, a herd of ponies, a tea party of monkeys, an office block of carpet.

Then, when the last race was over and we'd bet the last gold watch, it was back into the warm neon car park. And there was the Roller, big and burgundy, sitting in a space that was still 1979, chewing the cud of its memories. As I switched it on, it lit up, I kid you not, lit up, all its dials glowing with pleasure and pride. And I realised something profound: you don't take a Rolls-Royce any-where; it's the Rolls that takes you.

The next morning, I woke up and knew. Before I smelt the coffee, I knew. Before the duvet of want had slipped off the mattress of desire, I just knew. I had to have a greyhound.

Picture credits

The publisher would like to thank the following photographers, agencies and picture libraries for the permission to reproduce their work in this book:

12–13 Paul Lowe/Magnum; 14–15 Tom Stoddart/IPG Katz; 20–21 Paul Lowe/Magnum; 60–61 Peter Marlow/Magnum; 76–77 Paul Lowe/Magnum; 92–93 Paul Lowe/Magnum; 106–107 Peter Marlow/Magnum; 120–121 Chris Caldicott; 130–131 Peter Marlow/Magnum; 144–145 Paul Lowe/Magnum; 166–167 Peter Dench/IPG Katz; 184–185 Paul Lowe/Magnum; 200-201 Leticia Valverdes; 208–209 Robbie Cooper; 218–219 Terry O'Neill/Ed Victor; 266-267 Peter Dench/IPG Katz; 280–281 Jonathan Olley/Network Photographers; 294–295 Don McCullin/Mark George Agency.

"The end of the road"; "Out of their element"; "Game boy"; "I don't know what makes you angry . . ."; "Selassie come home"; "Awayday in a manger"; "The fatal shore"; "The city that Russia forgot"; "A short walk in the Hindu crush"; "Mad in Japan"; "Born to be riled"; "Sex and the city"; "Ride 'em chowboy"; "Hunforgiven"; "The Wilmslow boys"; "Look who"s stalking"; "To the manure born" and "Last exit to Whipsnade" originally appeared in the *Sunday Times* magazine. "The thin line" originally appeared in the *Sunday Times* "Style" section. "The return of the native" originally appeared in the *Sunday Times* "News Review" section. "When DD met AA"; "Dripping yarns"; "The coolest beauty contest in the world"; "Scumball rally"; and "Roller derby" originally appeared in *GQ* magazine.